THE

EVERYTHING®

GHOST BOOK

Spooky stories of haunted houses, phantom spirits,
unexplained mysteries, and more

Jason Rich

Adams Media Corporation
Avon, Massachusetts

An Everything® Series Book.
Everything® is a registered trademark of Adams Media Corporation.

Published by Adams Media Corporation
57 Littlefield Street, Avon, MA 02322
www.adamsmedia.com

ISBN: 1-58062-533-9
Printed in the United States of America.

J I H G F E D C B A

Library of Congress Cataloging-in-Publication Data
Rich, Jason R.
The everything ghost book / by Jason Rich.
p.   cm.   — (An everything series book)
Includes index.
ISBN 1-58062-533-9
1. Ghosts. I. Title. II. Everything series.
BF1461   .R48 2001
133.1—dc21   2001033546

Cover illustrations by Barry Littmann.
Interior illustrations by Michelle Dorenkamp, Barry Littmann, and Kurt Dolber.

This book is available at quantity discounts for bulk purchases.
For information, call 1-800-872-5627.

Visit the entire Everything® series at everything.com

Contents

Chapter One
Starting with the Basics
✻ 1 ✻

Chapter Two
Ghost Hunters, Parapsychologists, and Paranormal Investigators
✻ 21 ✻

Chapter Three
Real-Life Ghost Stories
∗ 83 ∗

Chapter Four
Mediums and Channelers
∗ 125 ∗

Chapter Five
Past-Life Regression and Contacting Your Spirit Guide(s)
∗ 169 ∗

Chapter Six

Ouija Boards and Automatic Writing: Let the Spirits Speak!

✶ 201 ✶

Chapter Seven

Near Death Experiences (NDEs)

✶ 217 ✶

Chapter Eight

The Skeptical Point of View

✶ 239 ✶

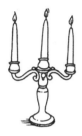

Acknowledgments

I'd like to thank everyone who is featured in *The Everything*® *Ghost Book* for sharing their knowledge and taking the time to be interviewed. I'd like to extend my gratitude to my family and close friends (especially Mark Giordani, Ellen Bendremer, the guys from B-Factor, Ferras AlQaisi and Thomas Wisdom), who have spent months listening to me talk about all kinds of paranormal-related topics. I'd also like to congratulate Ellen and Sandy on the birth of their first child, Emily.

—Jason R. Rich

Introduction

When it comes to discussions of the paranormal, people from all over the world and from all different religious beliefs all have questions. For example, do you believe in ghosts? Are you a firm believer that once we die, we travel to "the other side" and live on as a spirit? Do you believe there's an afterlife and all beings are ultimately reincarnated or reborn after death? Do you believe ghosts or spirits can communicate with the living? If you do, you're not alone. Millions of people have had firsthand unexplainable experiences that have led them to believe in ghosts and the paranormal.

If you've ever thought about things that go bump in the night or were alone in a dark room and felt a presence, perhaps you too have experienced something paranormal. Throughout history and around the world, people have always been fascinated by the paranormal and have looked for ways to communicate with the dead. In more modern times, the majority of people who seek out the services of mediums and channelers are grieving the loss of a loved one. These people often want to stay in contact or say one final farewell to a loved one who has passed on.

If you're already a believer, you'll probably find the information in this book reassuring and extremely interesting. If you're not yet a believer, well, after reading the interviews with all of the various experts and firsthand experiencers featured in this book, perhaps your mind will be opened to the possibilities that paranormal activity can and does exist, and that there are plenty of unexplained, paranormal, or supernatural things happening to everyday people.

Hollywood and the Paranormal

People are totally fascinated by TV shows like *The X-Files*, *PSI Factor*, and *Unsolved Mysteries.* Movies like *Ghost, Ghostbusters, The Sixth Sense, Casper, Poltergeist,* and *The Amityville Horror* have also captured our imaginations and opened our minds to the idea of life after death.

One of the highest-rated TV shows on the Sci-Fi network is called *Crossing Over with John Edward* (currently seen Sunday through Thursday nights at 11:00 P.M. EST). It features world-renowned psychic medium John Edward helping audience members communicate with loved ones on the other side. This show is probably one of the most credible in terms of how it handles conveying accurate information by actually showcasing demonstrations of ordinary people experiencing their own paranormal experience through the use of a medium (John Edward).

While some TV shows and movies do an excellent job entertaining us with stories of the paranormal, whether they be fiction or loosely based on fact, a huge portion of what you see on TV and in the movies is fake or greatly embellished for entertainment purposes. Even so-called documentaries about the paranormal tend to sensationalize the stories they're trying to convey in order to capture your attention. After all, the monster-like ghosts that ooze green slime, let out horrific moans, and rattle chains aren't typically what one sees or hears when experiencing something paranormal in real life. As you delve into your own research of the paranormal, don't expect to get dressed up like a character from the movie *Ghostbusters* and run around with weird contraptions strapped to your back that suck up ghosts from a haunted building. It just doesn't work like that.

How Hollywood misrepresents the paranormal is most obvious when you look at the work of actual parapsychologists and real-life ghost busters. The work these people do is absolutely nothing like what you saw in the movie *Ghostbusters* or in countless other films or TV shows. Many who saw the movie *Poltergeist* remember having nightmares for weeks afterwards, thinking that evil spirits were coming to get them through their TV sets. If these people had had a better understanding of what real-life paranormal activity is all about, they would easily have been able to come to terms with the fact that there are few well-documented cases of people being injured or killed by ghosts, spirits, poltergeists, demons, or other evil entities, but more on that later.

The Experts Share Their Experiences

Over the past year or so while writing this book, I have interviewed dozens of experts who study all aspects of the paranormal, including ghosts, hauntings, reincarnation, mediumship, past-life regression, the existence of spirit guides, and possessions. These experts include parapsychologists, real-life ghost busters, ghost hunters, psychologists, philosophers, psychics, mediums, channelers, hypnotherapists, educators, and a wide range of others, many of whom you'll read about in this book.

There are many people out there who firmly believe they have a special gift that allows them to communicate with the other side (also known as the "spirit world"). Most of the people who are "legitimate," however, don't have their own 900 telephone number and don't star in infomercials. Because of the way society looks upon them, often with disbelief, many people who possess a special gift tend to keep it to themselves and share it only with loved ones and close friends for fear of being labeled a freak or a fraud.

This book offers testimonials from a wide range of people who do believe in the paranormal and who have dedicated their lives to studying and understanding what many scientists currently classify as unexplainable. Just because something can't be scientifically proven certainly doesn't mean that it doesn't exist. There are countless examples throughout history where the general public, as well as scientists, frowned on certain areas of belief, simply because the scientific knowledge or necessary technology wasn't yet available to prove a specific theory or hypothesis.

More Sci-Fi Info

To learn more about this show, visit the Sci-Fi Channel's Web site at *www.scifi.com/john edward* or visit John Edward's Web site at *www.johnedward.net.* To become a member of the show's studio audience in New York, write to: Crossing Over with John Edward, P.O. Box 2175, Radio City Station, New York, NY 10019-2175.

The Shadowlands

If you are interested in beginning your research of the unexplained, The Shadowlands is a good place to start. This Web site (*www.theshadow lands.net*) offers a wealth of information on topics such as ghosts, hauntings, UFOs, aliens, and various other supernatural entities. Included are text files, photographs, video clips, sound clips, and first person accounts. Updated regularly, the Shadowlands provides the information you need to begin and continue with your paranormal research.

After all, until it was proven that the earth was round, the general consensus was that our planet was flat. Anyone who spoke out with different ideas was considered crazy or blasphemous. Perhaps the same holds true when it comes to the existence of ghosts, spirits, and other supernatural entities. It's totally conceivable that next week, next year, within the next decade, or sometime within this millennium it will be proven (from a purely scientific standpoint) that ghosts do exist and that there is definitely some form of life after death. For now, however, we're forced to rely on our personal belief systems, firsthand experiences, and the experiences of others.

What You'll Find in this Book

In writing this book, I have tried to compile as many facts as possible, and include as many interviews with experts as possible, so you can begin to understand what all of this paranormal phenomena regarding ghosts, hauntings, the afterlife, reincarnation, mediumship, and channeling is all about. Hopefully, you'll then be able to make up your own mind as to what you choose to believe.

Please consider *The Everything® Ghost Book* as a starting point into your exploration of the world of the paranormal and the unexplained. While this book can't provide hardcore, indisputable answers about the paranormal, it can offer many ideas and theories, and poses many questions along with potential (albeit unproven) answers.

I hope this book will capture your imagination and inspire you to learn more. Perhaps it will make you think about issues you've been afraid to deal with, or assist you in coming to terms with issues that have been plaguing you regarding the loss of a loved one. If you've spent your life being afraid of ghosts as a result of all those scary movies that have come out of Hollywood, maybe your perception about ghosts and the paranormal will change after reading these pages.

If you've purchased this book because you believe you've had some sort of paranormal experience and you're having trouble coming to terms with it—it's frightened you, or you simply can't explain what you experienced—I urge you to seek the guidance of a reliable expert and educate yourself as much as possible on this topic. Hopefully, this book will point you toward resources you'll find helpful and reliable.

It should be understood that many people have found comfort and solace using the services of a medium, for example, to help them communicate with a deceased loved one and come to terms with the loss. An entire section of this book is dedicated to the work of psychics, mediums, and channelers.

Countless other people have had their own experiences, either seeing ghosts or through a near death experience (where their physical body died and was later brought back to life while their conscious mind remained awake and alert, giving them a complete recollection of what transpired). Far too many well-educated, normal, hard-working people from all over the world have had these types of experiences. They can't simply be ignored, written off as being a by-product of a vivid imagination, or disbelieved because the experiencers are deemed nuts.

For those of you with access to the Internet, you'll find it an incredible resource not just for reading about the paranormal, but for communicating with other people from around the world who have had some sort of firsthand paranormal experience. As you read this book, I urge you to surf the Web and visit the various Web sites listed. If you're so inclined, you should also e-mail the various experts and witnesses featured in this book to help you obtain a better understanding of what the paranormal is all about.

As you'll soon see, *The Everything® Ghost Book* is divided into sections that focus on different aspects of the paranormal, yet all somehow deal with ghosts (or spirits) and one's ability to communicate with the other side. As you read this book, I invite you to visit my Web site *(www.jasonrich.com)* or e-mail me *(jr7777@aol.com)* to share your thoughts, ideas, and insights into this extremely fascinating topic.

Religious Beliefs

When studying the paranormal, it's virtually impossible not to take into account one's religious beliefs. However, *The Everything® Ghost Book* tries to keep the religious aspects of this topic to a minimum. If you want to discuss the religious implications of ghosts, hauntings, possessions, reincarnation, angels, spirit guides, and so forth, it is recommended you do so with a religious leader, such as a priest or rabbi.

Chapter One

Starting with the Basics

Unless you've already had a firsthand paranormal experience or you believe you've seen or interacted with a ghost, spirit, apparition, or poltergeist, chances are what you're about to read in this book will seem rather bizarre and perhaps a bit scary. The information may also contradict your personal or religious beliefs.

In this chapter, you'll receive a general introduction to paranormal activity relating to ghosts and hauntings. Later, you'll read interviews with professional ghost hunters, paranormal investigators, and people who have experienced paranormal activity. You'll learn what to do if you believe you've seen a ghost or experienced paranormal activity yourself, and discover places throughout America (and around the world) you can visit if you're interested in going on your own real-life paranormal investigation or ghost hunt.

While Hollywood specializes in films like *Poltergeist, The Exorcist, The Sixth Sense, Ghostbusters*, and *Casper* that typically portray ghosts as evil entities that go around scaring and killing people, the real-life paranormal experiences most people report having are absolutely nothing like what you see in movies.

As your quest to further understand the paranormal begins, it's important to have a basic understanding of the terms used by the experts to define and describe ghosts, haunts, and other paranormal activity.

There Are Many Types of Ghosts: A Vocabulary Lesson

According to *Merriam Webster's Collegiate Dictionary 10th Edition*, a ghost is defined as "1: the seat of life or intelligence. 2: a disembodied soul. The soul of a dead person believed to be an inhabitant of the unseen world or to appear to the living in bodily likeness. 3: spirit, demon. 4: a faint, shadowy trace. 5: a false image in a photographic negative or on a television screen caused by reflection."

Depending on whom you ask, a ghost is defined in many different ways. To keep things simple, in this book the term "ghost" or "entity" is used to define a wide range of paranormal activity, whether it's an apparition, poltergeist, floating orb of light, or a strange noise emanating from what's believed to be a "haunted" house or location.

A ghost may in fact be proof of life after death. As you'll read in this book, a ghost can also be the result of a strange electrical anomaly that causes what we believe to be paranormal activity, but that's not necessarily associated with an entity returning to earth (or one that's unable to leave the living realm, for whatever reason) after its death. Do spirits or souls survive after death? This question has been debated for eons. Even today, opinions on this topic vary greatly. One's religious affiliation often impacts one's belief in ghosts and a person's ability to return from the dead.

The fact is, in today's modern world where science attempts to answer all questions, even without absolute scientific proof, over half of the American and European population believes in some form of life after death, which includes the belief in ghosts.

Ghosts and Apparitions

What is a ghost, anyway? Many people use the word "ghost" to explain the visual appearance of a human being or creature that has died and passed on to the other side. Paranormal experts generally explain this as a visual manifestation of a soul, spirit, life force, or life energy. An "apparition," on the other hand, typically refers to the visual appearance of any spirit or unusual visual phenomenon that doesn't necessarily take on the shape of a human form or that doesn't show signs of intelligence or personality.

All too often, these terms are used interchangeably by nonexperts. In specific terms, however, all ghosts can be considered apparitions, but not all apparitions can be considered ghosts. To keep things interesting, people also use "phantom," "spook," "phantasm," "poltergeist," or "vision" to describe the visual appearance of a ghost or apparition. The term "collective apparition" is often used to describe an apparition that is seen simultaneously by multiple witnesses.

Supernatural Versus Paranormal

When people refer to ghosts and hauntings, they often use the term "supernatural." This word, however, is sometimes considered to have a religious, occult, or demonic significance. As a result, when describing unusual activity that involves ghosts, apparitions, spirits, hauntings, poltergeists, and so on, many experts prefer the term "paranormal." This defines anything within the range of normal human experience or for which there is no scientific explanation.

Where Do Poltergeists Come From?

There are many beliefs regarding the origins of poltergeists. One theory is that they are a manifestation caused by living people who unknowingly have paranormal, psychic, or telekinetic abilities and who unconsciously use these abilities to create the poltergeist activity. When a living person with any of these paranormal abilities undergoes excessive trauma, he or she may produce a force known as "repressed psychokinetic energy." So, for example, someone with telekinetic powers who is alive but under stress may be able to move objects with his mind, without consciously knowing what he's doing.

According to one of the world's leading paranormal investigators, Loyd Auerbach, and his Web site (*www.mindreader.com*), apparitions, which are better known as "ghosts," could be some form of the human mind (consciousness, personality, soul, spirit) that functions apart from the physical body. What is believed to be a ghost may be what survives the death of the body. Many reports indicate that apparitions act just like "real" humans. Some are even believed to have personality and emotions. Many eyewitnesses report the ghosts they see also act and dress like the person they were when alive. So, if a woman who lived in eighteenth-century England chooses to return to our realm and be seen as a ghost, she is likely to appear dressed in clothing from eighteenth-century England, not in an outfit from The Gap.

Auerbach believes there are four categories of apparitions:

1. "Apparitions of the Dead" are people who have been dead for more than twelve to forty-eight hours and who return to visit someone they knew when alive or return to a specific location that's currently inhabited by someone they knew when alive.
2. "Apparitions of the Living" (which is also referred to as "bilocation") involves a living person having an out-of-body experience.
3. "Apparitions from Another Dimension or Time" are apparitions that visit us from somewhere else or from another time and appear to be as confused and frightened of their visit to our world of the living as the people who witness them.
4. "Pseudo-Apparitions" refer to apparitions that actually haunt a location and may create poltergeist phenomena, which involves interaction with the physical environment. These apparitions, according to Aeurbach's Web site, don't typically show signs of personality or intelligence. Their actions or the sounds they create are repetitious "replays" of something that has already occurred, and those actions are repeated over and over.

Poltergeists

While a ghost is often seen, a poltergeist is more often experienced. A poltergeist will often "interact" with its environment or with people by moving objects, making noises, or by making itself known in other ways. Poltergeists have been reported to be responsible for starting fires, throwing stones, making objects appear and disappear, causing unexplainable sounds, and even levitating physical objects. In fact, the word "poltergeist" means "noisy ghost" when translated from German. They're typically not seen, however.

A poltergeist is also not generally considered to be the spirit of someone who has somehow returned from the dead. You'll soon read several theories regarding the origin of poltergeist phenomena. Some people believe poltergeists come from nonhuman origin, while others believe it is actually living humans with psychic or telekinetic abilities that create this phenomenon. Contrary to popular belief (and what's been commonly portrayed in horror movies), poltergeists aren't always evil. There have been very few reports of people actually being physically harmed or killed by poltergeists; however, they are considered by some experts to be more dangerous than ghosts or apparitions.

Ghosts: The General Consensus

There's a general consensus that a ghost is an energy-based entity, probably some form of a person's soul that continues to exist after a person dies. It's totally separate from their physical body. It's the part of the person that "lives" on.

Ghostly Behavior

Some ghosts are visible to the human eye and can take on a variety of different appearances, ranging from a floating cloud of smoke to the three-dimensional image of a human. In many cases, when someone sees a ghost, the ghost displays no intelligence and makes no attempt to interact with the witness(es). It just appears and then disappears, often at the same location over and over again. As you'll read later, some people believe these images have somehow imprinted or attached themselves to a specific location, sort of like a VCR makes a recording. The image somehow has the ability to keep replaying itself over and over again. This phenomenon is typically classified as an apparition.

Many people who report seeing ghosts swear that the entity they encountered communicated with them. Sometimes this communication occurs in a purely visual manner. However, there are also plenty of reports from people who have actually heard a ghost speak to them or who claim to have communicated with a ghost telepathically (by exchanging thoughts, not audible words). Any ghost that communicates clearly shows signs of intelligence and often has a specific purpose for making itself known.

Some witnesses of paranormal activity don't see or hear a ghost's presence, but feel it. In some occurrences, the temperature around the witness changes, often dropping dramatically; or an invisible presence is felt physically touching the witness. Some people hear strange noises or simply sense something around them that isn't normal.

While some people claim to see or hear ghosts, others have experienced ghosts actually interacting with them or the environment. Objects get moved, doors open and close for no reason, or other forms of interaction take place. This type of ghost is typically classified as a poltergeist. This term shouldn't be confused with what people often see in horror films, however.

According to the book *Ghost Watching* (Virgin Publishing, Ltd.) by John Spencer and Tony Wells, the spiritualist explanation for the poltergeist is that occasionally spirits do not leave the earthly plane for their proper place, and for several reasons this may cause disruptive activity. "The main reason for this is that the spirits may be irritated because living people do not recognize them or react to their presence. In their anger they may try to attract attention or simply discharge their aggression by typical poltergeist activity, such as throwing household equipment around. This belief, like all others relating to paranormal activity, is based on faith rather than explicit evidence." This is just one possible theory regarding the origin of poltergeists.

Helpful Resource

The American Ghost Society (888-GHOSTLY, *www.prairie ghosts.com)* is an excellent source for purchasing books and equipment used by ghost hunters and paranormal investigators. Whether you're looking to become a ghost hunter as a hobby or you're investigating possible paranormal events in your own home, The American Ghosts Society offers one-stop shopping for all the equipment you'll need.

Is Raley a Believer?

When asked if she truly believes in ghosts, Janis Raley (from the Ghost Preservation League) replied, "I can't see why we would suddenly lose our divine right to freedom of choice just because we die, and be doomed, with no say in the matter, to hang around one spot forever, or until some ghost hunter comes to save us. That seems a bit farfetched. Plus, I don't have any stats on hand, but I would guess that not too many people die in cemeteries to begin with. So, if we die tragically and unexpectedly, we are stuck. It would seem odd that we could truck on up to the graveyard, but nowhere else. If a ghost comes up to me and asks for help, I will change my mind. Until then, I will go with other theories. Being most interested in historical hauntings, we have, in the course of our investigations, run across what we call historical imprints. These seem to differ from other types of hauntings, or phenomena. We have gotten all varieties of the types listed as well as a recognizable apparition."

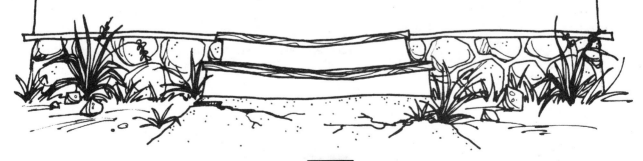

What Do Ghosts Look Like?

When many people think of a ghost, the image in their mind is of a human form that is somewhat translucent or that glows in the dark or floats in the air. However, many people also witness ghosts that appear as floating balls of light or as orbs of energy.

According to Janis Raley, cofounder of the Ghost Preservation League (a group of professional and amateur paranormal investigators), by far the most common phenomena caught on film is of an orb or sphere. "We have seen some that look like small bubbles, cinnamon buns, and a bad case of the hives. They can occur as single orbs, in clusters, in whirling clumps, be bright as stars, or be barely visible. They can look radically different but are recognizable as the same general type of phenomena."

What are these orbs that are captured on film? Some people insist they are trapped souls. Raley added, "We don't know for sure what they are, but we can hazard a few guesses about where they are found. You can almost always catch an orb or two in any cemetery. You can also catch them, however, where there are no burials whatsoever."

Mist and vapor are other forms of energy that some believe to have paranormal origins. Raley reports that based on her experience, "On occasion, they accompany, or cause, a cold spot. This is the feeling that you just walked inside a freezer, but it is contained in one generalized area. There are gadgets to measure thermal variance, but it seems pretty obvious when it happens. One minute you are just fine, and the next you are much colder, with the hairs standing up on your arms. There have been a few times when the very air around us felt electric, and a crackling sound was heard."

Aside from orbs and vapors, forces known as "vortices" are a very concentrated form of energy. These forces are often described as the kind that causes the hair on the back of your neck to stand at attention. A vortex is a mass of air, water, or in this case energy,

that spins around very fast and pulls objects into its empty center. Some believe that energy-based vortices have paranormal origins.

Electronic Voice Phenomena (EVP)

Electronic Voice Phenomena (EVP) refers to the noises and voices that are recorded on traditional audio or videotape, but that aren't audible to the human ear. Raley, like many paranormal investigators, has experienced this phenomenon firsthand. These noises that are recorded on tape, but can't be heard live, are believed by some to come directly from ghosts or "the other side."

She explained that under a controlled and monitored situation, a voice-activated tape recorder was left in what was considered the haunted front bedroom of a house. This was the room that was supposed to have the most paranormal activity, from apparitions to audible voices. The owner had already obtained several EVPs, which Raley politely listened to, but really couldn't understand. She left the recorder cushioned on the bed, and closed the two doors that entered the room. It was late afternoon, and all participants then discussed the haunting of the farmhouse outside, near a picnic table. The room was in plain view at all times through windows, and no one was out of sight. Raley gathered information, and in the meantime, the owner showed Raley and her colleagues different areas around the house where voices had been heard by many people. At all times, the "empty" bedroom could be seen.

"After a couple of hours, we checked the recorder. Indeed, the tape had advanced quite a bit. After rewinding, I heard the voice that changed my own perception of EVPs. Before the voice began, there was a series of loud electric pings. Then we heard the noises of something being scooted across the floor and children laughing. After that a deep black male voice said, quite clearly, 'Go on, get on outta here now.' Not only was I speechless, I felt a little shocked. This was my reaction to having my doors of perception blown open. The farm has been in the same family since its founding," said Raley.

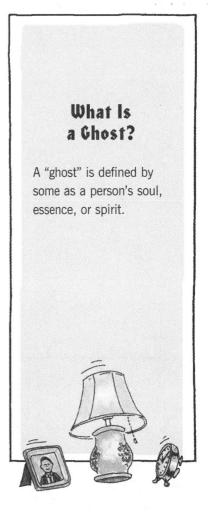

What Is a Ghost?

A "ghost" is defined by some as a person's soul, essence, or spirit.

Like many people who have studied EVP, Raley believes, "The voices of 'spirits' are just beyond our hearing, much like they are just beyond our vision. There seems to be a constant of magnetic energy associated with the unexplained, which would enable the magnetic tape of recorders to record that which we cannot hear, but can often feel. We have heard authenticated tapes, those in which we have ascertained that the participants aren't completely pathological, and don't speak through their other selves, that contain both present voices and voices of people not visually evident."

If you're looking to experience this phenomenon firsthand, Raley suggests leaving a voice-activated tape recorder within a cemetery or old deserted building. "Since we specialize in Civil War ghosts, my first choice would, of course, be a battlefield. If you are lucky enough to live near one, give it a try. There are rumors of EVPs from Gettysburg, for example, that caught military sounds such as bugles and gunfire, plus a few less pleasant sounds. Most of the national park properties are closed at night, so that is a consideration. Much of what is recorded sounds very mechanical, and not exactly human. The voices that sound very human are quite often preceded with electronic pings or blips," she explained.

Ghosts and Psychic Ability

As you'll soon see, people who experience paranormal activity often have a wide range of different experiences and interpret those experiences in different ways. Some people equate paranormal activity with psychic phenomena and believe only people with psychic ability can experience ghosts, hauntings, or other paranormal events. This may occur through telepathy (communication using the mind as opposed to your other senses), psychokinesis (the ability to move objects using one's mind), or clairvoyance (the ability to foresee the future or to see objects or events that others can't using only their eyes and ears).

It's certainly possible that ghosts do exist and that there's some type of life after death, but the proof hasn't yet been discovered. While researchers, investigators, and those who claim to have experienced paranormal activity make extremely convincing arguments about what they believe is fact, scientific proof regarding the existence of ghosts (as in entities that have somehow returned from the dead) doesn't yet exist.

Often, when people begin to explore or investigate paranormal activity, their religious beliefs deeply impact how they interpret anything unusual they witness or experience. For example, someone who believes in heaven and hell would most likely believe that a demon comes from hell, while a ghost is someone who has died and either returned from heaven or somehow gotten stuck here on earth among the living, but is trying to reach the other side (that is, the spirit world).

According to Loyd Auerbach, someone's "psi" (psychic ability or power) is the normal ability to communicate and interact with the environment in a way that is beyond our normal senses and muscles. "It is believed that perhaps this 'psi' [or psychic] ability can exist independently of our brains and bodies as a function of 'higher intelligence,' consciousness, soul, etc. Using this concept, someone whose body has died, or who is literally out of his or her body, could still be capable of communication or environmental interaction through psychic abilities."

Following this line of thought, an apparition could send a telepathic message that, if received, would cause us to "see" its form, "hear" its words, "feel" its touch, and "smell" its cologne or scent. These "sensations," according to Auerbach, are purely of the mental or psychic. They are transmitted by one mind and received by another.

More information about Auerbach's theories can be found both on his Web site and in his book, *Mind Over Matter*, published by Kensington Books. An interview with Auerbach is also featured in Chapter 2 of this book.

Where to Find Ghosts, Apparitions, and Other Paranormal Activity

Ghosts have been reported to appear or manifest themselves in many different locations—not just places where something evil or tragic has taken place (such as the site of a murder, suicide,

What Is a Soul?

A "soul" is believed by some to be the electro-magnetic energy field pattern or matrix that has intelligence, emotions, attitudes, and beliefs. Entities believed to be souls are self-aware. From a religious perspective (depending on the religion), one's soul is defined differently. It's believed to be the part of a person that is spiritual and that continues to exist in some form after the physical body has died. Some believe the soul is the part of a person that is not physical, but that experiences deep feelings and emotions before and after death.

or battle). Some experts equate ghosts, hauntings, and other paranormal activity with unusual energy fields located at specific locations. These energy fields might be natural—a result of metal deposits in the ground, a fault, or an underground water supply—or they might be the result of faulty electrical wiring in a house.

While it's been scientifically proven that many "haunted" locations are often in close proximity to electrical, magnetic, or geomagnetic energy fields, the exact correlation between the ghosts and these energy fields has yet to be determined. Some believe the electrical, geomagnetic, or magnetic energy fields open a doorway or create a portal that allows ghosts to make themselves known. Others believe it's the ghosts themselves that create the anomaly or cause the unusual energy field.

Whether or not you believe that electrical, geomagnetic, or magnetic energy fields have any relationship to the presence and manifestation of ghosts, apparitions, paranormal entities, or poltergeists, there are many types of locations where these phenomena have been documented to take place.

Popular Haunted Places

Some of the most popular places where ghosts seem apt to make themselves known include:

- Battlefields
- Cemeteries
- Crime scenes
- Sites of suicides
- Older educational institutions
- Homes
- Hospitals
- Hotels, motels, and inns
- Nursing homes
- Theaters

One of the best ways of finding haunted locations is to do research. Pay careful attention to local folklore. Research as much as possible the origins of that folklore. The majority of these locations have strange events or unusual stories associated with them.

Ghost Hunters and Their Equipment

A ghost hunter (or paranormal investigator) is someone who investigates and studies ghosts, hauntings, and paranormal phenomena. A ghost buster, on the other hand, is someone who visits a site that's believed to be haunted and uses any of a wide range of methods to eliminate the ghost or paranormal activity from that location. This might involve performing an exorcism or cleansing.

The Society for Psychical Research (SPR) (*http://moebius.psy.ed.ac.uk/~spr/*) was founded in 1882 and is based in London. This was the first organization established to investigate paranormal activity using scientific research. One of the Society's aims has been to examine the question of whether we survive bodily death, by evaluating the evidence provided by mediumship, apparitions of the dead, and reincarnation studies.

According to the organization, "The purpose of the Society for Psychical Research is to advance the understanding of events and abilities commonly described as 'psychic' or 'paranormal,' without prejudice and in a scientific manner. The Society does this by promoting and supporting important research, and by publishing scholarly reports of a high standard. It acts as a forum for debate by organizing educational activities, and by disseminating information about current developments."

The Society's principal area of study includes the psychical research concerning exchanges between minds, or between minds and the environment, which are not dealt with by current orthodox science. This is a broad topic of study that incorporates such

What Is a Spirit?

"Spirits" are believed to be electromagnetic entities, in the form of orbs, mist, vortexes, or shadows, that are the signature of a once-living person who has returned to a specific location to visit people he or she once knew. A "residual haunting" refers to a spirit that's trapped in an emotional loop that keeps repeating. For example, a spirit may cling to the scene of a crime in which he or she was suddenly and horrifically murdered in life.

The Spiritualist Movement

The Spiritualists believed that living people could communicate with the dead. The spiritualist movement spread in America in 1848, after the Fox sisters claimed that their home in upstate New York was besieged by strange noises and that objects mysteriously fell or were hurled off shelves. It was said that these events were caused by poltergeists with whom the Fox sisters were in communication. A group of mediums soon emerged claiming to possess paranormal abilities. Also during this time, séances (meetings for contacting the dead) and the use of Ouija boards became popular.

topics as extrasensory perception (telepathy, clairvoyance, precognition, and retrocognition); psychokinesis (paranormal effects on physical objects, including poltergeist phenomena); near death and out-of-the-body experiences; apparitions; hauntings; hypnotic regression; and paranormal healing.

The American Society for Psychical Research (ASPR) (*www.aspr.com*) is the oldest psychical research organization in the United States and is based in New York City. For more than a century, the ASPR has supported the scientific investigation of extraordinary or as yet unexplained phenomena that have been called psychic or paranormal. Over the years, investigators have found that upwards of 85 percent of all reported ghost sightings and hauntings have had other explanations. It's the unexplainable occurrences, however, that keep people fascinated with the paranormal.

When it comes to actually documenting paranormal events, professional ghost hunters, parapsychologists, paranormal investigators, and ghost busters use a wide range of fascinating (and at times technologically advanced) tools and equipment. Some of the equipment used during a paranormal investigation is extremely basic, while other tools are far more specialized and can be costly. This section explains some of the equipment used to document ghosts and paranormal activity.

- *Air ion counter*—This device (available from a company called AlphaLab, Inc., 800-769-3754, $580) can be used to detect natural and artificial ions. Natural ions can be generated by radioactive decay, radon gas, ions created by fires, lightning, and evaporating water. Artificial ions can be created as a result of using some types of electrical equipment. It's been documented by researchers that "ghosts" tend to either create ion fields or alter the ion fields in a location where they manifest themselves. Changes in the ion field are one way experts document the presence of paranormal activity.
- *Audio recorder*—A cassette, DAT, or Minidisc audio recorder can be used to record Electronic Voice Phenomena (EVP). Ideally, you'll want to use a recorder with a sound activation

system; otherwise, you'll need to leave the unit operating (recording) and then go back and listen to the entire recording to determine if you picked up anything unusual.

- *Compass*—While you can purchase several different pieces of equipment to detect magnetic or electromagnetic fields, a simple hand-held compass is a low-tech way of measuring this type of energy anomaly. If magnetic energy is present, the dial on the compass will go crazy.

- *Electromagnetic Field (EMF) Gauss meter*—This device can be used to detect and measure electromagnetic fields and electrical current located within an area that's believed to be haunted. Some experts have documented large fluctuations in the electromagnetic fields found in an area where paranormal activity is believed to be taking place. The Tri-Field meter is another device that can measure magnetic and electrical energy. It's portable, fast, and easy to use. Another device, the Tri-Field Natural EM meter, allows a paranormal investigator to measure the level of natural electromagnetic fields being generated from underground metal deposits, faults, underground water supplies, etc. Since it's believed that this type of energy may somehow be a conduit for paranormal activity, pinpointing areas that contain energy anomalies may be useful to paranormal investigators.

- *Geiger counter*—Paranormal investigators use this type of device to check the background radiation that's present at a specific location. A Geiger counter can measure radon gas levels as well as detect nuclear radiation and uranium. If ghosts are, in fact, energy based, this tool that measures certain types of energy that may be present at the site of a haunting may detect them.

- *Infrared proximity detector*—This type of device is used to detect even the slightest movements in an area by measuring changes in temperature and light. In come cases of paranormal activity, objects (such as furniture) are reported to move by themselves. This type of device can detect movement and help determine its cause.

- *Magnetic field detector*—This device pinpoints and measures the presence of low-level magnetic fields, which are often associated with ghosts and paranormal activity. These fields can be man-made or occur naturally.

- *Notebook and pen/pencil*—As you're participating in an investigation (even if it's in your own home), everything that's experienced should be documented in as much detail as possible. Keep track of dates, times, and anything unusual you see, hear, smell, or experience. Pay careful attention to all of your senses and what's happening around you, and take copious notes. If you happen to experience something unusual, write down details about your experience immediately, while the details are still fresh in your mind.

- *Photographic equipment*—Amateur and professional paranormal investigators alike use a wide range of photographic equipment, including 35mm cameras, basic point-and-shoot cameras, and Polaroid instant cameras. Video camcorders and digital cameras are also used in an attempt to document paranormal activity. Obviously, you'll want to use the best equipment possible. If you're using a traditional camera, be sure to have plenty of 400 ASA or faster speed film. Faster film speed allows you to take better pictures of fast-moving objects and to photograph in low light.

- *Temperature reading equipment*—Sudden temperature changes have long been associated with poltergeist phenomena. Being able to take ongoing temperature readings of an area will help you document these changes and possibly alert you to paranormal activity that's taking place but that isn't visible to the human eye. Specialized Products Company (800-866-5353) offers a device called the Raytek Raynger ST ($199), which can be used to take temperature readings in an area or of an

Videotaping Tip

If you're using a video camera or even a still camera, it's helpful to have a tripod on hand. If you do happen to witness paranormal activity, you don't want your hands to shake the camera. Even the most experienced ghost hunters and paranormal investigators get scared or overly excited when they witness something unusual.

object without making physical contact. To use the device, simply aim and pull the trigger. A temperature reading will instantly be displayed.

- *Stopwatch*—In addition to having a wristwatch or clock, a stopwatch is extremely useful for measuring and documenting how long a paranormal activity lasts.
- *Sugar or salt*—No, you won't be doing any baking when investigating paranormal activity. By sprinkling salt or sugar around objects that a "ghost" might move, such as furniture, you can easily determine if movement has taken place based on how the sugar or salt is scattered around the object. This is a very low-tech alternative to using a motion detector.
- *Voice stress analyzer*—When it comes to interviewing witnesses who claim to have experienced or witnessed paranormal activity, not everyone will be reliable. To help determine if someone is lying, a voice stress analyzer can be used.

Parapsychology, the Paranormal, and Beyond

Parapsychology is the study of phenomena, real or supposed, which appear inexplicable under presently accepted scientific theories. The older term "psychical research" is still commonly used in Britain, but in America the subject is generally called "parapsychology." According to The Society for Psychical Research, the field of parapsychology is growing rapidly as more people are becoming interested in this field and are dedicating their professional lives to working in it.

The definition of parapsychology makes it difficult to set rigid limits on the topics included, but in practice the focus of interest in recent times has been on the acquisition of information in unexplained ways (extrasensory perception or ESP) and on physical effects brought about in unexplained ways (psychokinesis, paranormal healing, etc.).

The contemporary scene in psychical research involves work being done by philosophers, psychologists, and physicists, many of whom are on the faculty of distinguished universities and colleges both in the United States and abroad. Some of the information in this book has been derived from interviews and research conducted by parapsychologists.

Most parapsychologists and professional paranormal investigators take their work very seriously. There are, however, plenty of individuals and groups that take a much more light-hearted approach to ghosts and paranormal activity.

For example, there's a service called Rent-A-Ghost (*www.rent-a-ghost.co.uk*) based in England that refers to itself as the world's first ghost installation company. This nonprofit organization works in just about every field of the paranormal. Among other things, the group specializes in the extraction of ghostly forms from various types of properties around the world. They report, "Due to the popular notion of having one's own ghost, we have found ourselves in the business of installing more apparitions than we extract!" The group receives a wide range of requests from clients interested in obtaining all kinds of manifestations, ranging from headless monks, the classic moaning chain-rattlers, gray ladies, and mythical and historical beasts, to cute, furry (albeit dead) animals.

According to Rent-A-Ghost, "Understandably this concept will seem from the outset to be absolutely ridiculous, even outrageous to many. Comments from those in 'the know' range from, 'It shouldn't be done' and 'It can't be done' to 'You can't create apparitions to order.' Rent-A-Ghost would like it to be known that we fully understand and totally respect everyone's view on this matter. At Rent-A-Ghost, we rely on our own judgment in morality, and tend to tread carefully in all that we do. To reassure anyone who may feel a little uneasy in the notion of creating a manifestation to order, we are not in the business of removing souls from the spirit world for any reason, basically because it is totally unnecessary!"

This Is Only the Beginning

This chapter barely touched the surface in explaining what people believe ghosts, hauntings, and paranormal activity are all about. From this chapter, you hopefully learned a few basic terms and gathered a general understanding of the type of people currently researching and documenting paranormal activity throughout the world.

The purpose of this book is not to convince you that ghosts exist, nor is it to convince you that they don't. Obviously, since you're reading this book, you have at least a mild interest in paranormal activity. The goal of this book is to provide you with information, offer different points of view and opinions, and then allow you to reach your own conclusions. As you'll see, each chapter contains phone numbers, addresses, e-mail addresses, and Web sites you can visit in order to learn more information on specific topics. Hopefully this book will tap into your imagination and point you in the right direction as you attempt to learn more about the unknown.

What Is an Apparition?

An "apparition" is the manifestation of a spirit that is visible to the eye. An apparition typically does not interact or directly communicate with its witnesses. It is simply seen.

Chapter Two

Ghost Hunters, Parapsychologists, and Paranormal Investigators

We're told at the beginning of each *X-Files* episode that "The truth is out there." When it comes to investigating ghosts, spirits, poltergeists, hauntings, and other paranormal activity, it's the work of paranormal investigators, parapsychologists, and a wide range of other scientists and believers who have dedicated themselves to discovering the truth behind whether or not ghosts and other paranormal activities are real.

There are many questions surrounding what ghosts, spirits, and poltergeists actually are and whether or not a house or specific location can actually be "haunted" or possessed. In an attempt to answer these questions and uncover concrete scientific proof, the people featured in this chapter have dedicated their lives and careers to finding answers. As you'll see, these people come from a wide range of backgrounds, live and work in different places throughout the country, and have varying opinions about the origins of paranormal activity.

One thing is certain, however: The people you're about to read about have had many incredible experiences that have caused them to become die-hard believers in ghosts and paranormal activity, whether or not scientific evidence actually exists. Each has had firsthand experiences with the paranormal. Many of these people maintain Web sites. They invite e-mail or phone calls from people who have questions or need help understanding experiences they themselves have had.

The purpose of this section is to expose you, the reader, to the wide range of ideas, hypotheses, and discoveries that "experts" in the field of paranormal studies have uncovered. Hopefully, the work of these people will help you to formulate or better understand your own beliefs.

Loyd Auerbach

Founder, Office of Paranormal Investigations
Web site: *www.mindreader.com*

Loyd Auerbach has been featured on numerous television and radio shows and been the subject of many newspaper and magazine interviews. He has become one of America's most renowned paranormal investigators. In addition to founding the Office of Paranormal Investigations in 1989, he's the author of several popular books, including *Mind Over Matter* (published by Kensington Books) and *Psychic Dreaming* (published by Barnes and Noble). The first book he wrote, entitled *ESP, Hauntings and Poltergeists*, was re-released in late 2000.

Aeurbach's Fascination with the Paranormal

Auerbach's interest in the paranormal began in high school, when he joined a parapsychology club. In college, Auerbach majored in anthropology, studying supernatural folklore. He ultimately obtained a master's degree in parapsychology from John F. Kennedy University.

It was when the movie *Ghostbusters* was released in theaters back in the early 1980s that Auerbach first began receiving national media attention for his work as a real-life ghost buster. Aside from his work researching paranormal activity, Auerbach is a professional magician and mentalist. "Performing magic is all about the psychology of deception. It focuses on how you can make one thing look like something else. Working as a magician has helped me to better understand how people who believe they've witnessed paranormal phenomenon can easily make mistakes," he stated.

Auerbach is currently based in the San Francisco Bay area; however, his work has taken him all over the world. "The paranormal itself encompasses a wide range of things. In parapsychology, when you talk about paranormal, you're really talking about psychic experiences. I've always been an avid science fiction reader, so believing in paranormal events wasn't difficult for me. While I've always believed that some people have psychic abilities, I wasn't sure if ghosts were real spirits of people who had died, or if they were instead a phenomenon related to place memory. In 1985, I was involved with an investigation, however, where I was actually able to communicate with a ghost, ask it questions, and obtained answers which dramatically altered my thinking," said Auerbach.

What's a Place Memory?

This phenomena works very much like a VCR. A location that somehow captures the right type of energy can record an image of an event that once happened there and later replay it. This causes a psydo-apparition to appear, but because it's a recording of something that happened long ago, there is no interaction between the witness and the three-dimensional image that's recorded. "An apparition can be a visual form, but it's more often auditory, in the form of voices, footsteps, or other unusual noises that can't otherwise be explained." added Dr. Nicholes.

Many ghost experts and people who study the paranormal believe that there are ghosts everywhere. "This simply isn't a theory I buy into," said Auerbach. "I believe there is place memory everywhere and hauntings everywhere, because the environment has the ability to store information that can seem like ghosts, but I don't believe that actual ghosts, that are intelligent and interactive, can be found everywhere. This is an extremely rare occurrence. For an intelligent ghost to appear and interact with the living, I believe the environmental factors have to be just right, plus the intent of the person who has died has to be strong in order for him or her to stick around."

How Auerbach Conducts an Investigation

The procedures Auerbach uses to study a situation or paranormal occurrence vary greatly for each investigation. "Generally, the interview process with the people who claim to have experienced something paranormal is the most critical part of the entire investigation. When I'm asked what it's like working as a paranormal investigator, the occupation I equate it most to is that of an investigative journalist. My job is to ask a lot of questions and do a lot of background research. As far as I'm concerned, a house or location can be labeled as being haunted, but unless there are credible witnesses who have experienced the haunting, there's nothing to investigate even if I can use my high-tech tools to obtain strange readings at that location." He believes the experiences of witnesses can be more informative and revealing than unusual readings taken using his equipment.

Once Auerbach begins an investigation, his first job is to eliminate any obvious or nonsupernatural reasons why a strange phenomenon might have occurred. This means checking out the structure of the house; for example, looking for faulty electrical wiring, checking for chemical leaks, or determining if there are pipe problems in the house. "I also ascertain if the witness has been or is on drugs. I sometimes also ask health-related questions. Unless I

Local Ghost Hunters: Tennessee

The Tennessee Ghost Chasers is a member of the International Ghost Hunters Society. It offers a handbook and tutorials for those interested in ghost hunting, free membership, and stories and photographs. For more information check out *www.tnghost.com*.

can eliminate the normal reasons why something might have happened, I won't even assume something supernatural has taken place," said Auerbach.

There are often normal explanations for many of the events people initially think have something to do with the supernatural. Auerbach believes that once someone has an unusual experience, that person begins to notice everything that happens in his or her physical environment. If someone believes she's seen a ghost, she often becomes sensitized to look at everything happening around her and begins to lump other experiences or observations in with her ghost or haunting experience. "If someone, for example, sees the cat swatting at something in mid-air, it might get interpreted as a ghost being present. In every case, I find that people group in normal events with paranormal events," he said.

Auerbach's Tools of the Trade

When asked about the tools he uses, Auerbach explained, "People have been seeing ghosts for thousands of years. I don't rely on my gadgets or photography as proof of a paranormal event, because a thousand years ago, these gadgets didn't exist and there was no such thing as a camera or camcorder."

During an investigation Auerbach uses many different tools. Aside from a standard tape recorder to record his interviews and various standard photographic equipment, he uses a Tri-Field Meter. "There are often unusual magnetic fields found in locations where people believe they have seen a ghost or experienced a paranormal phenomenon. Sometimes we can contribute unusual energy fields to electrical devices and we always look for those first, before assuming it's supernatural in origin. My job is to correlate an unusual energy reading with a specific paranormal experience someone has had," said Auerbach, who also occasionally uses microwave detectors and Geiger counters to measure unusual energy readings.

There are different methods for measuring events associated with place memories, which are when apparitions appear at the

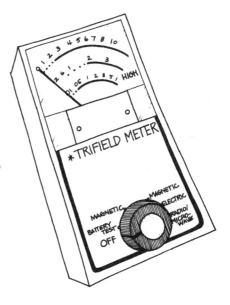

same time over and over again, show no sign of intelligence, and simply repeat the same movements.

"Apparitions are like recordings that are totally noninteractive. They tend to have higher-than-normal background magnetic fields present. We're not sure what causes this phenomenon, but it probably has something to do with the environment. Somehow, every once in a while, the unusual magnetic energy allows living people to see something that has happened at that location sometime in the past. The ghost someone sees in this situation is really an image from the past, not an actual ghost. I think the image someone sees is like a visual footprint left behind within the magnetic field that's present," explained Auerbach.

Auerbach's Theories and Philosophies

From a parapsychology standpoint, Auerbach believes that poltergeist phenomena is very different from what people see in the movies. A poltergeist isn't an evil spirit, according to Auerbach, but a manifestation of a living person's subconscious mind. "Objects move around, but this doesn't relate to ghosts. I believe poltergeist phenomena are caused by a living person whose subconscious mind is undergoing some type of stress and that person is basically blowing off steam. Very rarely does this type of phenomenon take on a physical form."

According to Auerbach, poltergeist phenomena typically involve objects moving, appliances turning themselves on and off, and strange noises. Most often when people see a ghost, however, it's not a poltergeist. "What they see is a three-dimensional image of something that looks human. Not everyone sees ghosts, however. Some people hear them, feel them, or smell them," said Auerbach.

If a ghost is actually seen, Auerbach believes the form it takes is somewhat reminiscent of what that person looked like when he or she was alive. "A ghost wears clothing, which is an unusual thing onto itself. Basically, ghosts look like people, although they're sometimes translucent or transparent. In some cases, people have reported a fog-like appearance, but these witnesses had the sense

Local Ghost Hunters: Ohio

The Ohio Ghost Hunters Society offers tips on hunting ghosts, a list of haunted places in Ohio, and photographs of local ghosts. For more information or to fill out a membership form, check out *http://toghs.virtualave.net.*

that the entity was in fact a person. Too many people see fog or an unusual mist and believe it's a ghost. These people don't, however, get the feeling that there's someone actually present when they see the fog or mist," said Auerbach.

Smells that are associated with ghosts often have to do with something related to the person who died. For example, the person seeing a ghost of a dead relative will smell that person's aftershave, cologne, or smoke from his favorite brand of cigar. "I had an experience with a friend of mine who died. About a week and a half later, I felt his presence in my car and smelled his cigar smoke. When alive, he had psychic ability, which is one reason why I believe he was able to return and make his presence known. It may feel like a ghost is touching you, but there's no physical touch actually going on. My theory is that ghosts are consciousness or pure mind, created from energy. Ghosts have no mouths with which to speak, because they are energy based. These are not physical manifestations. They are perceptual manifestations. Thus, the ghosts appear to us in the forms that they want to be seen in," he said.

Auerbach doesn't believe that there's a direct correlation between where ghosts appear and whether or not something tragic once happened at that location. One example he offers is a recent investigation he conducted aboard a United States aircraft carrier. The ghosts present aboard this ship didn't die on the ship. Upon doing research, it was discovered that the people involved died of natural causes at other locations and returned to the ship they had served on earlier in their lives. "In this investigation, the energy readings we took were totally useless because of the metal and electrical fields that are naturally present on the ship itself. What we had to do was rely almost totally on the human experience or witnesses," said Auerbach.

Unlike many organizations that investigate paranormal activity, Auerbach stated that the goal of the Office of Paranormal Investigations is somewhat different. "Our goal is to go in and help people understand what's going on, and not necessarily remove the phenomenon. We help people come to some sort of resolution

Local Ghost Hunters: Atlantic

The Atlantic Paranormal Society offers private investigations, documentation of the paranormal including photographs and stories, and tips for ghost hunting. For more information, photos, and stories, check out the Web site at *www.the-atlantic-paranormal-society.com.*

about what they're experiencing so that they're no longer afraid and can live with it. I see my work often as being an arbitrator between a family living in a house that they believe is haunted and the paranormal phenomenon itself," he said.

Often, when someone takes a picture of floating orbs or strange mist, Auerbach believes those photos mean absolutely nothing in terms of paranormal phenomena. He explained, "People take these strange pictures in cemeteries, however, based on my experience, ghosts that have intelligence and personality don't hang out in cemeteries. The orbs people photograph aren't ghosts. There is definitely some other phenomenon happening there. I think people have incredible expectations when they go out to photograph paranormal phenomena, especially in a place like a cemetery. They don't actually see anything unusual with their own eyes, but they're able to capture orbs or other strange images on film. I think people's expectations cause things to happen using psychokinesis or other psychic abilities they may or may not know they have. If they see strange mist, I believe that's a normal environmental phenomenon. Trying to take pictures in a dark place can cause a wide range of photographic errors to occur. It's these photographic errors that appear in prints or negatives, which people often interpret as being ghosts or spirits."

Based on his experience and research, Auerbach feels that ghosts make themselves visible in places where they had a strong connection when they were alive and they typically appear before people they were close to. "The ghost that I actually got to communicate with and ask questions of was female. She appeared within the house she lived in almost her entire life, but she didn't die there, nor did she experience a sudden or tragic death. She died of natural causes in a hospital, but later returned to her home as a ghost. Hauntings or apparitions, on the other hand, are highly emotionally charged images that are often a result of tragedy or violence," said Auerbach.

Incredible Firsthand Experiences

While it's possible to study the paranormal from a theoretical point of view, Auerbach and other investigators take their work into the trenches, so to speak, and conduct their own research. This often results in some incredible firsthand encounters with para- normal activity—not all of which can be explained.

When Auerbach had the opportunity to interview the female ghost he encountered, one question he asked was, "What is it like to be a ghost?" According to Auerbach, "The response I received was, that as far as she knew, she was a ball of energy, which was basically her mind. She attempted to communicate with others by somehow linking to their minds, but she was hesitant to make her- self known because she didn't want to scare anyone. This ghost was seen by multiple people, but for each person, her appearance was different. I asked her why that was, and her response was that her appearance had to do with how she felt about herself that day. If she felt like an old lady, that's how she appeared. If she felt like a child, she'd appear as a child. Her appearance was her own idea of self identity that day. She also was able to determine what type of clothing she would be seen wearing. When people visualize themselves, they typically think of themselves with clothing on. Thus, ghosts think about their appearance in much the same way. When asked why she was present, she stated that she had no clue about why she stuck around as a ghost, but when she died, she didn't want to go to hell. Since she wasn't a religious person when alive, she didn't know if she'd wind up in heaven or hell, so she stuck around in a place that was familiar to her."

During his investigations, Auerbach refuses to allow himself to get scared by the paranormal phenomena he experiences. He does, however, get scared by some of the living people he meets who are experiencing paranormal phenomena and request his help. "Ghosts don't carry guns and knives. There is nothing that I know of, except for my own fear, that can harm me during an investiga- tion or an interaction with a ghost. However, there is plenty that can hurt me on the human side. There are plenty of angry and disturbed people who are living out there who I have had to deal with," said Auerbach, who believes that ghosts were once people and that people in general are good.

"Someone's personality does not dramatically change after death. I also don't believe that the truly evil people have the mental

Local Ghost Hunters: Massachusetts

The Massachusetts Ghost Hunters Society offers private investiga- tions and photographs of the paranormal, as well as membership for those interested. For more information, check out *www.homestead.com/ mghs/ghost.html*.

Where Can Ghosts Be Found?

According to the Ghost Preservation League, almost anywhere! Cemeteries, abandoned town sites, historical sites, and sites of emotional upheaval are common places where paranormal activity takes place. The organization reports, "If you are just starting out and need some results in a hurry, try an old cemetery, unless you live near a battlefield of some sort, or a place where a tragic situation occurred. It is always important, however, to respect private property and no trespassing signs."

wherewithal to stay around after their death as ghosts. In poltergeist cases, there are objects that fly around at random and there is at times danger involved, but I don't believe poltergeist phenomena are caused by ghosts or spirits. I have seen instances where living people who are causing the poltergeist phenomena actually wind up hurting themselves," explained Auerbach.

According to Auerbach, parapsychologists don't go around looking for or studying demons. The idea of a demon is completely mythological and has a religious connotation. Demons have nothing to do with science at all. "If you wanted to say there are evil entities out there, that's possible, but I don't believe in demons. Evil is a human construct. What is evil depends on a lot of things, including a society's ethics and morals. There don't seem to be truly evil forces out there. Nuclear power can be used for good or evil, for example, but it is not inherently evil. It is just there. There is energy out there that can be used for good or evil, but it is not inherently evil. This is a common misconception," explained Auerbach.

Another common misconception, Auerbach stated, is that ghosts can possess people without permission. "Channeling and spirit mediumship is a very permissive thing, where people allow themselves to supposedly be taken over by a ghost or spirit. Most of the time, however, people who experience this phenomenon aren't channeling ghosts or entities. There's an entirely different process going on. They're either being psychic or they're basically allowing themselves to shift into an altered state so that their subconscious can begin speaking for them," said Auerbach.

Tips for People Who Have Had Paranormal Experiences

If someone believes his or her home is haunted, Auerbach suggests first looking for other possible reasons why the strange events are taking place and then keeping detailed notes over a period of time as to what exactly is happening. He suggests calling experts for advice, but not jumping to the immediate conclusion that there's a ghost present. "You should be curious, not afraid. Don't assume whatever you experience can or will cause you harm. If you do see, feel, or hear a ghost, ask what it wants. Sometimes, you'll actually get an answer. Most people aren't of the mind to ask the ghost questions, so they never receive answers. I consider ghosts, spirits, and consciousness to be the same thing," he said.

Auerbach warns that if you believe you've experienced paranormal activity and seek out the help of a professional, it's important to be sure you're dealing with someone who is credible. He suggests contacting an established organization, such as the American Society of Psychical Research (*www.aspr.com*), for a referral.

"There are many people out there who charge a fortune for their services who are absolute frauds. People who do paranormal investigations for a living and who are credible don't do this for the money and don't typically earn a living doing it. Beware of any promises someone makes. Nobody can guarantee the removal of any type of paranormal phenomenon. Anyone who does is either misrepresenting himself or is an out-and-out fraud. The other thing to watch out for is someone who immediately says 'It's evil.' If they use the word 'evil' right off the bat, that's an indication to me that the person is a fraud."

Denise Jones

Founder, Foundation for L.I.F.E.
P.O. Box 1112, Manchester, CT 06045-1112
E-mail: *djones1315@aol.com*
Web site: *www.paranormalhelp.com*

Denise Jones has dedicated her life to this field for a very personal reason—to help and protect her son (whose story will be summarized shortly). She is a native of Connecticut and has been helping people in one way or another as part of her livelihood for more than fifteen years. Until the early 1990s, she worked in the geriatric field; however, she was forced to leave her job once the paranormal situation with her son began.

Jones's Fascination with the Paranormal

In the process of seeking help for her son, Denise Jones ultimately founded the Foundation for L.I.F.E. (Living In Fear Ends), which was formed to be a free resource to help others in dire need, just as she was in need in 1992. "At that time there weren't any organizations we could turn to. After our ordeal was resolved, I formed the Foundation to prevent others from having to go through years of fear and loneliness that my family did."

Through her own research and experience, Jones has learned, "Paranormal phenomena are a universal experience. It is not specific to any race, geographical area, or religion. Stories and events associated with hauntings and possessions have been recorded since man has been able to write. In every corner of the world, since the days of the caveman up through today, the type of events associated with the paranormal are essentially the same. It is only the way we deal with it that may have changed during the course of history."

Incredible Firsthand Experiences

While her own story sounds like the premise for the movie *The Sixth Sense*, Denise Jones and her son have lived it firsthand. According to Jones, her story began with a scream from her then-five-year-old son, Michael. He was "afraid of the man who kept trying to touch him." This "man," however, would disappear, or was not visible to Jones or anyone else (other than her son). As the years progressed, so did the haunting activities her son and later she experienced. Constant whispering or talking was heard by all of her family members, whether they were alone or together. Events began to deteriorate as Denise witnessed her son being slapped or hit by unseen hands. "Consider the anguish of watching your child scream and thrash around as cuts and scraps appear of their own volition," she said.

Once Jones became determined to find help for her son, she described a sense of helplessness, because she didn't know where to turn. She was considered crazy by people around her and by many of the people she contacted. Jones first turned to her church, only to be turned away. In the beginning she was afraid everyone would think she and her son were nuts. She knew, however, it wasn't their collective imaginations that were shaking the beds, smashing their possessions, moving pictures, throwing objects around rooms, or banging and pounding on the walls at night. The activity finally got to the point where it was keeping her and her son awake night after night. "And so, we continued in our search for help," she explained.

After searching for over five years, Jones finally came across two paranormal investigators who agreed to offer their assistance. "They did substantiate our claims and were successful in photographing several ghosts as well as capturing on audiotape recordings of three separate demon entity voices. The investigators gathered all the information from the medical testing that was done on us. All of these tests only confirmed what we knew all along: Michael was completely healthy. The medical testing and the results of the photos and tapes finally got the attention of the local Bishop, who agreed that Michael was in the early stages of possession. From that point on, things began to move rapidly," she recalls.

Jones's son eventually underwent an exorcism. While her son still has a special gift, the evil entities that seemed to interact with him appear now to be under control. "At this point, the investigators who up until now had proved to be so helpful suddenly changed. They asked me to sign away the rights to our story. Upon refusal to do so, they withheld the photos and tapes of my investigation, and I am still unable to obtain even copies of this very private information. Although we were still experiencing activity to some extent, the investigators completely ignored our pleas for help. They appeared to be unhappy about the fact that there had been no formal closure in the case and would not respond to us or the attorney who represented us. We had trusted them with our very lives, but were ultimately hurt and confused by their reactions. Again we were alone with the remainder of our ordeal."

Local Ghost Hunters: Texas

The South Texas Paranormal Society offers investigations and documentation of the paranormal including photographs, EVPs, and stories. For more information, check out *www.angelfire.com/sk2/stparnormal.*

With the help of the public, media contacts, and her attorney, Jones has gathered many reputable paranormal investigators, psychics, and parapsychologists throughout the United States and formed the Foundation for L.I.F.E. "We investigated each of their credentials before asking them to come aboard. People can be confident that any investigator recommended by us is of the highest reputable quality and will function in a completely professional and discreet manner," she said.

"Michael still has a gift. He sees ghosts walking around. No matter where we are, if there's a ghost in the area, he can see it and often communicate with it. He's twelve years old now, but still sometimes gets scared at the things he experiences. Most of the time, however, he has learned to deal with his gift. He has the ability to sense if a ghost is good or bad," stated Jones, who wrote her own book describing her son's ordeal. The book, entitled *The Other Side*, was published in October 2000 by Horizons Press.

Tips for People Who Have Had Paranormal Experiences

"Unfortunately, someone who is experiencing paranormal activity and who is bothered or scared by it can't simply open the phonebook and seek out help. This was my experience and the reason why I founded the Foundation for L.I.F.E. When someone writes, calls, or e-mails me, I am able to provide them with a resource in his or her area. I have gathered a database of over 300 paranormal investigators who have met my criteria for being reputable and knowledgeable," said Jones.

Since launching the Foundation for L.I.F.E., Jones has accompanied several investigators on paranormal investigations. Between these experiences and her own, she has learned a lot about paranormal activity. "If someone believes his or her home is haunted, it's important to learn as much about the history of the location as possible. It's also helpful to determine if other people have had similar experiences at that location," said Jones.

Based on her experience, Jones believes that ghosts, spirits, apparitions, and poltergeists can take on a variety of appearances.

Reliable Help for Paranormal Problems

The Foundation for L.I.F.E. maintains a database of trustworthy resources that people who are experiencing paranormal activity can turn to. Denise Jones states that everything within the Foundation's power has been done to assure that any representative sent as a referral from her group is highly professional and utterly moral. A good investigator cares for the client and helps him or her through the entire ordeal until it's over. Keeping this in mind, she offered the following advice:

- Never give money to an investigator who states that he is from the Foundation for L.I.F.E. The people working for the Foundation typically do so on a volunteer basis.

- Do not disclose any personal information concerning money or valuable items.
- Do not sign a contract with any investigative group or individual unless you contact the Foundation first.
- Do not follow any advice that goes against your better judgment.
- Make sure the investigator has credentials and that those credentials are real. This can often be done by contacting the organization or university he or she works for. Referrals are also useful for checking credentials.
- Report any and all unprofessional or unethical behavior by an investigator or investigative group to the Foundation for L.I.F.E.

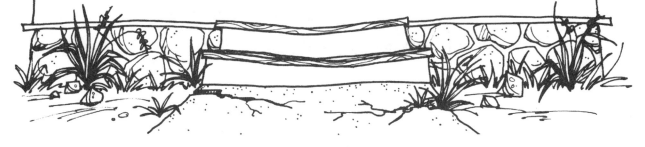

"We've seen it all," she says. "We've seen them take the form of lightning-like flashes and we've seen them take on a full human-like form, for example. My son has also seen demons who start off looking like cute little boys and then transform into grotesque-looking older men. I don't think ghosts only appear in places where a tragedy has occurred. I believe they go where they want to go. My son has talked to his former best friend who passed away. This communication happened in my son's bedroom, but his friend didn't die there."

Jones's Theories and Philosophies

When asked if she believes a ghost is the same as someone's soul, Jones stated that she believes ghosts (not poltergeists or demons) are in fact what remains of those who have died.

While nobody has been able to explain exactly why Jones's son has the ability to see and communicate with ghosts and other entities, Jones believes it has something to do with the fact that her son actually died during childbirth several times and was brought back to life. This ability to communicate with ghosts, she believes, is a trait that her son shares with many other people who have had near death experiences. "I think people who have had a near death experience [when someone dies and is brought back to life] tend to develop some type of psychic or supernatural ability that allows them to somehow tap a portion of their brain that most people can't or don't use," she said.

Lucy Keas

Professional Ghost Hunter/Investigator
Founder, The Michigan Ghost Hunters Society
E-mail: LKeas@tmghs.com
Web site: www.tmghs.com

Ghost hunter Lucy Keas has been preparing for her job for her entire life. She is in her early-thirties and has been living in the

Michigan area for about three years; however, she grew up in the Chicago area in a home that she firmly believes was haunted. While growing up she lived near her best friend, whose house was also haunted. Keas has since returned to her friend's home and performed a complete paranormal investigation, during which she confirmed the house is, as far as she's concerned, haunted.

While in college, Keas studied biology and currently earns a living as a professional Web site designer as well as a ghost hunter/paranormal investigator. In May 1999, she founded the Michigan Ghost Hunters Society after dating someone who also believed deeply in the paranormal and had a strong interest in it.

The Michigan Ghost Hunters Society has been growing extremely quickly and currently consists of several hundred members. The Web site Keas created continues to be bombarded with individuals in the Michigan area who request help in trying to get rid of a ghost that's haunting their home or who want to put a stop to other paranormal activity that's been happening around them.

Over the years Keas has obtained a wide range of photographic, audiotape, and videotape evidence of paranormal activity, using a variety of high-tech gear to obtain unusual energy and temperature readings in areas she believes to be haunted.

Local Ghost Hunters: South Carolina

The Paranormal Search and Investigation Group offers investigations of the paranormal. For more information, check out *www.angelfire.com/ct2/PDIG/ PSIG1.html.*

Keas's Fascination with the Paranormal

Keas's interest in the paranormal began at an early age when she experienced unusual events taking place in the home she grew up in. "I grew up in a large family, with three brothers and a sister. One of my brothers also experienced paranormal activity while growing up; however, none of my other siblings or my parents ever believed me. I would experience lights and electrical appliances, such as the television, turning on and off by themselves. This became a regular occurrence while growing up," she recalled.

Although a wide range of unusual things happened to Keas during her childhood, she never actually saw a ghost, spirit, or apparition appear before her in her own home. However, she did hear and feel a presence. She believes everyone has the ability to be an open portal to hear, see, or feel ghosts or spirits, but people have to practice becoming attuned to what's happening around them. "I have had entities throw temper tantrums in front of me. This included making loud noises and moving objects around me," Keas said, although she is the first to say that she doesn't hold conversations with ghosts on a regular basis.

Over time, Keas feels she has developed the ability to hear and communicate with ghosts and spirits. "Growing up, I had many paranormal experiences in my best friend's house. My friend and I would have slumber parties and wake up to stuffed animals waving at us and moving. We'd also see candy flying out of dishes, for example. While I haven't been able to do an investigation in the house I grew up in, I have returned to my friend's home and conducted a full investigation. What I found was what I believe to be many spirits or ghosts living there. As it turned out, the house is very old and has a lot of good and bad history associated with it," she said.

For Keas, experiencing fear is all part of her job when she embarks on an investigation. Like so many other investigators or ghost hunters, Keas begins every investigation with a thorough prequalification interview that she conducts with people seeking her help.

Incredible Firsthand Experiences

In 1991, Keas had her scariest experience to date. It happened on Easter. She explained that her grandmother had recently passed away and had died in Keas's bedroom. She had been bedridden prior to her death. Within a five-minute period, Keas experienced three different events happen in her home that ultimately sent her out of her house terrified. "Boxes were being thrown, for example. We heard pounding and pacing coming from the upstairs which we knew was empty. It was as if someone was stomping through the house," she said. Despite having had many scary experiences, Keas has never felt as though her life was in danger as the result of a ghost, spirit, poltergeist, or other form of paranormal activity. Some of her clients, she stated, haven't been so lucky, although she hasn't heard any reports of anyone ever being killed by a supernatural event.

When going into an investigation, Keas takes several precautions to protect herself and her team. "A spirit mainly consists of energy. We can counteract their effects with our own energy. I use white light and salt as a protection device. Salt is also used to cleanse an area that's believed to be haunted. Every one of our clients has a different religious or spiritual belief. These people often use religious objects for protection. It doesn't matter what object or relic they use, because it's someone's religious or spiritual belief that gives an object or relic power against evil. As a result, we adapt our practices to take into account the beliefs of our clients. If someone has requested my help, they already believe in the paranormal," she said.

Keas's Theories and Philosophies

As to why ghosts and spirits make themselves known to living people, Keas's beliefs coincide with many other people who have studied this type of phenomenon. She believes there are three primary reasons why ghosts make themselves known. The first is that the entity doesn't know it's gone. The second is that the entity is very angry and didn't want to go, so it's purposely staying. The third reason is that they have strong emotional ties and it's their living family members or loved ones who keep them close by, often unknowingly.

How Keas Conducts an Investigation

Whenever Keas embarks on an investigation, after conducting her preinterview, she sets specific rules for the people

Local Ghost Hunters: Utah

The Utah Ghost Hunters Society offers results of investigations, true ghost stories, and maps of paranormal activity in the Utah area. For more information, check out *www.ghostwave.com.*

who requested her help. Most importantly, she won't permit children to be present during the investigation. She also insists that the house be quiet and that only the adults actually living in the home or people who are directly involved in the case be present.

"I have the client accompany me throughout the house and the surrounding property as I conduct my investigation. I typically invite a team of several qualified people to also accompany me. This team consists of two to four individuals. At least one of the team members will be as open as I am, so I can receive help picking up vibes from the location. My other team members will have other skills or specialties. One person will be in charge of temperature gauging throughout the site. Another team member will be in charge of the photographic equipment and taking pictures, while a third person will handle analog or digital audio recording," said Keas, who has spent considerable time developing a team she trusts. This team is comprised of people she describes as totally reliable, dedicated, and whom she works well with.

After an investigation, if Keas determines some type of paranormal activity is present, she offers her clients several options. "Once someone understands the phenomenon they're experiencing, they often don't mind living with it. Many of my clients, however, are having problems with evil spirits or events that are disrupting their lives. In these situations, they want the entities, whether they're good or evil, removed from their home. In a few cases, the people find themselves to be in physical danger. For example, one client had a butcher knife fly at him. It was clear this person wanted the entity removed," she said.

To remove an entity from a location, Keas "bans" it from a location. "After an investigation, you can usually get a good sense of who the spirit or entity is and hopefully find out why they're making themselves known. When we decide to remove an entity from a location, we create a protection circle in order to keep the evil energy out of our space. We then undergo a series of

Local Ghost Hunters: Missouri

The Ghost Hunters of St. Louis Transcendental Society offers investigations of the paranormal, guidelines for investigating, and links to other resources. For more information, check out *www.ghosts.veryweird.com.*

procedures to remove the entity. Once it's removed, I follow up with the client in two weeks, two months, and then in two years to ensure there are no longer any problems," explained Keas.

While Keas has had experiences where an entity didn't want to leave a location, she has always managed to force them from the location using her methods. She said, "I have had entities follow me back to my home. I need to cleanse my own home at least once per month. Sometimes, it gets pretty weird."

One of the problems Keas sometimes runs into during an investigation is that the entities she's investigating drain the power from the battery-powered equipment she's using. This, she believes, happens because the entities are energy based and have the ability to steal energy. "When a fully charged battery pack suddenly goes dead on a camcorder during an investigation, for example, that's usually evidence to me of a very agitated spirit. There have been times when I get so pissed off at an entity that I tell 'em off. I know people think I'm crazy when I do this, but this type of verbal and mental communication with an entity often is effective in getting a situation under control," said Keas. "I consider entitles to be like children. If they're going to have a temper tantrum, I let them. I do my best to avoid getting too angry or too scared, so that I'm not providing energy that the entities need to manifest themselves. I've actually had an entity call me a bitch once during an investigation."

When communicating with ghosts or spirits, Keas uses a combination of verbal communication and telepathy. She seldom, however, receives an audible response from the entities she's communicating with. "Entities can sense the emotional state of the people they interact with. Sometimes, they use this to their advantage," explained Keas.

If someone believes their home is haunted, Keas encourages the person to do extensive research into the history of the home and property. She also tells people to evaluate what's happening in their own lives.

"Things that happen out of the ordinary always happen for a reason. This often means that the emotional and mental state of the person experiencing the paranormal phenomenon has changed in some way. This could be for good or bad reasons and involve positive or negative emotions. If I can establish what's happening in someone's life, it often helps me to determine how I can best help with the situation. If nothing has changed in someone's personal life, but paranormal events start to happen, that's when a full investigation is often needed to determine what's going on," said Keas.

There is no doubt in Keas's mind that she continues to experience a wide range of paranormal activities and that some areas she visits are in fact haunted. "I don't know, however, if the ghosts or spirits I am dealing with are the souls of human beings who have died. I have seen no conclusive proof either way," she said.

Keas's Tools of the Trade

As part of her investigations, Keas uses a variety of different pieces of high-tech gear. "One of my favorite 'toys' is an infrared thermal scanner which can take measurements in very low-light areas. In less than a tenth of a second, I can gauge the temperature of an area and measure any sudden temperate changes. A

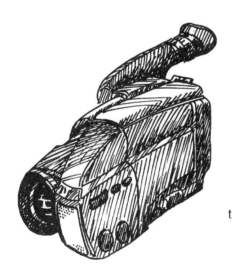

drop or increase in a room's temperature usually indications the presence of some type of paranormal activity. I also use digital photography equipment as well as more traditional 35mm cameras. I have at my disposal high-end analog audio recording equipment. I usually use analog audio recording devices because I have discovered that transmissions from cordless telephones in the area, for example, can alter a digital audio recording," she said.

Keas also uses several different types of camcorders for capturing video documentation during her investigations. She admits that the results are totally different for each investigation; however, the most common paranormal activity she has documented are floating orbs of light. "These look like cells under a microscope. They're all ovular or circular shaped and pretty transparent. They look like balls of light. I have captured this phenomenon in both still photographs as well as on video. On rarer occasions, I'll capture ectoplasm or some kind of apparition. Whenever I do capture this type of phenomenon, I always determine if the orbs could have been caught on film as a result of strange lighting or reflections in the area or if the film could have been tampered with," she explained.

There are many possible explanations for why orbs are the most common form of paranormal phenomenon people see and are able to capture on film. Keas believes that these forms are newly formed souls, created from energy, that haven't yet learned how to form themselves into more recognizable shapes, such as that of a human. "When you hear stories about full apparitions roaming throughout an area, these are often entities that have been around for a very long time. These entities have learned how to control their energy and form it," she stated.

Once data is gathered from an investigation, Keas uses several different computers with specialized software packages to filter the audio, video, or photographic data in an attempt to analyze it and compare it to other data, from other locations or investigations, that has already been obtained. "The first objective is to ensure the data we gathered is legitimate and that it's not a hoax or something that we ourselves somehow created by accident," said Keas, who explained that analyzing traditional 35mm film is difficult, because anomalies that appear on the film or negatives can be a result of bad film, improper processing, or errors that occurred while taking the photographs. For this reason, Keas prefers analyzing data that was compiled digitally, because the chances of error or bad film are greatly reduced or eliminated. The quality of the data—whether it's audio, video, or photographic—is also typically much more detailed and

Local Ghost Hunters: Pennsylvania

The Pennsylvania Ghost Hunters Society is a member of the International Ghost Hunters Society. It offers workshops, photographs of ghosts, and investigations of the paranormal. For more information, check out *http://users.desupernet. net/rfisher/pghs.html.*

can more easily be analyzed using computers, because the data is already in digital form.

Tips for People Who Have Had Paranormal Experiences

In conclusion, Keas stated, "Paranormal events do happen. The best thing people can do is arm themselves with knowledge. The biggest problem people have if they think they're experiencing something paranormal, is that they hire an investigator or psychic who isn't legitimate to investigate the situation, and they wind up with poor information. Don't invite someone into your home unless you know the person is legitimate. Ask for references and try to obtain referrals. Do your research. The Web is an ideal resource for tracking down information."

L'Aura Muller

Co-Founder, New Jersey Ghost Hunters Society
Ghost Hunters, Inc.
P.O. Box 2672, Westfield, NJ 07091
(908) 654-7502
Web site: *www.njghs.net*

Jeff and L'Aura Muller are a husband-and-wife team of more than sixteen years who have been ghost hunting together for more than six years. They are members of the American Society of Psychical Research (ASPR) and the International Ghost Hunters Society (IGHS). Additionally they have been recognized as Inner Circle Society Award Members of the IGHS, and members of the Cosmic Society of Paranormal Investigators. Their experiences have led them to investigate cemeteries, private homes, businesses, and even college dorms. Together they have founded the New Jersey Ghost Hunters Society (NJGHS). The group's Web site offers a list of haunted locations within New Jersey that the organization has investigated as well as other information of interest to ghost hunters.

The Mullers' Fascination with the Paranormal

Their interest in ghosts and the paranormal began when L'Aura Muller and her husband went on an organized ghost tour. After the tour, they started discussing what they experienced and discovered they both had a strong interest in this subject matter. "We started doing our own research and participating in other groups comprised of ghost hunters and people with an interest in ghosts. In 1998, we attended the International Ghost Hunters Society's annual meeting. While at this meeting my husband and I learned that no local chapters of the organization had yet been formed in the New Jersey area. Shortly thereafter, we founded the New Jersey Ghost Hunters Society," recalled Muller.

Thus far in her career, Muller has participated in over a hundred investigations. For her, an investigation begins with a telephone interview with witnesses of paranormal activity, during which she asks a few key questions to determine the legitimacy of the call. If a call sounds legitimate and captures the attention of the Mullers, they will gather a team of between six and eight people and launch an investigation.

How the Mullers Conduct an Investigation

"The first thing we do when we reach the site of an investigation is an in-person interview with each of the witnesses. I ask the people to have a chronology of events that have already occurred written up for us. I audio record all of my interviews, asking each person involved the same questions. We then go on a walkthrough of the location and begin taking pictures and measurements. Once everything is set up at the location, we do a lot of watching and waiting. During this time, we'll take 35mm photographs, shoot video,

The New Jersey Ghost Hunters Society Mission Statement

According to the New Jersey Ghost Hunters Society, its mission is: "To search out and obtain definitive proof of the existence of life beyond the grave and other paranormal activity." L'Aura Muller added, "Things that go bump in the night are more prevalent than you might think. Ghosts are here and there. We, the founders of NJGHS, have witnessed their existence on a firsthand basis. We have obtained proof on 35mm film. We have been on investigations of various places, from historic sites to modern-day dorm rooms on college campuses."

record audio, and take EMF readings at the location. We also use a video camera capable of shooting infrared images, a thermal scanner, motion detectors, as well as a digital camera," said Muller.

"We later analyze our results, summarize what we found, and present it to the people who originally contacted us. Out of all of the investigations I've participated in, one stands out in my mind. There was a house in Plainsboro, New Jersey, that contained a staircase where years ago, the woman of the house was believed to have fallen to her death. One night, it was getting late and I was sitting on those stairs resting while several other people on my team were taking various types of readings. As I was sitting there, I started to get very cold on my right side. My husband took thermal measurements and found that the area on the right side of me was eight degrees cooler than the area on my left side. We then took pictures all around me. In the photos, orbs were appearing all around my right side. This was the first time I actually felt something firsthand and was able to obtain physical proof that something unusual was happening," said Muller.

There have also been times, according to Muller, where a ghost has been detected but not seen by her team. She has, however, been able to record voices on audiotape. "In some of these circumstances, the ghosts say short sentences, usually in response to something that was taking place in the room. For example, there was one instance when I was talking with the person living in the house we were investigating and she said that the hauntings typically take place between 9 P.M. and 3 A.M. On the interview tape, however, there was a second voice that stated, 'Yes, 9 P.M.,'" said Muller.

Muller's Theories and Philosophies

Muller believes there are many reasons why a ghost may remain earthbound after its death. One reason, she hypothesizes, is because relatives are grieving so strongly, it prevents that spirit from crossing over. The strong emotions from the living generate an energy that somehow forces the spirit to stay in our realm. "There are also spirits or ghosts that simply don't know they are dead, and others that are somehow tied to a specific location where something tragic has occurred. I have seen photos of ghosts and spirits that have taken on many different forms. I have taken photos of floating orbs and vapors and have taken audio recordings of what I believe to be ghosts or spirits. I have yet to see an actual apparition, however," she said.

While Muller admits to have gotten scared during a few of her investigations, she never believes she has been in any danger from the ghosts, spirits, or paranormal activity taking place at the sites she's investigated. "Many of the people I have met co-exist with ghosts or spirits that exist within their homes and have no real problems. If someone believes his house is haunted, I suggest that he bring in experienced investigators as opposed to conducting his own investigation. Some of the common things people experience are cold spots, objects being moved, doors opening or closing, strange noises, or flickering of lights. Electrical appliances, such as TVs, will sometimes randomly turn on and off or switch channels. It's much less common for someone to actually see an apparition or some other visual manifestation," added Muller.

Tips for People Who Have Had Paranormal Experiences

Over the years, people from all walks of life—including doctors, lawyers, law enforcement officers, homemakers, and teachers—have contacted the Mullers with very credible stories of experiences they've had. "I think anyone with an open mind has the ability to see ghosts or experience paranormal activity. If someone is living with a ghost they'd like to get rid of, there are several methods of cleansing that can be done at a location," she said. Once people living with a ghost understand what they're experiencing, the living people can often live in harmony with the ghost or paranormal activity.

Local Ghost Hunters: New Jersey

The New Jersey Ghost Hunters Society is a member of the International Ghost Hunters Society. It offers investigations of the paranormal, a listing of haunted sites in New Jersey, and membership to the society. For more information, check out *www.njghs.net.*

Crisis Apparitions

According to Dr. Nicholes, "Apparitions, better known as 'ghosts,' appear to be some form of the human mind (consciousness, personality, soul, spirit) that functions apart from the body and may survive the death of the body. Reports indicate that apparitions indeed act like 'real' humans. They have the personality and emotions and act and dress like the people they were when alive. Crisis apparitions— apparitions of the dying or recently dead (usually fewer than twelve hours, but as much as twenty-four to forty-eight hours)—are the most frequently reported kind of apparitions."

Dr. Andrew Nicholes

Psychical Research Foundation, Inc.
P.O. Box 142193, Gainesville, FL 32614-2193
(352) 371-7363
Web site: *www.afterlife-psychical.org*

Dr. Nicholes is a psychologist by training as well as a professional parapsychologist. He is a professor of both psychology and parapsychology in Gainesville, Florida. His particular area of interest and expertise is in haunting and poltergeist investigations, which he's been pursuing for more than twenty-five years. Thus far in his career, Dr. Nicholes has been an active participant in several hundred investigations both in America and abroad.

Dr. Nicholes is a lecturer and active member of the Parapsychology Association, which is the only professional association for parapsychologists in the world. He's also the founder of the Florida Psychical Research Foundation (PRF). He currently has a research grant that he's using to study the neuropsychological and electromagnetic aspects of hauntings and poltergeists.

Dr. Nicholes's Fascination with the Paranormal

Dr. Nicholes's interest in ghosts, hauntings, and poltergeist activity stems from an experience he had at the age of twelve, shortly after his younger sister was killed in an automobile accident. This traumatic experience led to the young Nicholes having nightmares. About four months after his sister's death, he recalls having an apparitional experience during which he saw his younger sister standing in his bedroom. Since childhood, Dr. Nicholes has always been interested in science, however, it was this experience of seeing an apparition of his sister that captured his interest and imagination, causing him to dedicate his career to better understanding supernatural phenomena.

How Dr. Nicholes Conducts an Investigation

According to Dr. Nicholes, every investigation begins with a detailed telephone interview. "The very first step is to do an extensive telephone interview with the person or people who have experienced something unusual. Our goal is to weed out people who aren't serious or who have psychological problems," he said.

"Due to financial and time constraints, generally, I won't take a case and pursue an investigation unless there's more than one witness involved. I also look for cases where there are multiple witnesses who aren't related. During the course of the interview, I determine if the person's experience is along the lines of what's been experienced by other people, from other cases I've investigated. Obviously, my goal is to eliminate the possibility of fraud or mental instability. If I determine that an onsite investigation is warranted, the first thing I ask people to do is create a floor plan of the site and indicate all of the places where something unusual has occurred," he said.

Upon arriving at the site itself, Dr. Nicholes begins by doing a detailed in-person interview with the primary witnesses involved with the case. "I try to interview everyone separately and determine if all of the stories coincide with each other. I then follow up these interviews by giving the people a series of psychological tests, in the form of written questionnaires. I have found that people who experience something supernatural are prone to having these types of experiences, and typically they've had them, in one form or another, before. One of the things I look for as I evaluate a witness involved in an investigation I'm working on is a condition called temporal lobe labiality. People who have psychic experiences frequently tend to have a particular brain configuration which is a hypersensitivity of the temporal lobes of the brain to very subtle energy fields, particularly electromagnetic fields," said Dr. Nicholes, who also does a personality test on each witness.

Once his interviews and tests of the witnesses are complete, Dr. Nicholes and his team begin a detailed examination of the site itself as well as the surrounding grounds. For this portion of each

investigation, Dr. Nicholes uses electromagnetic field detectors, geomagnetic field detectors, and ion density meters. "What I'm looking for are unusual electromagnetic or geomagnetic fields. Over the course of my career, I have discovered that cases involving poltergeist activity typically involve certain types of witnesses who have certain characteristics living or working in places with specific energetic characteristics. Specifically, there are often electromagnetic or geomagnetic anomalies associated with the locations, and the people who experience these things have brains that are particularly sensitive to these fields," said Dr. Nicholes.

He believes that every house isn't haunted because these electromagnetic or geomagnetic fields aren't present. In addition, he has found that even if someone moves into what is believed to be a haunted location, he or she might not experience anything unusual unless the brain is sensitive to these fields. "Living in an environment with unusual energetic characteristics can sensitize the brain, so someone can actually become more psychic over time. This phenomenon is like an allergy in many ways. Someone with an allergy is sensitive to minor levels of chemical or biological agents, whereas these people are sensitive to subtle levels of energy that have no impact on others," he explained.

Dr. Nicholes's Theories and Philosophies

Having found a specific correlation between someone's brain configuration and the specific location, one of Dr. Nicholes's goals is interpreting the impact of his discoveries. He added, "There is no question in my mind that there are genuine haunted sites. But, how does someone define the word 'haunted'? There is very little evidence to substantiate the presence of a particular spirit or spirits at a location. What I do define as a haunted location is anyplace where people repeatedly experience paranormal phenomena. There is no question that people experience these things and that some people experience them more than others. Exactly what the phenomena are, or 'who' they are, is another matter. Is there any evidence of survival of consciousness after death in any of these cases? Based on my experience, the answer is yes, but not always. There are several types of ghosts. The ghosts that seem to indicate an intelligence or conscious presence of some type are generally spontaneous aberrational experiences that occur at or near the time of death or within a few months after death. These are often a one-time experience, and involve the witness seeing an apparition of someone he or she knew or who was meaningful to the person. In these cases, it's not unusual for there to be some form of communication between the person and the apparition, either verbally or telepathically. These ghosts often indicate intelligence."

Not all ghosts or apparitions demonstrate intelligence, however. There are many haunt cases that Dr. Nicholes has investigated that involve pseudo-apparitions. In these cases, the ghost or apparition doesn't interact with the witness. "They tend to repeat the same movements over and over again. I think that in some cases, locations can be imprinted with place memories or object memories. Some places hold impressions of past events, particularly emotionally charged events. In cases where there's an electromagnetic or geomagnetic anomaly at the location, I believe these energy fields act as a containment zone for the imprints themselves, or these fields impact a person's ability to actually see or experience these imprints," he said.

The most common type of haunting Dr. Nicholes has come across during his investigations is what he refers to as a psy-projection. These are thought-forms that certain people can have. They're most common with poltergeist cases. According to Dr. Nicholes, a poltergeist becomes a manifestation of the witness's hostility or anger, which is often otherwise repressed. The images and sounds people see in a haunting are externalized expressions of the emotional needs or fears of the witness. The haunted location somehow allows these thought processes to become projections. "I believe they are a mirror of the unconscious mind that is somehow triggered by energy anomalies present at the location. Some ghost hunters who measure electromagnetic fields at haunted sites

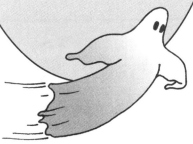

Local Ghost Hunters: Michigan

The Michigan Ghost Hunters Society offers ghost hunting tips, a gallery of investigation photographs, private investigations, and membership to the society. For more information, check out *www.tmghs.com*.

attribute the energy anomalies to the ghosts themselves, however," he said. In this situation, a thought-form is something that someone thinks about, often on a subconscious level, that somehow comes into being.

Dr. Nicholes's Psychical Research Foundation reports that two other phenomena produce "ghosts" or apparition-like phenomena that are often confused with true apparitions. These are haunting apparitions and poltergeist phenomena. Haunting apparitions, at first glance, may appear very similar to apparitions of the dead. However, upon observation it becomes clear they do not seem to possess intelligence or personality. Whereas a haunting, and the "images" seen or "sounds" heard, are repetitious "replays' of a past event that was somehow "recorded" by the environment of the location where it occurred, true apparitions allow for two-way communication and display self-awareness.

In a pseudo-apparition situation, Nicholes believes that the haunting apparition appears to be part of the event "recording," and communication or interaction with such a ghost is not possible (just as communication or interaction with a character you watch on TV is impossible).

Poltergeist phenomena involve physical disturbances caused by a living person (the poltergeist agent). The agent, due to unresolved emotional or psychological stresses, unconsciously uses a form of psychokinesis (mind over matter) to cause the physical disturbances. In rare poltergeist cases, apparitions may be seen or heard. He stated, "These apparitions are believed to be an unconscious telepathic projection from the mind of the agent that is 'picked up' by some participants. These apparent mental projections of the agent do not display independent intelligence or personality. Often, such apparitions do not look human, but rather appear to be an archetypal reflection of the inner stress of the agent."

In Dr. Nicholes's experience, the cause of the energy anomalies can often be traced to faulty electrical wiring, the presence of nearby high-voltage power lines, or in the case of geomagnetic fields, the energy comes from the earth itself. Underground water sources, metal deposits, and geologic faults can all cause geomagnetic anomalies.

When an unusual energy source is present, people with unusually sensitive brains begin to experience supernatural or psychic phenomenon, such as ghost sightings. "If you look at the experience itself and analyze it, what you often find is that what the witness experiences is very similar to dream-type imagery. These experiences can be analyzed and evaluated like a regular dream or nightmare, and often eliminated in the same way that someone would overcome recurring nightmares through therapy. Most hauntings involve sounds and visual imagery, which I believe are created by someone's mind in an environment that's impacted by electromagnetic or geomagnetic energy anomalies," he said.

Once Dr. Nicholes begins an investigation of a haunted location or someplace where something supernatural has taken place, his on-location work typically lasts for three or four days and can cost several thousand dollars. "To pay for some of these investigations, I use funds from my grant or ask the witnesses to contribute. In some instances, I've worked with television programs, such as *Sightings*, and the producers pay for the investigation," explained Dr. Nicholes.

Thus far in his experience, Dr. Nicholes has found no indication that ghosts are actually dangerous to living people. He has found, however, that the energy fields often associated with paranormal activity can be dangerous, especially if experienced over a long period of time. "Exposure to strong energy fields can cause an increase in depression and/or aggressive behavior. This has been proven in laboratory studies. We have recommended that if someone is living in an area the person believes to be haunted, and that area turns out to be surrounded by a strong or unusual energy field, the person should consider moving, not because of the ghost, but because of the health hazard associated with exposure to the energy. In many cases, these unusual energy fields have been present for a very long time. As a result, if the haunting is

The Psychical Research Foundation (PRF)

The Psychical Research Foundation is a nonprofit parapsychological research center founded in 1960. The Foundation conducts scientific studies into the continuation of consciousness beyond death. It is the oldest organization in the world devoted specifically to that purpose. The PRF investigates mediumistic communications, reincarnation memories, transpersonal consciousness, dream states, ESP, hauntings and poltergeists, out-of-body experiences (OBEs), and near death experiences (NDEs).

believed to be a result of a violent death, for example, the energy field could have created an imprint of that event, which is now being triggered," he said.

Dr. Nicholes recalls a case that took place in an army base. Two families had been driven out of the house by a series of ongoing paranormal activities that couldn't be explained. The witnesses reported hearing voices, feeling as if they were being touched in a sexual way, and at times they also saw apparitions. When Dr. Nicholes and his team were called in, they pinpointed a very strong geomagnetic field over a certain area of the building. This field was not found in other houses or buildings in the area, and was believed to have been caused by a nearby fault zone or underground water source.

The army ultimately shielded the bottom of the building's floor with an alloy that blocks magnetic and energy fields. This stopped the energy field from reaching the main area of the affected house. Upon doing this, the unusual phenomenon within the building abruptly ended.

While Dr. Nicholes believes and has proven to some extent that energy fields somehow impact a person's ability to experience paranormal activity, he can only hypothesize about what each witness is actually experiencing. Unusual energy anomalies can cause a wide range of things to happen, including the movement of objects by so-called ghosts or poltergeists.

Participating in paranormal investigations can be a scary experience at times. "Very rarely does anything truly frightening take place in the course of an investigation. This really isn't anything like what people see in the movies. I have seen apparitions myself and have experienced poltergeist phenomena. One time I became frightened of a poltergeist during an investigation when a large piece of wood located at the bottom of a staircase flew up the stairs. It barely missed my head and bounced off a nearby wall. That was the most physically threatened that I've ever been," recalled Dr. Nicholes, who wound up temporarily leaving the area but returned later to investigate.

Another of Dr. Nicholes's more incredible experiences happened in Denmark in 1999. "I saw an apparition of a woman in white. This was only the third visual apparition I've seen firsthand in my lifetime."

In most of the cases Dr. Nicholes has investigated, there has been little evidence of a surviving consciousness. "If you're defining a ghost as a surviving spirit of the dead, then I have found little evidence to directly support this. What I have found, however, is that there is a lot of interaction between people's minds and the environment around them, especially when an energy anomaly exists. That's what parapsychologists study. It's not about demons and spirits, but about the mind and the interaction of the mental world with the physical world and how the two meld together. Houses or locations that are believed to be haunted are places where the mind and the physical world interact the most."

Within a laboratory environment, Dr. Nicholes stated that when people are exposed to pulses of magnetic fields across their temporal lobes, it can cause them to see apparitions, sense a presence, feel cold, or become scared, which are common traits among those experiencing unusual phenomena within haunted locations. When investigating a haunted location and photographing it, what Dr. Nicholes believes he's capturing on film is the impact of the unusual energy field that's present.

There have been many experiences that Dr. Nicholes has not been able to explain. While he does believe in ghosts, he also believes that unusual energy fields can and do impact what people see and hear in many haunted locations, and these strange paranormal activities aren't necessarily being caused by ghosts in the traditional sense, but by how the human mind reacts to the presence of the unusual energy fields.

Local Ghost Hunters: New England

The Southern New England Ghost Hunters Society is a member of the International Ghost Hunters Society. It offers investigations and documentation of the paranormal, as well as resources for further study. For more information, check out *www.atlanticghost.itgo. com/sne.html.*

The Psychical Research Foundation Tries To Make Sense of Some Paranormal Phenomena

The Psychical Research Foundation described several experiences a witness to an apparition might have. "Though most commonly seen or sensed (as in sensing a 'presence'), apparitions are also reported to be heard, touched, and smelled. When seen, they usually look solid to the touch, although they are sometimes reported as slightly transparent or with blurred edges. They may also be monochromatic or incomplete (visible only from the waist up, for example). Often, the apparitions appear so lifelike that, unless the apparition is known to be dead, there may be no indication that he or she is a ghost until he or she vanishes."

Often, an apparition will look just like the person did when alive. The apparition can also change his or her age, style of dress, and emotional mood in a way that seems to relate to the self-image the apparition desires to project (for example, when asked to mentally picture ourselves, we all tend to do so fully clothed).

According to the Foundation's research, not everyone present in a given location can perceive the apparition. This may be due to the sensitivity of the witness, the intent of the apparition, or a combination of both factors. Keep in mind that since perception involves both the physical senses and information processing by the mind/brain, what is "seen" or "heard" may not have a truly physical external form (and thus can't be photographed or recorded by technology).

"When more than one person sees the apparition simultaneously, the different angles at which the apparition is observed are such that the apparition seems to be physically present, 'correctly' occupying three-dimensional space. Apparitions appear to be capable of using the full range of their own psychic abilities. Thus, because they have no physical speech apparatus, they communicate via telepathy. On rare occasions, apparitions have been known to interact with the physical environment (via psychokinesis)," reports the Foundation.

The group's theoretical explanations of this phenomenon state, "If psi is our normal ability to communicate and interact with the environment in a way that is beyond our normal senses and muscles, then perhaps this psi ability can exist independently of our brains and bodies as a function of 'higher intelligence,' consciousness, soul, etc.

Local Ghost Hunters: Maryland

Ghost Hunters of Baltimore offers a training course in ghost hunting, a listing of haunted sites worldwide, and investigations of the paranormal. For more information or to join this society, check out *www.ghostpage.com.*

Using this concept, someone whose body has died or who is literally out of his or her body could still be capable of communication or environmental interaction through psychic abilities.

"Thus, an apparition could send a telepathic message that, if received, would cause us to 'see' his or her form, 'hear' his or her words, 'feel' his or her touch, 'smell' his or her cologne or scent, etc. However, these 'sensations' are, again, purely of the mental or psychic. They are transmitted by one mind and received by another. They are not physical in the sense that a person's body stands before you and speaks. As such, they do not reflect light or create sound waves and thus cannot be photographed or recorded. In the same way that people use psychokinesis (PK) to move objects mentally, so could the apparition theoretically use PK to do the same thing—although reports of such occurrences with apparitions are rare."

The movement of objects, however, if performed via PK, could be photographed. This is in contrast with a telepathic hallucination of something moving, which could not be captured on film, because in reality, no movement happened. Several alternative models of understanding have been proposed to explain these situations. Some suggest that apparitions have nothing to do with dead people or "consciousness outside a body," but are the result of telepathic transmissions and PK by living brains (those in their bodies). According to this theory, poltergeist activity is caused by living people with unusual powers, not the dead.

There are many different beliefs as to what makes ghosts and apparitions appear. Some propose that apparitions are subjective mental images triggered by psychological stress or by geomagnetic or other environmental influences. The parapsychological model defines an apparition as a consciousness without a body.

Dr. Nicholes reports, "I have seen objects move, float, and fly across a room. I know these things take place and are real. They can be observed and photographed. The experience of ghosts also exists, but whether or

not ghosts actually exist in the physical world is unproven as far as I'm concerned. There are types of poltergeists that suggest some type of externalized intelligence is at work, but even this can't be proven. I don't know if these events are triggered by the mind of the person experiencing them or by the mind of the person who has passed away that has somehow been contained within a specific environment," he said.

Dr. Nicholes is quick to state that what people see in fictional movies about ghosts, haunted houses, and poltergeists has little to do with reality. "I have spent thousands of hours investigating paranormal activities, but it's very rare for me to be in the right place at the right time to experience something firsthand. Even if something does take place, the event usually only lasts for mere seconds. This isn't as intense or as frequent of an experience as Hollywood would lead us to believe. I believe that a few TV shows, like *Unsolved Mysteries*, do an excellent job in retelling someone's actual experiences without adding too much dramatic flair. I believe the A&E television network did an excellent job with its special *Beyond Death*, in terms of presenting ghosts in a scientific and rational manner."

Dr. Nicholes believes that his hypothesis regarding how energy fields impact the human brain explain many of the haunted houses, ghosts, and poltergeists that people experience; however, he's the first to admit that this theory doesn't explain every paranormal event ever documented. "People who experience hauntings of any kind need to learn how to incorporate these experiences into their lives without being afraid of them. Most of the fear relating to this type of phenomenon is a result of what people have seen on TV or in the movies. I have never known a case where someone was actually physically harmed by a ghost," concluded Dr. Nicholes.

There are many ways to evaluate the work of Dr. Nicholes. Some experts and researchers believe that the energy fields he has found present at many of the haunted sites have caused the witnesses to hallucinate. These fields could also allow witnesses to experience an alternate reality and actually be responsible for "opening a door between the physical world and the one in which ghosts or spirits (people who have died) exist."

Dr. Nicholes stated, "I don't pretend or claim to have any absolute answers about this," he said. "Whether or not we'll ever have any absolute answers about survival of consciousness or alternate dimensions of reality, I don't know. I think we are developing a good understanding, however, of the mechanism that allows many of these paranormal events to take place."

Janis S. Raley

Founder, Ghost Preservation League
E-mail: *didyouseethat@hotmail.com*
Web site: *http://members.nbci.com/ghostleague*

Janis S. Raley founded the Ghost Preservation League (GPL) after a firsthand ghost experience she had on the Vicksburg battlefield. Raley is a Civil War historian and has been researching and documenting ghosts and energy anomalies for over twenty-five years.

She explained, "The term 'ghost' is an archaic term, since it is usually interpreted as some type of apparition with a recognizable human form. In twenty-five years of researching and documenting ghost activity and sites, I have seen such an apparition once. I have witnessed many events that would be classified as ghost encounters, without seeing anything close to the Hollywood variety of a flowing, see-through figure, shrouded in mist, glowing with otherworldly light, beckoning with one crooked finger. The GPL uses the term 'ghost' very loosely. We still use the term since it is instantly understood that we are talking about something unusual. Frankly, there isn't a better term at this time."

The Ghost Preservation League investigates paranormal events through documentation and research. It has been locating haunted sites and what are believed to be sacred or energy sites for over twenty years. Raley stated, "I founded the GPL to differentiate what we do as a group from the many other people involved in the investigation of the ghost phenomenon. The members of our group follow specific guidelines and adhere to a strict code of conduct that involves adhering closely to our mission statement at all times.

Survey Says . . .

The Psychical Research Foundation is currently collecting firsthand information on haunted buildings or buildings where paranormal experiences have been reported. If you have experienced seemingly paranormal occurrences in your residence or other building, you're invited to take a few minutes and fill out the group's survey by visiting the PRF's Web site at *www.afterlife-psychical.com*.

The Ghost Preservation League's Mission Statement

According to the Ghost Preservation League, its mission is: "We are dedicated to the impartial documentation of paranormal activity, and the locating of sacred sites. We strive for a high level of professionalism and respect the privacy and property of all individuals involved in our investigations. . . . We document through research and advanced technology to better understand the evolving world around us. It is our goal to share any information and photographic evidence wherever and whenever possible, but we do not presume to know all the answers."

The group does not have an open membership. Our members include historians, writers, photographers, laboratory specialists, architects, and one rocket scientist. The co-founder of our group, Barb Lloyd, and our Apollo Mission engineer serve as our skeptics, keeping us from getting too far from the mark and making sure our documentation is sound."

Raley's Fascination with the Paranormal

Raley approaches her work as a ghost hunter/investigator from the point of view of an historian and preservationist. Like many people who have dedicated their lives to investigating paranormal phenomena, her interest began after a firsthand encounter while visiting the Vicksburg battlefield in Mississippi, a location that dates back to the Civil War. At the time of her encounter, she was in her early twenties. "A lot of people say that when you have one of these encounters, it throws open your doors of perception and your life changes. That's pretty much what started me on my quest to see what's really out there. I wanted to determine if what I saw on that battlefield was a fluke," she said.

Incredible Firsthand Experiences

Her first experience with paranormal phenomena happened after dark near a monument on the battlefield. Out of nowhere, a large black dog with bright red eyes appeared. Just as quickly as it appeared, however, it began to disappear in sections, according to Raley. "I have since learned that a black dog represents a guardian. It's not that uncommon, but I didn't know it at the time. I have since had other encounters on the battlefield. When I had my first encounter, several of my friends were with me and saw the same phenomenon," she said.

After completing graduate school, Raley began participating in paranormal investigations on a full-time basis. She admits that at various times thus far in her career she has become frightened by her discoveries and experiences. "There are a couple of places that I would never go back to. When I visit a high-energy location that's believed to be the location of paranormal activity, I tend to have physical reactions as a result of the negative ions and different magnetic energies that are present. There is this one location along a river that dates back before the Civil War. When I visited there, I got a very sick feeling in my stomach. It was a horrible and depressing feeling, and I had difficulty breathing. The area was surrounded by a sickly green and yellowish color. All I saw was some sort of unusual light, not an actual ghost or apparition, but I'll never go back there," she recalled.

It was after many years of participating in investigations that Raley actually saw another apparition. This one appeared in a park in Dallas, in an old plantation house. Raley was upstairs setting up some equipment just before dark. "Out of my peripheral vision, near a window, I saw what looked like someone in a gray suit. When I turned my head, I saw nothing but a tree out the window. When I looked again, just a second later, the apparition appeared again. What I saw this time was a three-dimensional figure wearing a turn-of-the-century gray suit. It was there for a few seconds, then disappeared once again," she explained.

It was during an investigation at a tavern in Mississippi that Raley had an experience that convinced her that ghosts really do exist. She says she actually had a physical encounter with a ghost that left a dime-sized welt on her body. "There is no doubt in my mind that I had an encounter with a ghost. I also have witnesses to the event. I think ghosts have the ability to interact with living people, but I haven't encountered anyone who claims to truly have been injured by a ghost or apparition."

She explained, "About two years ago, I actually recorded voices of what I believe to be a ghost on audiotape. That was very convincing for me as well. I was invited to a haunted ranch in south Texas where a registered nurse told me about hearing voices and being able to record them." As part of her investigation she captured a man's voice on tape, however, there were no men present anywhere at the location.

Raley believes that people are attached to emotional things when they're alive; she doesn't see any reason why emotional attachments can't continue once someone passes on. "I think energy attracts energy, which is why many haunted locations are sites where something tragic or extremely emotional took place, such as a battle, suicide, or murder. The more energy that's concentrated into an area, the more readily ghosts can manifest themselves. That's why I think they flicker the lights, for example, because that deals with energy," she said.

Raley's Tools of the Trade

In the process of conducting an investigation, Raley believes in using only basic equipment, including several types of cameras. "I use a basic 35mm camera, a point-and-shoot camera, and a digital camera. I also have a video camera with a 'night shot' feature that captures infrared, night vision images. I also use motion detectors and thermometers that set off alarms. On occasion, I also use a Gauss meter that measures electromagnetic changes. I also pay careful attention to my own senses, which often work better than the equipment," said Raley.

It's often a result of a telephone call that Raley finds sites to investigate; however, she has also pinpointed several battlefields to investigate based on her own historical research and stories she hears about strange things happening at those battlefields. "I try to learn as much as possible about the history of a site by speaking with as many people in the area as I can. I take many of the stories I hear with a grain of salt, especially when the stories sound as if they've been embellished for dramatic flair. When I interview people, I listen carefully for those little details about something bizarre, but that they think is trivial. After learning what I can through interviews and research, I visit the area itself, both during the day and at night," explained Raley, who begins every on-site investigation by taking photographs of the area.

Since photographic or scientific proof doesn't typically make itself available in the early stages of an investigation,

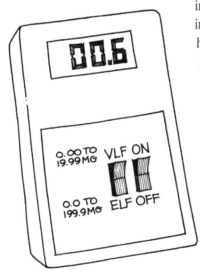

Raley admits she often chooses exact places to investigate based on how they feel. "Often, I'll investigate a site or a haunted house over a long period of time. Sometimes I get results, sometimes I don't. If there's a site I consider to be worthwhile, I'll spend six months to several years investigating it. One thing I pay particular attention to is how the lunar cycles impact the area," she said.

Even when she gathers photographs and scientific readings, Raley admits she has yet to obtain actual proof that ghosts exist. "You can't really come up with hard evidence, even though we have proof that something unusual is taking place. My approach is that I make available my findings and let people make up their own minds about it. I have taken some incredible photographs, but I don't try to define what exactly appears in the photos. I don't say, 'here is a ghost or some sort of paranormal experience.' What I capture on film is some form of unusual energy that could very well be a ghost, but I don't know. There are many theories about what the energy might be. I will, however, state that certain sites that I've investigated are, in fact, haunted," she said.

Tips for People Who Have Had Paranormal Experiences

If someone believes his or her house is haunted, Raley states it's important to keep a journal and document the experiences as much as possible. "Pay careful attention to the sights, sounds, and smells. Write down as much detail as possible and look for patterns. Also, take lots of pictures. Be sure to keep track of exact dates and times when events or observations occur. I personally believe you can communicate with ghosts simply by speaking with them. If someone tells me they believe his house is haunted, because he's being kept up at night by noises he believes are coming from ghosts, I tell him to talk to the ghosts and set boundaries. If there's something disturbing you, say out loud, that you

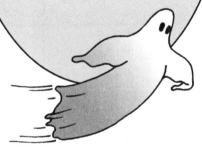

Local Ghost Hunters: Pennsylvania

The Philadelphia Ghost Hunters Alliance offers investigations of the paranormal, tips for ghost hunting, and documentation of the paranormal including photographs, EVPs, and stories. For more information, check out *http://members.aol.com/rayd8em/index.html.*

need your sleep and that whatever is keeping you up should not be allowed to happen at night," she said. In other words, Raley suggests openly talking to ghosts and setting boundaries about behavior when necessary. It's also appropriate to ask questions if the situation arises.

For people who have been living for a long time at a site they believe is haunted, Raley suggests going through old pictures to seek out physical or visual proof. "A lot of people go back and see smoke, mist, or swirls of light in their pictures that previously went unnoticed. I think anyone has the ability to see ghosts or experience paranormal phenomena as long as they open their mind to the possibility," she concluded.

Troy Taylor

Paranormal Investigator
President, History and Hauntings Book Company
Founder, American Ghost Society
888-GHOSTLY
E-mail: *ttaylor@prairieghosts.com*
Web site: *www.prairieghosts.com*

For his entire life, Troy Taylor has been fascinated by the unknown and specifically by what he believes to be paranormal activity, such as ghosts and hauntings. It was about a decade ago, however, that he began to take his interest in this subject matter seriously and dedicate a considerable amount of time to actually doing research and performing investigations. It was through this research and hands-on investigative work that Taylor began to realize there was actually something to his beliefs and that ghosts and paranormal activity aren't just a matter of folklore or legend.

Taylor's Fascination with the Paranormal

"I became involved with a group of people who were active paranormal investigators. I was fascinated by the fact that these

Local Ghost Hunters: Indiana

The Ghost Hunters Society of Indiana offers documentation of the paranormal including photographs, video, and EVPs. For more information, check out *http://members.nbci.com/GHSOI.*

were well-educated people looking to obtain real evidence of paranormal activity as opposed to simply believing all of the stories about ghosts, hauntings, and the paranormal that people are so fond of telling. I am certainly fascinated by all of the stories and by people's personal anecdotes, but I'm also interested in the real, genuine phenomenon. I have seen many circumstances where totally unrelated people have had similar unusual experiences at a specific location, and none of these people knew anything about what the other people had experienced until later," said Taylor.

While Taylor may consider himself something of a skeptic when he hears other people retell stories about paranormal experiences they've had, based on his own firsthand experiences, he has come to believe that such phenomena actually do exist. "I am a skeptic, but I'm not one of these people who doesn't believe in anything. The true definition of a skeptic, I believe, is someone who maintains an open mind and who is willing to look at both sides of everything. That's the way I always approach an investigation into paranormal phenomenon. On the other hand, before I can be convinced that something is truly genuine, I have to be satisfied that there can be no other possible explanations," he said.

Taylor considers people who don't know one another but who have similar experiences at one location to be a form of proof that paranormal activity exists. This is because there's no way, he believes, for people who have never been in contact with one another to have independent experiences at different times, but that involve the same location, that all turn out to be similar. "It's my own personal experiences, however, that have really convinced me that paranormal phenomenon can and does exist." What Taylor means is that people who have never met one another but who have visited the same location at different times have had the same paranormal experiences without the knowledge that others have had the same prior experiences. Taylor feels this can't be coincidence and that when this type of situation occurs it serves as excellent circumstantial evidence of the paranormal.

How Taylor Conducts an Investigation

Normally, Taylor begins an investigation by conducting in-depth telephone interviews with the people who have witnessed or experienced something unusual. "There isn't typically anything we can do if someone describes a one-time experience. I recommend to people that they keep a personal journal and see if a pattern develops over time in regard to having unusual experiences," said Taylor. "If someone experiences paranormal activity on a regular basis, there is more of a chance we'll launch a full investigation. Early in an investigation, I gather a team of no more than eight people, each with different skills."

During an on-site investigation, each person on Taylor's team has his or her own well-defined job. One or two people will interview each witness separately. For this, he tries to select the people on his team who develop the best rapport with the witnesses. Taylor stated that an investigation can often be extremely invasive into someone's life. Thus, it's critical that the people involved become comfortable sharing very personal information with the person or people assigned to interview them.

"When I launch an investigation, I literally move in. I bring a team of people with a lot of equipment, and this can be disruptive. Aside from the people who interview the witnesses, someone else on the team will be in charge of creating diagrams and maps of the entire location. We'll carefully pinpoint where each instance of paranormal activity has taken place. One person on the team will be in charge of photographing everything, while someone else will videotape what transpires. We usually also have people use various pieces of equipment to look for fluctuations in energy or magnetic fields that may be present," said Taylor, who uses his high-tech measuring devices to search for natural or supernatural energy anomalies that may be present at a location.

Typically, the people in charge of using the measuring equipment will take many sets of readings throughout the location that are spread out over time. Each person on the team will then mark on the maps locations where they believe something unusual is

Local Ghost Hunters: Kansas

The Kansas Ghost Hunters Society is a member of the International Ghost Hunters Society. It offers investigations of the paranormal, tips on ghost hunting, and a list of haunted sites in Kansas. For more information, check out *www.ksghosts.com*.

going on. Each person does this totally independently, without discussing it with other team members. "I encourage team members to go with their gut feelings if they believe there's something weird about a particular spot or area," explained Taylor.

Once all of the initial work is done, Taylor describes a typical investigation as involving a lot of sitting around and waiting. He admits that all too often, nothing unusual takes place, but there are times when his team does experience something strange at a location. Before Taylor even begins to consider the idea that a ghost may be present at a location, he goes out of his way to rule out every other possible explanation. He doesn't go into an investigation expecting to find a ghost.

Taylor's Tools of the Trade

While Taylor has access to a wide range of high-tech equipment, he tries to take a more old-fashioned approach to his paranormal investigations. "I use cameras a lot, and I use audio and video recording equipment, especially to record people's testimony and eyewitness accounts. When I do use other high-tech gear, more often than not it's to rule out any kind of natural or artificial interference at a location. I use EMF detectors to pick up disruptions in the magnetic field. I am mainly interested in anomalies that are a result of geomagnetic energy, which means that the anomaly is coming from the earth itself. Another tool I use is a thermal scanner, which is an infrared thermometer that is pointed like a gun at an area. When you pull the trigger, you get an instant temperate reading. This is helpful for picking up cold spots, which are a manifestation of some type of energy that may or may not be ghost related," said Taylor.

Incredible Firsthand Experiences

When asked which of his many cases actually convinced him that ghosts exist, he quickly recalled a case that he participated in which took place in Indianapolis, Indiana. "It was an old house that was being moved from one location to another. As the house was being moved, since it was an historic home, the local newspapers took pictures of the event. When the pictures were published, people reported seeing a little girl in the pictures who was looking out the window of the house," he recalled. A friend of Taylor's was a police officer in the area and got permission for Taylor and his team to investigate the house and the original location where it was built.

When Taylor got to the house, it was sitting on a trailer and had no electrical wiring attached to it. The sewer lines and water pipes had also been disconnected from the house. "It was basically a wooden shell of the house," he said. "We went inside and used a variety of different types of equipment to pinpoint unusual energy fields. We initially didn't pick up anything. When I got to the upstairs bedroom, however, I picked up a really strong electrical field, which didn't make any sense. As I began to measure and analyze the energy field, it began to move around the room. I called to my other team members to come see what I was experiencing, but they too were experiencing strange things in a different location in the house. One of the other team members was near a light in the hallway that was hanging from the ceiling on a chain. Suddenly, the light started moving back and forth all by itself. It would swing up at an angle, stop in mid-air, and then start moving again. This phenomenon continued for about ten minutes, allowing us to videotape it," said Taylor.

"Before we went into the house, we purposely didn't do too much research into its location or the house. After we had these experiences, I asked my police officer friend to tell me more about the house itself. It was then that I learned the house was believed to be haunted, and many people over the years had experienced paranormal phenomena originating from the upstairs bedroom."

Another experience that helped to convince Taylor that ghosts really exist happened in a theater located in Springfield, Illinois. He was investigating the theater because he had heard many stories that it was haunted by an actor who had committed suicide years earlier. "Every old theater seems to have a ghost story attached to it, but these stories are rarely anything more than just stories. This time, however, I was exploring the theater myself and in one of the old dressing rooms, I began to smell Noxzema. It was a very overpowering smell that only lasted for about ten seconds before it disappeared. This wasn't something I thought too much about until later," he said.

Taylor had assumed that the actors used a lot of Noxzema skin cream to remove makeup, so he didn't think the smell was anything unusual. "During the next few hours, I did a bunch of interviews with people who worked at the theater. The last person I spoke with was the theater's manager. I asked her why she thought the theater was haunted. Sure, a lot of unusual things were reported to have happened to various people, but I wanted to know why she thought the ghost was that of Joe, the actor who committed suicide. She stated that whenever anything unusual happens, they always start smelling Noxzema. I then learned that for many years after Joe's death, because people started equating that smell with Joe, they totally stopped using Noxzema anywhere in the building. When Joe was alive, he had psoriasis on his leg and always used a lot of Noxzema. Wherever he went, people remember him being surrounded by a cloud of Noxzema," said Taylor, who stated he had no idea about the tie-in with Noxzema in regard to the paranormal events happening in the theater. This was something he experienced first-hand, without knowing it was related.

Over the course of his various investigations, Taylor recalls feeling as if he's been touched by ghosts. He has also experienced cold spots that shouldn't be present. While more often than not, unusual events don't take place during an investigation,

Local Ghost Hunters: Georgia

The Georgia Haunt Hunt Team offers private investigations and documentation of the paranormal including case summaries and photographs. For more information, check out *www.geocities.com/gahaunt*.

Taylor says he usually winds up with some good witness testimony, but little or no hardcore proof that anything unusual took place. "In ninety percent of the investigations we do, nothing happens. Paranormal activity just isn't that common. It's not like in the movie *Ghostbusters,*" said Taylor.

After an investigation, if any type of photographic or video documentation was gathered, Taylor always has both photographic and paranormal experts independently evaluate the footage. "Nine times out of ten, when globes or orbs are captured on film, it's the result of a lens refraction, which means light that was present in the location bounced off the camera's lens and made a strange impression on the film. In the past, I have, however, sent pictures to Kodak's laboratories and have been told by their experts that they couldn't explain or account for the images that appeared on film that I shot. Despite having this photographic evidence, I'm the last person to say that what I have pictures of are ghosts. I just don't know. There are times when I don't have an explanation for something, but I never jump to the conclusion that it's a ghost," said Taylor.

Taylor's Theories and Philosophies

At this point in our scientific knowledge, Taylor says there isn't a way to ultimately prove whether or not ghosts exist. "We can believe it. We can provide evidence or circumstantial proof of it, but we can't ultimately prove that ghosts exist. Just like evidence in a courtroom that's presented during a case, it's up to the individual viewer to decide if each piece of evidence gathered during a paranormal investigation is authentic. I have not yet seen evidence, beyond a reasonable doubt, that ghosts exist. I have seen a lot of great circumstantial evidence, but that's all it is. The evidence can almost always be interpreted in different ways, based on someone's personal belief," said Taylor, who honestly doesn't know if concrete proof will ever exist that ghosts are real. If such evidence were to be discovered, he believes scientists would have to take a much different view on this topic.

Local Ghost Hunters: Kentucky

The Western Kentucky Ghost Hunters Society offers summaries of investigations, tips for ghost hunting, and photographs of the paranormal. For more information, check out *http://westkentucky ghost.homestead.com.*

John Zaffis

Professional Ghost Hunter/Investigator
Founder, Paranormal Research Society of New England
E-mail: *jzaffisjr@snet.com*
Web site: *www.presne.com*

When it comes to ghosts, spirits, poltergeists, possessions, and haunted houses, John Zaffis has seen it all. He has more than twenty-six years of experience studying and investigating the paranormal and has had the opportunity to work with several prominent investigators in the field, including Ed and Lorraine Warren, Malachi Martin, and a variety of priests, ministers, and Buddhists. His research has taken him throughout the United States, Canada, England, and Scotland, and has included well over 2,000 investigations. Through hands-on research with other investigators and clergy, he has obtained a great deal of knowledge and understanding of the paranormal and is considered one of the foremost authorities in the field today.

Early on, ghosts and poltergeists were among some of his first-hand paranormal experiences, as well as those that he believes involved the demonic and diabolical. He has since worked extensively with both spiritualists and psychics concerning how their knowledge is used for channeling (communicating with the dead), reincarnation (past-life regression), or the "calling of the spirits" (another form of channeling) for information and how they use meditation to acquire the information that they are seeking. Because of his personal and painstaking experiences with hauntings, ESP, near death experiences, and other paranormal activities, he is firm in his conviction that such phenomena do exist.

Zaffis's Fascination with the Paranormal

When asked how he became interested in the supernatural, Zaffis is quick to answer that it's in his blood. He says this because he's directly related to Ed and Lorraine Warren (*www.warrens.net*),

two of the world's most prominent paranormal investigators, who were responsible for investigating the Amityville Horror. "Ed is my uncle by blood. Since I was a little boy, I always looked forward to visits from Ed so I could hear his ghost stories. When I turned eighteen, I was allowed to participate in actual investigations," he recalls.

Despite having relatives in the paranormal investigation field, Zaffis believes it was an experience he had as a six-year-old that has been the primary driving force behind his interest in the paranormal. "My grandfather had passed away several years before this event took place. My grandmother, who was still living, became very ill. I remember seeing my grandfather appear before me at the foot of my bed. He was shaking his head back and forth. While I don't know what it meant, this event has stuck in my mind, as clear as day, even after all of these years. That experience really intrigued me to become a paranormal investigator in an attempt to determine if what I experienced was real or simply something that happened in my imagination," he says.

Incredible Firsthand Experiences

Throughout the years Zaffis has been working as a paranormal investigator, he's had many different and highly unusual experiences. He's also heard many witnesses convey to him what many would consider to be extremely bizarre experiences. "I don't believe anything unless I witness it myself. I certainly believe what people tell me and I believe that *they* believe what they tell me really happened, but I personally need to see things firsthand. So many things have happened to me over the years that I believe, without a doubt, that ghosts do exist. I have seen things form in front of me. I have felt cold spots suddenly be created. I have seen solid objects move, and I have actually communicated with ghosts, spirits, and poltergeists," he said.

"The very first thing I ever experienced as an investigator happened when I was in the living room of someone's house. It was in a mutual friend's home. The house was believed to be haunted. All of a sudden, the drapes began to move from side to side, not in and out as if the wind were blowing them. I remember the lights began to flicker and then the temperature in the room changed dramatically. I was eighteen years old at the time [it was about twenty-five years ago] when I witnessed what looked like the spirit of a human, in terms of its appearance, actually doing something," said Zaffis, who describes himself as extremely analytical, especially when it comes to his research and field work.

Out of all the poltergeist phenomena he's studied, one case came to mind as being the most incredible for Zaffis. He witnessed a woman who was about five feet tall and no more than 90 pounds have an exorcism being done on her. She was believed to have been possessed. He recalls, "There were five large guys holding her down during this process. She was also placed in a straight jacket. This event was taking place inside of a church. Right before my eyes, this woman tore apart the straight jacket and pulled the pew out of the floor of the church."

For Zaffis, his worst experience was seeing a demon fully form in front of him. This happened about twelve years ago. He was investigating a haunted funeral parlor at the time. "I saw this demon form and come down a flight of stairs. At that same moment, the entire room became ice cold. I was calling out to people I was working with who were in other rooms, but nobody could hear me or respond. This event scared me. I wouldn't return to the site for three days. When you're at a location and dealing with negative energy or demons, fear is certainly part of the job. I believe that demons are not human spirits. When dealing with human spirits or ghosts, I don't believe these paranormal events are meant to cause harm," he said.

Zaffis's Theories and Philosophies

When asked why he believes ghosts and spirits make themselves known to living people, Zaffis explained that it could be for many reasons. "If someone sees a loved one who has passed away, I often believe that the spirit is trying to convey a warning or is trying to protect the living person. There are many instances when someone was killed tragically, but they don't realize that they are dead, and they never crossed over properly. Sometimes ghosts or spirits will stay dormant for many years, then something will act as a trigger causing them to make themselves known," he said.

According to the reports of people who claim to have seen ghosts or spirits firsthand, these entities can take on many different forms. "I have seen a grayish, light figure of a person. I have seen tiny balls of light appear and then take the form of a person. To actually see a full form of a person who has passed on, this hasn't happened since I was a child and saw my grandfather."

Zaffis also says he has witnessed many shadows and visible energy forms over the years that he believes were good ghosts or spirits. However, he doesn't know why ghosts and spirits take on so many different forms. "I believe it has something to do with the environment, the people you're with, and the level of energy that's somehow created. Living people can create and give off energy. Likewise, some areas contain higher levels of energy. When these energies are combined, I believe it allows us, as living people, to see paranormal activity, such as ghosts or spirits," explained Zaffis, who believes that ghosts and spirits need energy to be able to appear and cause things to happen.

Some experts believe that excessive levels of electromagnetic or geomagnetic energy need to be present at a location for a ghost to appear or for something paranormal to happen. Others believe it's the ghosts themselves that create the energy anomalies investigators are able to measure when paranormal activities are taking place. Zaffis stated, "I agree that certain areas have energy fields associated with them that somehow allow ghosts to appear. I also believe that some ghosts have the ability to pull energy from locations and individuals in order to make themselves known."

According to Zaffis, while many ghosts and spirits are considered "good," there are also evil spirits and poltergeists that can make themselves known to living people. "From the point of view of

a researcher, poltergeists are among the most fascinating cases to investigate, because when you can see something that's solid move or levitate for no apparent reason, or see a solid object instantly break up in front of you, that's an incredible experience. I have worked on several poltergeist cases and these always pique my interest. My belief system tells me that when spirits or poltergeists are evil, it's more on the demonic level. I have seen wounds appear on people as a result of an evil spirit. I have also seen people begin speaking in foreign languages they never studied," said Zaffis.

Zaffis certainly finds his investigative work exciting and interesting; however, he believes his first priority is to help the people who are dealing with these strange phenomena to better understand and deal with what they experience. "When people experience something paranormal, they typically don't know what to do. They don't know how to get the help they need, and they often think they're going crazy. One of my responsibilities is helping people come to grips with what they've experienced. Sometimes, as a result of research, I'm able to find out why certain things are happening, and I'm able to help put the paranormal activities to rest, allowing people who experienced them to go on with their lives," said Zaffis.

When Zaffis perceives that there could be danger involved in an investigation, the primary precaution he takes is relying on his own strong belief system. He believes there is a universal God. "As long as I believe in God and his power, I will be protected. In every religion, not only is there a good, there's also evil. By believing in the good, I believe I'll be protected from that evil. It's my strong belief that keeps me safe," he explained.

It's a common theory that ghosts, spirits, and apparitions tend to manifest themselves more frequently in locations where a tragic event took place. Zaffis believes that if a spirit is earthbound, it will always go back to the scene where its death occurred. "It's as if the ghosts or spirits are trying to figure out what happened to them or why they died. The ghosts in these situations tend to keep coming

Local Ghost Hunters: California

The Southern California Ghost Hunters Society offers investigations and documentation of the paranormal including stories, photographs, EVPs, and videos. For more information, check out *www.scghs.com*.

back, over and over, like a continuous rerun. A lot of times, you can feel a presence in these locations, even if the ghosts or spirits don't make themselves materialize for the human eye to see. I personally don't know for sure if only ghosts with some type of unfinished business are able to return to earth; however, I believe that spirits have the ability to communicate with living people if the person is in danger or needs to be warned about something. Too many people have told me stories about dead loved ones instantly appearing to warn them of something, even if that loved one has been dead for a while and has never before made him- or herself known. It's been my experience that if someone suddenly sees or feels the presence of a loved one who tries to communicate, it should be taken seriously and not dismissed," explained Zaffis.

Based on Zaffis's experience, people don't have to possess psychic ability in order to experience paranormal phenomena. "I do believe, however, that people with psychic ability are more apt to make contact with ghosts, spirits, or other paranormal activities, because for some reason, their minds are more open to this type of event or experience," he said.

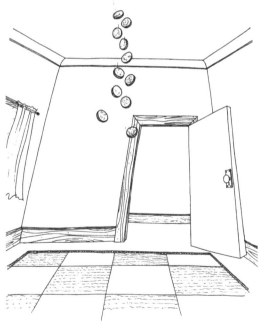

For most people, what they know about ghosts or hauntings is what they see in the movies or on television. Zaffis has, of course, seen many of the movies dealing with hauntings, ghosts, and possessions, and believes that while many of these films have a basis in reality, they often take artistic license when showcasing the event.

"I've seen all sorts of objects appear right before my eyes, such as ectoplasm, little pieces of metal, feathers, and even coins dropping from the ceiling. Some of these phenomena are absolutely amazing. I've been sitting at a table and saw a teacup and saucer move around. The woman whose house I was in started getting excited during our conversation. Her teacup first started to rattle, and then it moved across the table, directly toward me. Most of this really exciting stuff that happens in real life that you also see hyped up in the movies happens rarely and when you least expect it," said Zaffis.

Having participated in so many investigations and through extensive research, Zaffis has found that children are extremely open to paranormal activity. Many of the reported cases involving ghosts and other phenomena somehow involve children. Zaffis urges people to believe their children any time they report something unusual happening. "Don't just write off whatever your child says as something from an overactive imagination. If your child claims to hear or see something, don't be alarmed, but make a point to investigate it. Every time I investigate a case that involves children and it turns out to be legitimate, the parents always tell me that they wish they had believed their child sooner when he or she reported strange things happening. This is probably the most important piece of advice I can offer," concluded Zaffis.

For someone who believes his or her own house may be haunted, Zaffis encourages the homeowner to investigate all of the possible explanations for what is being experienced, especially if the person has just moved into the home and isn't yet familiar with the natural noises the house makes. "Many older houses have plumbing or flooring that makes noise. This is almost always a natural occurrence that has nothing to do with the paranormal. If there's a problem with lights flickering, for example, have an electrician come make sure the electrical wiring throughout the house isn't malfunctioning. If you can't explain what you're experiencing, begin by doing a historical check on your home. Determine who lived on the property before you and whether or not any tragedies occurred there. Find out what was on the property before your home was built. If possible, speak with the people who lived in the house before you to determine if they experienced anything unusual. Many people don't like to discuss this type of thing if it's happening to them, because they're worried that other people will think they're crazy," explained Zaffis.

In Zaffis's opinion, someone's soul and what ghosts are believed to be could possibly be the same thing. "I believe we all

Local Ghost Hunters: Southern Ohio

The Southern Ohio Ghost Hunters Society offers a listing of haunted sites in Ohio, membership to the society, and a newsletter. For more information, check out *www.ghost hunters.topcities.com*.

have this essence within us. Some people call this a soul. Nobody has yet disproved this theory," he said.

How Zaffis Conducts an Investigation

Zaffis is often contacted to participate in investigations throughout the country and abroad. At the start of any investigation, he always begins by making contact with the people who are reporting the paranormal activity. He tries to obtain as much information from the witnesses as possible. He also tries to learn about the home life and belief system of the witnesses, and gather as much detail as possible about what they believe they're experiencing. "I also ascertain if there have been multiple witnesses to specific events and determine how long the paranormal activities have been going on. It's always helpful to discover if the witness knows why the paranormal activity might be taking place. During this process, I ask a lot of questions and evaluate whatever evidence or documentation the witness has gathered," he said.

The first thing Zaffis tries to do is come up with logical explanations for what the witness believes is paranormal activity. He has found that it's often faulty electrical wiring or the natural settling of a house that someone has recently moved into. "If I determine there is something worth investigating, I'll travel to the actual site and begin with on-site, in-person interviews of the witness(es). Most of the time, however, I can tell if a story is legit simply by speaking with the person on the telephone. When I visit a location, such as someone's home that's believed to be haunted, over ninety percent of the time, I won't experience anything unusual firsthand," explained Zaffis. "It often takes two or three visits to a location before I will witness or experience something."

Based on Zaffis's experience, paranormal events happen at a very fast rate and in an unpredictable way. Thus, while it's totally possible that something is in fact happening at a location, the odds

Local Ghost Hunters: Alabama

The Alabama Ghost Hunters Society offers tips for ghost hunting, investigations of the paranormal, and photographs. For more information, check out *http://ghostinvestigator.tripod.com/ghostinvestigators*.

of him seeing it during an investigation are slim. "This is one of the more frustrating aspects of my work," he said.

Zaffis's Tools of the Trade

During every investigation, Zaffis uses a traditional camcorder, audiocassette recorder, and 35mm camera. He also brings holy water to every investigation as well as his rosary and several other relics that have strong meaning for him. On occasion, he'll use more high-tech equipment, such as EM or Gauss meters, in order to verify events. An investigation can take anywhere from one hour to many weeks, months, or even several years. He spends a lot of time helping witnesses and the people he works with understand what's happening around them. Upon completing an investigation, he strives to wind up with a good collection of photos, videotapes, and audiotapes. This isn't always possible, however. The primary result of Zaffis's work is that the people who experience paranormal activity ultimately develop a better understanding of what happened and they're better able to deal with it. He is able to walk away from an investigation knowing that he's truly helped them. "I am often able to make a huge positive impact on someone's life," he said.

Anytime Zaffis winds up with any type of physical documentation from an investigation, whether it's photographs, videotape, audiotape, or anything else, he always has his documentation verified and analyzed by independent professionals. Typically, Zaffis only trusts evidence he has personally gathered. "Many different things can happen during the process in which a photograph is developed. If I spot something in a photo, I always have the negatives examined as well. While evidence can't always be explained, it's important that I'm able to ascertain if it's been tampered with on purpose or by accident," he stated.

Zaffis's Web site offers samples of photos and EVP recordings he's obtained as a result of his investigations throughout the years.

For some reason, he's been able to obtain many EVP recordings at cemeteries. This type of evidence requires many hours to obtain and then analyze, he explained.

So, Who Ya Gonna Call?

What you've just read are interviews with real-life ghost hunters, parapsychologists, and paranormal investigators who have dedicated a great deal of time and energy to their work. While many of their stories and experiences seem incredibly compelling and could very well be real, virtually all of the information you just read that relates to ghosts, hauntings, spirits, poltergeists, apparitions, and other types of paranormal activity is based on opinions and hypotheses formed by people who are dedicated to discovering answers to questions that may in fact have no definitive answers.

When someone believes he or she has seen, felt, heard, or somehow interacted with a "ghost," is this simply a figment of an overactive imagination, an event that has happened sometime in the past that has somehow been imprinted at a location and is now being replayed, or is the witness actually seeing, hearing, feeling, smelling, or interacting with an intelligent entity that was once a living person?

Obviously, the paranormal experiences people have vary greatly. It's certainly possible that on rare occasions, when the situation is just right, people can communicate with entities. Perhaps the people who have this ability are psychic or have special powers. Maybe the experiences are a result of natural energy fields or energy anomalies that somehow act as a portal between the world of the living and those who have died. It's also possible that ghosts simply exist and roam freely among the living, but only those who decide to open their minds and believe are able to experience this phenomenon.

Believing that your own home is haunted or that you've seen the ghost of a departed relative or loved one can be a very traumatic and life-changing experience. If you're overwhelmed by the paranormal phenomena you've experienced (or continue to experience), or you need or want to obtain a better understanding of what you're actually experiencing and why, consider seeking the assistance of a parapsychologist or paranormal investigator. When searching for guidance, however, make sure the people you turn to and decide to trust are credible and knowledgeable. Obtain a referral from an established organization.

The people you just heard from in this section of *The Everything® Ghost Book* are among the best known and most credible experts in America when it comes to ghosts and the investigation of related paranormal activity. In the next chapter, you'll read about ordinary people who have had extraordinary encounters with ghosts and the paranormal.

Local Ghost Hunters: Great Lakes

The Great Lakes Ghost Hunters Society is a member of the International Ghost Hunters Society. It offers investigations of the paranormal, tips for ghost hunters, and a listing of haunted sites in the Great Lakes area. For more information, check out *http://glghs.tripod.com*.

Chapter Three

Real-Life Ghost Stories

Have you ever seen a ghost? If so, you're not alone. Extraordinary sights and chilling, inexplicable experiences are far more common than you might think. This chapter offers many firsthand encounters with ghosts that have happened to ordinary people, just like you. As you'd expect, people who experience these things are often leery about going public with their experiences for fear of being called crazy. Many of these people are well-educated individuals with steady jobs. To ensure the privacy of the individuals who have chosen to share their experiences here, all names have either been omitted or changed.

Some of these stories have been reprinted from the Archive X Web site (*http://simplex.wirenot.net/X/),* which offers a "virtual library" of ghost stories and other paranormal experiences submitted by people throughout the world.

Ghosts in the movies and on TV have been portrayed as being everything from flat-out terrifying (such as the ghosts in *The Shining* or *Poltergeist*) to disgusting and silly (*Ghostbusters*) to fun and friendly (*Casper, Ghost Dad*). The ghosts you'll read about here are often a little spooky, somewhat scary, but are not the ghosts you're used to seeing on TV or in the movies. Sure, some of these people were frightened by their experience, but as you'll see, the majority of the encounters these people had with ghosts were harmless.

The Warning

Have you ever done something stupid, like start cooking something and then forget about it? Maybe you've left the iron on or the water running in a sink until it overflowed. Hopefully, you remembered your mistake before a disaster happened. This short story involves someone who was reminded of something by her dead grandfather.

One day I was boiling some tea on the stove. I had walked off and started to do something else. Well, of course I forgot about the tea on the stove. A while later, I heard buttons on the microwave being pushed. I knew I was home alone so I went in there to look.

My dead grandfather's birthdate was displayed on the microwave screen. I saw the pot on the stove and remembered. The water had evaporated and the tea bags were about to catch on fire. My grandfather was watching over me.

An Inherited Gift

Are psychic abilities and the power to communicate with ghosts inherited? Can this ability be passed down from parent to child? The following story took place when this person was in his late teens. It explains some of the unusual experiences he has had as a result of having a special "gift."

My father always had what we believe is ESP. He knew when things were going to happen. At Christmastime especially, he could always guess what was in every wrapped present, even ones that were sent from family and not purchased from our household. I feel that I have inherited this sort of talent but in a different manner. I seem to feel things that some people don't. For example, a friend and I were going to go out to a club, yet for some reason, I just knew that I should not drive that night. I decided to ignore my "feelings," so I drove anyway. We got on the freeway and not twenty minutes later, we were in a car accident.

It's funny because during that twenty minutes before, I kept either hearing an outside voice or hearing my own thoughts (I'm not sure which). It was telling me I should not drive, over and over and over. Well, I also can walk into a house and know that either something bad happened in it or something was in that house that was not happy.

To go on to another story, my aunt's grandmother had passed away in her home, which was built I'd say in the early 1930s, if not before. My aunt made some needed repairs to the house and moved in. One night I stayed over, choosing to sleep by the fireplace. I woke up, however, with an uneasy feeling. I looked up and the door to the kitchen opened and shut, then opened and shut again.

This was in winter and no windows were open and no breeze was in the house. I knew something was there, but I saw nothing.

Famous Ghost Stories

The Canterville Ghost by Oscar Wilde puts a new spin on the classic ghost story. Canterville Chase, a well-known haunted property, is bought by an American minister and his family. Having no fear of ghosts, the family pays little attention to the performances of the Canterville ghost. In fact, they scold and punish him as if he were a living being. A humorous tale of the failed attempts at haunting, the reader is led to feel sorry for the ghost.

I jumped up and ran into my aunt's bed and woke her. I told her what happened. She said it was most likely her grandmother.

After I ran into her bedroom, I did shut the door. A few minutes later, it opened. My aunt and I just looked at the empty doorway. She said "go away" very loudly and the door shut. I never had any more occurrences in that house again.

The Premonition

Have you ever gotten a creepy feeling and somehow knew something bad was about to happen? Some people have this ability. Others have received warnings from the other side. The young woman in this story was warned in her dream about an upcoming disaster. She later wrote about her paranormal experience.

One night, at about 8:00 P.M., I was waiting for my live-in boyfriend to come home from work. He was three hours late and I was worried. He liked to drive fast and often had to travel long distances. I was so scared he was in a car wreck. I prayed so hard for him to make it home safe.

At 9:00 P.M., he finally walked in the door. I was so glad to see him I began to cry. He asked me what was wrong and I told him what I thought happened. Joking, I told him I thought I was going to have to buy a black dress. He laughed at me, then threw his paycheck at me and told me to go buy one if I wanted a new dress, but black wasn't a good color for me.

That night we went to stay at the home his parents were buying. They asked us to be there and wait for the cable guy to come the next day. His parents couldn't be there because of work schedules, so we said we'd do it for them. It was closer for my boyfriend to travel to work from there anyway. The next morning, I got him up for work just as I did every other morning. I kissed him goodbye and sent him out the door.

Then, I remembered I forgot to tell him to make sure he picked me up after work. I ran out the door to try to catch him before he left, but I was too late. Oh well, I thought, he'll

Famous Ghost Stories

Author Henry James begins his story *Turn of the Screw* by describing a group of people telling ghost stories. One member of the group, Douglas, claims to have a true story of ghosts. Douglas reads from a manuscript written by a governess that tells the tale of the haunting of her two charges. The story describes the governess's fears that the ghosts of the houses's former valet and governess are seeking to possess the innocence of her two charges, a ten-year-old boy and an eight-year-old girl.

remember to pick me up. I tried to go back to sleep, because it just was 4:00 A.M., but I had a hard time getting to sleep.

When I finally did get back to sleep I dreamed of him. In this dream, he forgot his lunch, so I took it to him. He was painting a subway station and I could see him [in the dream] up high. Before I could get too close, a man stopped me and told me I shouldn't be there. I was told I had to leave. I remember trying to explain that my boyfriend forgot his lunch, and that all I wanted to do was give it to him and leave. The man, however, was saying something to me, but I can't remember what it was. I was watching my boyfriend. All of a sudden, he began falling!

I got all panicky and started to shout at the guy to get help. The man, however, ignored me. I then felt calm. I could see my boyfriend getting up. He then started to walk away. He called to me and said I should hurry up if I was going with him, but the man kept talking to me. I remembered my mother telling me it's rude to walk away from someone when that person is talking to you, so I stayed and listened to the man.

The whole time, my boyfriend kept telling me to hurry up, because he had to go. If I was coming, he said, "Let's go." Finally, I turned away from the man and started running after my boyfriend. I was too far behind him and couldn't catch up. As I passed where he fell, I noticed he was still lying there. This scared me so badly I jumped up and was again totally awake.

It was now 8:10 A.M., according to my clock. I tried to go back to sleep, but I couldn't, so I called his mother so I'd have something to do while I waited for the cable guy. There was no answer, so I called my sister. I knew she'd be asleep, but I thought I'd wake her up to talk. When I called, she answered on the first ring.

I asked what she was doing awake at the early hour. She told me that my boyfriend had fallen at work. I asked if he was okay, but she said she didn't know. It took a while before I could find someone to come get me and tell me what happened. If you haven't guessed, my boyfriend did fall at work. The official time of death was 8:08 A.M., the same time I saw it happen in my dream.

A Young Child Visits

It's believed that some ghosts have emotions and personalities. This next story involves a young married couple and the ghost of a child that apparently wanted to be adopted by the couple.

I should explain first that this ghost of ours is a child, with a child's sense of humor. Some of these things that have happened scared me a lot, but other times I have thought the ghost's actions were cute.

Sometimes it's funny, sometimes it's not, but each time he plays a joke you can nearly hear him splitting his sides laughing. I recently spoke to my uncle about this. My uncle is very psychic, and he told me that this is a child who wants desperately to be born and become part of our family.

I don't know how to explain this, but the minute he said this, I felt it to be true. I swear that all of this is true, but I don't pretend for a minute to understand any of it. My husband and I have experienced a lot of strange happenings since we got married and moved in together two years ago. It started with lights and candles mysteriously being turned on or lit.

Sometimes, I would have to turn off the back porch light three or four times. I know it sounds strange, but there was a ghost at my parent's house, so I was pretty used to just ignoring this type of thing. Obviously being ignored was not what this particular ghost wanted, so it started to play with other electrical devices.

One day, I wanted to watch a video, so I pressed play on the VCR and thought that I'd let it play through the previews while I made a cup of tea. Suddenly, I stopped hearing the audio on the tape and wandered in to find that the tape was playing, but like I had pressed fast forward to get to a certain point.

I stopped the tape and pressed play again. This time, it fast forwarded itself three times. Then, I fast forwarded the tape to the beginning of the feature and stopped it. I went back to the kitchen and made my tea, but when I pressed play again, the tape was back at the beginning of the previews. I went to the feature, but I couldn't watch it because the tape kept fast forwarding itself.

I got annoyed, then I asked for him [the ghost] to please stop it and either sit down and watch the video or go away. On that day, I stopped watching the video and went for a walk. That night I got the video out to show my husband and it worked perfectly. A little while later, we were awakened at midnight by the CD player in the living room turning itself on and blasting loudly. I have never been so scared!!!

The week that we were moving houses, I had left a plate on the bedroom floor and had lost my eyeglasses. I got home from work to find the plate on the bed with my glasses on it. The knife and fork were on the plate, like the meal was finished. We laughed, thinking this was our goodbye gift from the ghost. We moved houses, and for a few weeks nothing happened.

Then, one night, our new housemate came home late and suddenly started screaming, "Who's there?" She was terrified and crying, saying that someone had opened the door from the inside and then refused to let her in. The door was open two inches, but when she went to push it open all the way, it wouldn't budge. She said she truly felt that someone was going to kill her.

My husband and I, who are quite sensitive, didn't feel the least bit worried, but she was nearly having a heart attack. My husband felt that our ghost had thought it was me coming home and got scared when he saw her instead of me. Another night, I was at home by myself and was feeling pretty uncomfortable. I heard singing coming from the living room. Being very scared, I ran straight into the living room to find nobody there. Not even the radio was on.

Since moving to this house, things go missing and turn up in strange places. One day, I was cleaning up and put my husband's dice in our wall unit, which is where we always used to keep them. Later that night, he was looking for dice and I pointed him to the wall unit but they weren't there. The next day he found them in the pencil case that he had been keeping them in lately. Apparently I was the only one of the three of us who didn't know that the place for the dice had changed from the wall unit to the pencil case.

Famous Ghost Stories

A Diagnosis of Death by Ambrose Bierce tells the story of a man, Hawver, who comes in contact with the ghost of a doctor. Hawver plans to spend time with a relative in Meridian. Upon his arrival, he finds the relative to be ill. So he takes up residence in a vacant house formerly owned by Dr. Mannering. The doctor was rumored to have the power of foretelling a person's death. Hawver recounts his encounters with the doctor to friends only to find out the doctor died three years ago.

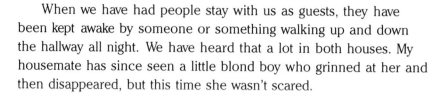

Famous Ghost Stories

Narrative of a Ghost of a Hand by J. S. Le Fanu tells the story of, not an entire ghost, but only the hand of a ghost. Mr. and Mrs. Posser lease the Tiled House. Shortly after their arrival, strange occurrences take place. Apparently a hand wants admittance to the house. Knocking incessantly on all windows and doors, the hand nearly drives the household crazy. Mr. Posser, thinking it a practical joke, finally opens the door to confront the jokester. The hand gains admittance to the house and disrupts the lives and sanity of those living within the house.

When we have had people stay with us as guests, they have been kept awake by someone or something walking up and down the hallway all night. We have heard that a lot in both houses. My housemate has since seen a little blond boy who grinned at her and then disappeared, but this time she wasn't scared.

A Local Legend . . . or Is It?

Some local legends, even the ones that sound bizarre, are based on the truth, only the events get exacerbated or changed as the story gets passed from one person to the next. This story involves a visit to a small town and an urban legend about a ghost that roams the town.

This experience with a ghost takes place in a small town and involves the ghost of a man, named Moody. The reasons that he still hangs around after his death vary from person to person, but here's the story I got during my short visit.

The Moody family was murdered except for the father. Moody the father now roams the countryside, near where his house used to be. He appears to be looking for the murderer of his family. On the road that is there now, called Moody Road, there is an old tree. If you stop your car underneath the tree, where its branches would be, and flash the car's headlights three times, a light appears to the north. The light seems to come from a farmhouse at the end of Moody Road, but I know the family that lives there and there is nothing luminescent or reflective there.

Saved by a Premonition

There are many documented cases where someone alters his or her plans at the last minute due to an unexplainable feeling that disaster is about to strike. In this story, a teenage girl changes her plans at the last minute and winds up avoiding death.

In the early 1950s, my mother was a teenager. She was completing her senior year of high school. At the time, she was dating my father. They had an argument one day and my mother was not talking to my future father. At some point later, my father slipped my mother a note saying that he would like to meet her after play rehearsal. It was a play in which my mother was participating, along with a number of her close friends.

According to my mother, she had every intention on getting a ride home that evening with her friends in one of their pickup trucks, but at the last minute, she decided to meet my father instead. They went to a small restaurant and had sodas.

At one point, they noticed their friends racing by in the pickup truck. Ten minutes or so later, a police car and ambulance raced by. On the way home, my mother and father came upon the accident. Their friends had been drag racing and had a head-on collision into a steamroller, instantly killing three of them. My father stopped and wound up helping to load the bodies into an ambulance.

Upon reaching my mother's house, my future father went in with her to wash his hands. As they entered through the door, they were greeted by my frantic aunt. Terrified, she exclaimed that she too had a premonition about the tragedy, as my aunt had seen the image of a funeral wreath appear at the top of the staircase, but didn't know what the vision meant.

A Visit from an Old Friend

When a loved one dies, it's often a traumatic experience. In cases where two people—one living and one who has passed on—are linked emotionally, sometimes a paranormal bond is created. In this story, a woman describes a relationship with a man whom she was involved with on and off for twenty years. After the relationship ended, she made the decision to see him again, but before she had the chance, the man died of a heart attack. For this couple, there was unfinished business.

For about two weeks, I was running into things that were relevant to an ex-love and thought that I should call him and tell him about these things that I knew were of interest to him. But I didn't.

On a particular Thursday, on my way home from work, the feeling that I should call this guy was getting stronger. I felt as if I needed to call him. Being in a new relationship that I didn't want to ruin, I thought better of it, so I didn't.

But, I thought, since in two days I was going to be in the area where he works, maybe I would just wait until then, drop by to say "hello," and then leave. There was never any real closure to our relationship, so I was extremely apprehensive about it. Still, I figured this would be what I'd do.

That same (Thursday) night, I had a dream that I walked into a dimly lit room. It was kind of what old bus terminals used to look like, maybe fifty to sixty years ago. He is sitting on a bench-type seat in front of me. In this dream I sat down next to him, and he said, "So, what's new, kid?" (Kid is what he always called me.) I went on to tell him that I was keeping busy, working, etc.

He said, "Good," and I proceeded to tell him that I was now in a relationship. He asked if the new guy was being good to me. I told him, "Yes, but you wouldn't like him." He asked why, and I explained that it was because he had long hair, a beard, and was Irish. He just smiled.

The only thing I remembered about the dream after that was that I was feeling very warm and comfortable. There was a door behind him and you could see light around the door, as if there was a bright light on in the next room and it was shining through.

The following day, I received a phone call that this guy had died from a heart attack. I had had the dream within an hour of his death. Other weird things happened after that, but all of the incidents stopped at the time he was cremated.

Accepting Death with Help from the Other Side

One of the most difficult things in life is dealing with the loss of a loved one. Grief is a terrible thing to live with, and saying goodbye to someone who is about to die can be an incredibly traumatic experience. In this story, someone finds solace with some help from the other side.

This is a true story that includes three events that happened to me around the time of my father's death. I am in my fifties, do not have a vivid imagination, nor do I tell stories.

The week before my father's death, on a Sunday morning, I was in church during Mass, praying for strength and comfort as we reached the end of my father's illness. I wasn't quite ready to let him go yet. As I finished my prayer and looked up, I saw three men in white clothes standing behind the altar.

As I continued to look, I noticed a casket in the center aisle, and my father standing beside the casket. He then started to walk toward the three men, and the man in the middle opened his arms to my father. At that point I experienced a wave of incredibly intense feelings that I have never had before. These feelings all happened at once, and included love, joy at seeing each other again, welcoming, and total acceptance. The experience left me breathless.

My reaction was, "If that's what he's going to, how can I be so selfish and try to keep him here when he's so sick?" After that, my attitude became more calm and accepting of my father's pending death. The following Saturday night, my father insisted on going to church, but I was unable to help my mother, so we persuaded my father to wait until Sunday. My father had become very ill the day before and was really too ill to go out without a great deal of assistance.

I had been at their house all Saturday afternoon, leaving at 5:00 P.M. to go home and change. I then went to my brother's house for a while. He lives very close in the other direction from me than my father did. I was at his house a brief time when my mother called to say that my father had collapsed. We both rushed over, finding my father had already passed away.

It was 6:00 P.M. I called the paramedics, then called my church and left a message with the secretary to have a particular priest come to our house directly after the 6:00 P.M. Mass that he was conducting. When he arrived, his first words to me were, "What was your dad doing at Mass by himself? I saw him in the back by himself, but when I went to talk to him after Mass, he was gone."

Famous Ghost Stories

To be Taken with a Grain of Salt by Charles Dickens is a first-person account of the narrator's interaction with the ghost of a murdered man. As the story begins, the narrator is fascinated by a newspaper article about a murder. He is later summoned to sit on the jury for the trial of that very same murder. Throughout his account, the narrator repeatedly describes the visits he receives from the ghost of the murdered man and the influence this ghost has on the fate of the murderer.

I told him my father couldn't have been there because he had died around that time.

A few days after the funeral, I was awakened in the middle of the night by a sound downstairs. I wasn't afraid because I have a huge dog with a very deep bark that will not let any strangers near our house. As I got out of bed, I went to the steps and started to look down the stairwell. I saw my father come to the top of the steps.

I started to touch him, but he told me that I couldn't. However, he gave me a hug and told me everything was all right, and not to cry or be sad for him. When I told my mother what happened, she asked why he had not come to her. The only reason I can give is that we had always had discussions about life after death. He told me if there was any way to come back and let me know, then he would do that. I believe he did.

Face-to-Face with a Ghost

What was the scariest experience of your life? Chances are you remember it as if it happened yesterday. In this story, an older man recalls an event that happened to him and his friend when they were teenagers.

This occurrence happened to my friend Frank and myself in 1959. At the time, we were both about thirteen years old and still attending junior high school. The time was about 8:00 P.M., but the month I no longer remember. I believe it was in autumn or winter.

I lived in the County of Worcestershire, located roughly in the middle of England. The area was a housing estate owned by the local council; it was then a respectable area as it was only eight or so years old. I believe the area is now more of a slum, but I haven't been there in over thirty-three years, as we moved in the middle 1960s. I later relocated to Australia in 1967.

On the street where we lived, the rear of our houses backed onto undeveloped bush land, which went on into some pretty, unspoiled countryside in most directions. However, the area just to the rear and to the south was called "The Burlish Camp."

Famous Ghost Stories

Hamlet by William Shakespeare tells the story of young Prince Hamlet whose life is turned upside down after seeing his father's ghost. The ghost reveals the story of his death—murdered by his brother while sleeping. The ghost prompts Prince Hamlet to avenge his murder and thus is the catalyst for the events shaping the story.

This Camp was built during WWII as a repatriation hospital for U.S. servicemen. After WWII, it was used to house Polish war refugees. As children we played, mixed, and were schooled with their children. In the mid-1950s, the people were relocated and the whole area was knocked flat, except for one lonely structure, called the "Water Tower."

As the name suggests, it was exactly that, a very large brick tower, from childhood memory, about fifty feet by fifty feet by at least eighty feet high, with a giant water tank on the top. It was used to supply the camp with water. There were eight windows, including four in the rear and four in the front.

The first pair of windows were about thirty feet from the ground. The next pair were another thirty feet up. There was a steel door on the southern side, but it was bricked up in the mid-1950s. There was never any electricity to it and it was inaccessible.

Frank and I were just hanging out, at the end of our street under a streetlight. This streetlight was at the junction of our tarred street and a wide dirt track (which led over to the camp, straight past the Water Tower and onto another small town, about four miles farther on). During our conversation, Frank said, "Hey, look at those lights in the Water Tower." The tower was probably a quarter-mile away, but could be made out in the moonlight.

I was quite surprised, because we could see some form of moving or blinking light in the window area of the tower. The light color did not appear as normal. This light was very shallow white, almost opaque. A short time later, about twenty yards from us on the dirt track, at an angle of about 45 degrees, we could see a light, the same color light that was in the tower.

I remember we thought it was someone on a bicycle, because the light seemed to fall to the ground. We started giggling, saying it must be someone drunk who fell off their bike. In the next instance, I remember myself drawn and staring wide-eyed at the figure of a man. I remember looking at his face. It had very distinguishable features, including a vertical flat forehead, long pointed nose, and sunken, very staring eyes. Because my concentration

was so intense, I did not seem to observe any body detail, except the lack of normal motion movements. He appeared to float along. He was also transparent. We could see right through him.

I then picked up a stone and threw it in his direction. Frank was pulling at my left arm screaming at me not to throw it. The stone, I estimate, fell short, but was in line as it hit the soft grass with a thud. The man brought up his arm as if to protect his face, and my own legs went to jelly. I fell to the ground and the vision disappeared. Frank stumbled off running, holding his ears and screaming.

The next thing I remember was lying on the ground. A lady was standing over me asking if I was okay. I ran home very scared. Frank lost his hearing for two days. We made a pact not to tell what happened to us, for fear of ridicule. As time went by we told, and we got laughed at. This occurrence left an indelible mark on me.

Many years later, my dad and I were passing the time talking about our family, being kids, where we lived, neighbors, and the like. My father told me how in the post-war years, times were hard. Back then, five or six of the local ladies would work continuous night shifts in an electrical insulator manufacturing plant, in the next town over from ours. He said they would bicycle eight to ten miles to work each way, instead of using the four-mile-long shortcut through the Burlish Camp.

When I asked why, my father told me none of the women felt good about going that way. It always seemed very still and eerie, especially when they went past the tower. When they'd come home in the morning, the birds were singing but up there by the tower it was always still and quiet.

Well, in the mid-1960s the tower was removed to make way for a communications repeater station. The local news was there to cover the event. Apparently, it took three days of drilling and massive explosives to finally collapse the tower.

The experts were scratching their heads, because they couldn't understand how it stayed up through so many explosive attempts.

This Old House

Growing up, do you recall living near an old, dilapidated house that just looked haunted? Did you and your friends trade stories about the ghosts that could have been living inside that house? When it comes to haunted houses, it seems that the older they are, the better the ghost stories become.

There is this old, rundown plantation house located along this old road with roughly ten houses on it. My boyfriend's family used to live there. The old house had stables, barns, and slave quarters. Throughout the inside of their old house, there are hidden quarters and passages where I suppose the "masters" hid the slaves when the authorities arrived.

My boyfriend told me that he recalled an event that happened when the entire family was home. His mother was upstairs vacuuming his little sister's room and the rest of the family was watching TV downstairs. His mother had turned off the vacuum cleaner to straighten out the shoes in the closet.

The vacuum was an old-time one, with the hose attached to the heavy base that follows behind. Anyway, while she was bent over, the vacuum turned back on and started moving toward the hallway. She figured it was just one of the kids playing games. She went downstairs and asked the family who did it. While she was downstairs, the vacuum turned on again; this time it convinced her that it wasn't any of the children playing a prank.

My boyfriend also says that he experienced a couple of things, like having someone walking around the house while he was home alone. His family moved from there several years ago, so nobody lives there anymore. A couple of my friends and I decided to go in the house one night. I will never forget it. We went in through the back door. It was pitch dark in there and I had no clue where anything was.

We went through the kitchen and the cabinets began to shake. We came to the conclusion that the floors were just weak. We walked into the hallway. There was a large antique mirror set up against the wall. We stopped and stared. I swore I had seen an

image. It wasn't my reflection in the mirror. It was a blurred, dark, fuzzy image. I didn't know what it was. I couldn't ask my friends, because I was afraid they'd accuse me of being high or something.

We then went upstairs. This is where I really got freaked out. We went into this one room where the ceiling was falling out, the floors were weak, and trash of all sorts was everywhere. My friends had walked out ahead of me and I suddenly felt a warm wisp of air go past my neck. It couldn't have been a warm breeze, because it was the middle of February.

I turned around and saw nothing, but there was some strange noise coming from the corner. It was as if something was approaching. I freaked out and ran down the steps and never returned. I've told my boyfriend about it and he backs me all the way. He claims to have experienced similar occurrences. I don't know what did happen. All I know is I never have and never will go in there again.

Two Guests for the Price of One— One Living, One Not

It's common for people not to believe in ghosts or haunted houses—that is, until they experience a paranormal event firsthand. In this case, a young woman was visiting her boyfriend's house. For a long time, her boyfriend claimed his house was haunted, but his girlfriend didn't believe him.

This experience happened to me at my friend's house. It isn't very scary in writing, but to experience it firsthand was something else. My friend was always telling me that his house was haunted, but I never believed him. I simply didn't believe in ghosts.

One night, we had a get-together at his house. It was just the two of us. The rest of his family was on vacation. We watched television until about 1:30 A.M. We had just gotten settled down in the den to go to sleep when we heard the back door open and close.

We thought it was his parents getting home early, so we were pretending to be asleep.

Then we heard footsteps. They started at the back door and went across the kitchen, stopping at the entry to the dining room, which is connected to the den by another entry. We knew that something was wrong because those footsteps didn't belong to anybody that lived in the house. We both looked as the footsteps stopped at the dining room. There was no one visible where there should have been. The footsteps then proceeded to walk into the den. At this point, I was ready to walk ten miles to my house in my pajamas, but I found that I couldn't move.

At the exact moment the footsteps entered the den, I turned as cold as an ice cube. That surprised me because I was in my winter sleeping bag that kept me warm in weather that was below zero. The footsteps stopped right next to me and for the next ten or fifteen seconds, it felt as if we were being watched. It's a feeling I can't explain. I guess it has to be experienced firsthand.

My friend's dog ran upstairs when the cold entered the room. He didn't just casually get up and leave, he jumped up and bolted out of the room. The footsteps then left the room and went upstairs, stopping in every room for a few seconds. We then heard them come back down, and head into the basement, where they stopped for the rest of the night. We searched the basement the next day, but found nothing. My friend said it must have been a ghost just checking up on his house.

Bad Luck Blamed on an Old Man (or Maybe His Ghost)

This person's paranormal experience involved an encounter with an old man, possibly a shaman, who placed what the experiencer believed was a curse on her and her friends as they embarked on a mountain biking expedition. Is this story about bad luck blamed on an old man, or is there really some paranormal force at work?

Famous Ghost Stories

The Phantom Coach by Amelia B. Edwards tells the story of a young hunter who loses his way during a snowstorm. Luckily he comes across an old man who leads the hunter back to his master's manor. Anxious to get back to his wife and quell her fears, the hunter dares to go back out into the snow, hoping to catch a ride with a mail coach the master spoke of. The coach, however, has no intentions of returning the hunter to his wife.

This event occurred in 1998, in Moab, Utah. After a tough day of mountain biking, my group of nine friends decided that the following day would consist of an easier ride. The weather had been quite nice thus far, around 85 degrees every day.

After finding what looked like a good trail, located about fifty miles out of town, we loaded everyone, along with the bikes, in the 1993 Suburban. My husband, an experienced 4×4 driver, took us up the desolate, curvy road toward our destination.

The terrain was harsh and desert-like. The road began climbing up in elevation. About thirty miles into our trip, we spotted an old man with a six-foot wooden cane. The cane had feathers hanging off the top. The man looked very old. We thought he was hitchhiking.

With nine people plus bikes, we did not have room for him. Someone made a sly comment, "Like we're going to make room for some old hitchhiker, we barely have room to breathe as it is." As we drove quickly past him, we all noticed that he stopped, shook his cane at us, and appeared to say something. I spoke up and said, "He was probably a shaman, putting a curse on us for not picking him up."

While determining how much farther we had to go, someone noticed that the road we were on led to basically nowhere. It was at least fifty miles back to town if we continued on. There were no homes or other cars for as far as we could see. We all felt odd about the man, and wondered where he could have been headed on foot.

Before we knew it, there was snow on the ground. We had been climbing in elevation quite quickly. We were all in shorts and were shocked. There was disagreement as to what we should do. We had to either turn back or continue on. It was interesting that no one at the bike shop warned us about the snow.

We decided to continue on. Well, before we knew it, the Suburban overheated. We had the Suburban checked prior to our trip, so we were quite perplexed. Anyhow, we let the truck cool down, then tried to find a place to turn around. This was not easy, considering the road was now down to one narrow lane. We made the U-turn, but shortly thereafter, we started sliding off the road.

With everyone yelling, the driver slowly gained control. After that, we were all very uptight, but we turned the music up and tried to relax. Well, the CD player suddenly stopped working. The stereo was brand new, however. I spoke up again and stated, "Well, it appears we've been cursed by that old shaman. When we see him on the way back down, let's make sure to smile and wave." Well, guess what, there was no old man in sight the entire way back.

We had been camping up the river up until this point, and decided we should continue to camp, considering the weather was so great. We had made hotel reservations, however, just in case. So, after returning to town, we dropped off some of the gang at their vehicle. We told them that we would cancel the hotel reservations and meet them back at the campsite.

We pulled in to the hotel, turned off the Suburban, and all went inside. After canceling the reservation, we hopped back in the truck, and again, just our luck, it wouldn't start. It appeared the starter was shot. At this point, I told my husband, "That's the third bad luck incident. Hopefully, this is the end to our curse." Four hours later, we pulled up to the campsite. One of the bikers walked up, cussing that we had her bike on top [of the Suburban] and that she had been waiting for several hours to ride. She grabbed her bike and took off. Again, too much tension for this gang.

No one slept well that night, but the next morning was beautiful and full of hope. We all laughed about the bad luck we had endured the previous day. Part of the group decided to sightsee, while the others decided to go on another mountain bike ride.

While touring around, no one seemed to get along. As the day came to a close we noticed storm clouds quickly rolling into town. Then the rain started. Not just a light sprinkle, but a full-on down-pour. On the way to camp, we decided we'd grab some of our gear and do the hotel thing for the night. We arrived to our worst luck yet.

Our campsite had flooded. A flash flood had obviously stormed through. My husband and I had been sleeping in the Suburban, so most of our belongings were okay. It was pitch black out, but with

our flashlights, we could see camp gear floating away. We couldn't have imagined anything worse that this. Everything at the campsite was gone or destroyed.

Instead of getting angry, we all decided that we would band together for the night and salvage what we could. Luckily, some kids from a higher camp had pulled some of our gear up to shore before the deep water set in. Hours later, nine wet ex-campers headed to the last hotel room in town.

From that point on, our trip was terrific. We're not sure what exactly stopped the curse. Maybe it just ran its course. We didn't really dwell on that. We do all agree, however, that we had been cursed, for whatever reason, and don't wish to be cursed ever again—forty-eight hours of pure bad luck was plenty!!

A Haunt at Sea

We've all heard about haunted houses, haunted battlefields, and haunted graveyards, but what about haunted ships that are part of the U.S. Navy? This sailor tells the story of his encounter with a ghost while serving in the navy. His encounter happened aboard a ship where many sailors had died years before in a tragic fire.

Hurricane Andrew had ripped through Florida, but the U.S.S. [name deleted], stationed in Pensacola, Florida, had pulled away from the pier to minimize any damage from the storm. The ship had been underway for three days. I was an airman at the time, out smoking a cigarette on the port quarter of the fantail with two of my friends. I looked up toward the entrance of the port quarter and noticed another person standing there.

The man wore a white sailor hat and blue dungarees. After a second of looking at him, I answered my friend's question then looked up again, but the person wasn't there. This all took place in about two seconds, not enough time for anyone to get off of the port quarter, let alone a sailor with bell bottoms.

The reason I looked up again was to say "hey" or "hi" or something like that. The pause between me looking back at my friend and looking back at the person standing there was so brief, I couldn't believe that he wasn't there when I looked up again.

When I looked back, a chill ran down my spine and I high-tailed it out of there. My friends also got a scare, but they didn't see what I saw! Why did they get creeped out? Now that I remember, I ask myself questions like: Why was he wearing a white hat while underway, especially when they aren't authorized any-more? Why was he wearing a blue dungaree (chambray) shirt, when we wear turtleneck jerseys now? Why did I feel the sudden need to get off of the port quarter? Why did my friends feel the same as me when they didn't even see what I saw?

Later, I learned a little more about the U.S.S. [name deleted]'s tragic fire in the 1960s. It killed more than 160 sailors. The fire had also affected the port quarter of the ship, and the ghost I saw isn't the only ghost that's been seen. Now the ship is decommissioned, and the ghosts may never be investigated, but just ask anyone who was on the U.S.S. [name deleted] after the fire if they heard about the ghosts, and I guarantee that you will hear an interesting story.

Two Ghosts Drop in for a Visit

In this story, a woman encounters what turns out to be two ghosts living in her home. At first, this was no big deal, but when the ghosts started scaring her kids, she took action.

This story is totally true and there are several witnesses. When I purchased my home, it was only three years old. My family would hear strange noises coming from our upstairs. At first, we thought the noises were the results of maneuvers or practices conducted by the Marines at the Quantico Marine base. It soon became obvious that this was not the case.

The noises seemed to start in my teenage daughter's bedroom and "walk" across the floor into the bathroom. We could sometimes hear footsteps or chairs being dragged across the kitchen floor. I placed an open Bible in each room of my house to let these visi-tors know that we had faith in God, and to deter any bad spirits.

Famous Ghost Stories

A Ghostly Duel by Jack London opens with a dis-cussion between young men of the existence of ghosts. Two of the men, Damon and Pythias, are disbelievers and entreat their friend, George, to provide proof. The men agree to explore the Birchall mansion that night, which is suppos-edly haunted. Damon and Pythias look about the mansion and upon not discovering anything supernatural, decide to play a game of chess to pass the time. That game leads to a possession that may end up costing one of the men his life.

This, however, did not stop the activity. Finally, one day I was upstairs after hearing a lot of noises. (It was during the day.) I spoke out loud, "I don't mind your presence here, but I wish I knew how to help you. You are, however, frightening my children. Please don't scare my kids."

The noises immediately subsided for a few days, but started back up again and even louder this time. My daughter was fifteen years old at the time. She was sleeping soundly one night when something grabbed her by the arm and was dragging her off the bed. Now we were all very scared.

I contacted a psychic who was located in Orange County. She told me that I had the spirits of a father and his young daughter residing in our home. They had been killed at the same time and were afraid to go on to the other side because they were afraid of what life in the spirit world would be like. She worked with these spirits, however, and eventually led them over to the other side. I felt as if a good deed had been done. There have been no noises or activities since.

Meeting the In-Laws

Meeting your future in-laws can be a bit scary, but imagine if you were in the bathtub when your deceased soon-to-be father-in-law (if he were still alive) suddenly appeared for a visit. Yup, the guy was a ghost. He'd been dead for years, but apparently wanted to meet the woman his son planned to marry.

It was June 1974. I had been living with my then-boyfriend (now husband) Joe for about five months. Our apartment was in an old building with a door going into the bathroom from the hall (which ran through the apartment) and another door that came off an odd little room that also opened onto the living room.

The night this event happened I was alone. Joe was in school. I was minding my own business taking a bath when I looked toward the door into the odd room. I saw a luminescent green swirling cloud up near the top of the doorway (the door was

open). A little surprised, I looked back at my bath. If I ignore it, it will go away, I thought.

When I looked back, there was a face in the cloud. It was narrow, like Joe's, but it looked more like the face of his brother. I looked away, then back. This time, the cloud had transformed into the shape of a person. It was taller than Joe, but with the same thin build.

I knew who it was, though I'd never even seen a picture. Joe's father had died when Joe was only four. It couldn't be anyone else. So there I was, wet and naked, with the ghost of my future father-in-law right near me. His eyes were politely averted.

I dried myself rapidly, wrapped the towel around me, and fled the bathroom. I stopped in the living room to get the phone, then ran back, past the bathroom door, toward the bedroom. As I passed the bathroom, I glanced in to see the ghost had turned as if to follow. I ran into the bedroom, jumped into bed, pulled the blankets over my head, and placed the phone against my belly. I didn't know, however, whom I was going to call.

A short time later, the ghost was gone. When Joe got home, I asked him what his father looked like. As Joe gave me a description, I was able to fill in the details. I then told him the whole story. Months later, I finally saw a picture of his father. That confirmed to me whom I had seen, but I haven't seen the ghost of my father-in-law since.

Our New Home

Would you move into a house knowing someone had committed suicide there a few years earlier? This elderly couple was shopping around for a home in which to enjoy their retirement. When they came upon one particular house, they chose to purchase it, even after learning what had happened there.

My husband and I moved to Fresno, California, in 1990. We were purchasing a cozy three-bedroom home in a quiet and well-kept neighborhood. The house had been built in 1985, yet after only five years we were the third family to have lived there.

Rather than having to ask why this was so, our realtor (who was also a friend of ours) came clean with us. She was giving us one more look at the place when she paused in the living room. "The couple who had this home built was young. This was their first house together. They had a pool table right here in the middle of the formal living room. By all accounts they were happy, and doing well in every way. They hadn't even been here for two years. It was around Christmas when the husband stood at the end of the pool table and fired a shotgun into his mouth. He never even left a note to explain why," said the realtor.

Without thinking about it, my husband and I reached for one another's hands. Our friend went on, "I'm telling you this simply because I want to give you a choice, and I don't want you to hear the news from your neighbors. Some people are uneasy about these matters."

I knew about the stigma attached to places where suicide has been committed, but hearing the story, I felt mostly a loss for this young couple, especially the wife. I squeezed my husband's hand, not able to imagine what the pain would be like if I lost him. The story did not shy me away from the house, but drew me to it. I knew then that we would buy it and transform it into the warm and welcoming home for friends and family that it was originally meant to be.

We soon settled in and started our new life, pleased with our decision. As far as strange occurrences go, every now and then some small item would turn up missing, only to reappear in some unlikely place. We blamed this on the move, on being forgetful, or on our smaller grandchildren.

Then on one morning, after we'd been living in the house for about two months, I got out of the shower, wrapped a towel around myself, and suddenly got the urge to play the piano that was in the formal living room. With the doors locked and the blinds shut, I had no worries about being caught half-naked.

I sat on the bench and played for about five minutes. Once finished, I replaced the cover over the keys. It was absolutely quiet. Then, from the kitchen, loud and clear, I heard an unmistakable whistle, the type that construction crews are fabled to blast at passing young women. Embarrassed and somewhat shaken, I investigated. But I knew from the start I would find no one there.

I suppose that this event "broke the ice," so to speak. From then on, on the few occasions I was alone in the house, I never felt alone. Often, I'd hear a soft whisper in my ear, or have the sensation that someone was passing me in the hallway. My husband and two of my grown daughters had the feeling of always being watched, as did I.

The days before Thanksgiving found me cleaning from floor to ceiling as I prepared for a house full of company. On the afternoon before the holiday, I cleaned the spare bathroom and asked my husband not to walk on the neatly vacuumed rug until after the guests arrived. A few minutes after I said this, I heard him call me from the hallway.

My husband stood at the bathroom doorway, pointing inside as I approached. It took me a moment to see what had caught his attention. On the carpet in front of the toilet were the indentations of a man's footprints. They were slightly spread apart and facing toward the bowl. There were no other footprints in that bathroom, nor had the carpet been disturbed other than that. What's more, the toilet was on the far side on the bathroom, about fifteen feet from the door. Unless my husband could fly, or his feet had suddenly grown two sizes, I knew we had a ghost.

We decided to spend Christmas at a cabin in the Sierra foothills (in no way due to our "visitor"). Before leaving, we did a careful walk-through of our house, making sure all windows and doors were bolted and the burglar alarm was set. We were gone for over a week, and despite the chilly air, the first thing I did when we returned was go through the house opening drapes and windows to get rid of the stuffiness.

As I pulled open the drapes on the sliding door in the family room, the sun reflecting on the glass drew my eye to the

Famous Ghost Stories

The Bowmen by Arthur Machen is a tale of paranormal intervention during a war. This story is believed by many to be fact. It is up to the reader to decide. British troops are surrounded by Germans and have no hope left for survival. A British soldier, for a reason undiscovered, remembers having seen a picture of St. George with a motto beneath. Uttering the motto, the soldier witnesses the downfall of the German troops at the hands of St. George's bowmen.

Famous Ghost Stories

The Escort by Daphne du Maurier is yet another tale of supernatural intervention during wartime. A British ship is heading home through the dangerous waters of the North Sea. The captain falls ill just as a German submarine is spotted. As the crew lies in wait of action from the enemy submarine, a ship appears alongside their own and offers to escort them to a port of safety. The merchant ship escapes danger with the protection of the mysterious ship. Once reaching safety, the escort disappears and the identity of its captain is revealed.

mark of a handprint. It belonged to a man. I ran my finger across a small portion of it, and it smudged. It was on the inside of the door.

Like a typically obsessive neat freak, I had cleaned the house the day before we left, so that we could come home to perfect order. This included washing the glass on this particular sliding door. Since our departure, my husband was the only man who'd been inside the house. Furthermore, his hand was smaller than the print. Nobody had a key to our home and nothing had been disturbed during our absence.

Had there been a break-in, the alarm would have sounded, and we would have been notified by our security company. There was no logical explanation, and I wanted there to be. After seeing the handprint, the only thing I could imagine was the phantom of this young man, staring sadly through the glass at the outside world, trapped inside this home where he had, without explanation or reason, taken his own life.

The thought of this saddened me to the point where I called our priest to come and bless the house, and to commend this man's spirit to the world beyond. The service was beautiful and brought a stronger feeling of peace to our home and to my heart. More than anything, though, I hoped our "locked-in" guest had found peace and freedom.

The week after our priest's visit, I awoke in the middle of the night for no particular reason. There was absolute quiet, both in and outside of our bedroom. As I shifted to my other side, I caught a glimpse of the bedroom doorway, and saw standing in it the form of a man. My husband was snoring at my side. Besides, the pitch black silhouette did not match my husband's shape. I knew what I was looking at was not made of flesh and blood. I could not believe my eyes, but I was not scared. I watched, unblinking.

The figure faced me, unmoving. The name "David" drifted through my mind. I spent roughly the next thirty seconds trying to identify his features, but he lacked detail. The figure seemed only to be a shadow. Finally, without noise, he faded into the darkness. Somehow, I sensed he was leaving forever, and for some reason he felt compelled to say goodbye to us. I appreciated him for that, since goodbyes seemed to be difficult for him while he lived.

My Cat Saw a Ghost

It's widely believed that animals, such as cats and dogs, have the ability to sense ghosts and can often see, hear, or feel a presence that is invisible to humans. In this ghostly encounter, a woman is staying at her aunt's house. She is quietly reading, with her aunt's cat purring on her lap. All of a sudden, the cat becomes very excited.

I have an aunt who used to live in Kansas City. About five years ago, I flew to Missouri to visit her. She lived in an older plantation-style house, which had been divided into two halves, duplex-style. My aunt lived in one half. I was sitting in a reading room on the second floor, adjacent to one of the sealed doors that separated the two "apartments." My aunt's cat was sitting in my lap.

All of a sudden, the cat began arching its back and hissing in a way that I had never heard. It was terrified but refused to leave or be consoled. I looked around for what was bothering the cat, but we were alone in the room. Then I took a deep breath, and almost choked. I could smell a very strong, very putrid perfume. It was almost overwhelming. It seemed as if the air in the room was getting tight . . . as if the pressure was increasing. I looked at my aunt's cat, which was still going crazy. Its attention seemed to be wandering to various parts of the room.

At one point, the cat grew frantic, backing away from whatever it sensed, and screeching loudly. By this time I was covered in goosebumps, my heart was pounding, and I could almost feel my hair turning gray.

Eventually, the cat calmed down. The smell seemed to weaken and finally vanish. The room "felt" empty once again. When my aunt came upstairs and looked at me, she saw my hair standing on end, and at first was shocked. Then, she seemed to realize what happened. She said, "Did my cat introduce you to our ghost?"

A Reunion with Grandpa

This is a short story that describes a man's reunion with his deceased grandfather. The encounter happens when this man stays alone for the night at his grandparent's house.

My grandfather died in 1988. In 1992, I was offered a summer placement with a law firm in Miami and decided to accept it. I arrived in Miami from Jamaica on a Sunday evening. I can't remember the exact date. It was sometime in July. I decided to stay at my grandparents' house for the night. The house was empty. My grandmother was on vacation and my grandfather was deceased.

I was tired when I got to the house, but I couldn't sleep because my adrenaline was going crazy at the excitement of beginning my new job the next day. I decided to watch TV in bed, hoping maybe I would nod off. I soon began hearing this strange ticking sound and thought it was a fan that had gotten stuck.

The sound became louder. I got up to check. Someone may have broken in, I thought. Then I heard a bell sound. It was the type of sound that a typewriter makes when the return carriage is pressed. I froze. The skin on my hands pulled tightly up into goosebumps. My grandfather would always spend long hours in his study typing away at night.

The sound was so familiar that when I realized what it was, it was almost comforting. I was scared but relieved. I crept to the door and looked out. I could smell his cologne everywhere.

Grandfather's Ghost

Some people believe they are regularly visited by deceased loved ones. In this encounter with a ghost, a girl is staying at her best friend's house. Her best friend's family, however, has another frequent guest—the ghost of their grandfather who died years earlier.

When I was a preteen growing up in Bloomington, Indiana, I had a very close friend with whom I would "sleep over" frequently.

One night over dinner, my friend's mother rather calmly stated that my friend's grandfather had been to see them the previous night. My friend seemed a little uncomfortable about this. After dinner I asked why, and was shocked to find out that her grandfather had passed away in 1972, which was four years earlier.

Since that time, her mother claimed to have been regularly visited by him via what she believed to be a dream. Although my friend loved her grandfather dearly, she was not comfortable with the concept that the dead could visit the living. She also was afraid that her mother might be a little nuts.

When Saturday arrived, I was asked to sleep over as usual. I had completely forgotten about the "visit" from "Papa." When her parents left for a party at 7 P.M., we were left in the care of my friend's older brother, who was more into listening to music than paying attention to a couple of twelve-year-old kids. At around 11 P.M., my friend and I unfolded the sofabed in the family room as we always did.

By around 11:30 P.M., we were both ready to turn out the lights and get to sleep. At about 11:45 P.M., a large recliner directly to the right of the sofabed opened up and reclined on its own. I was jolted awake and looked over at my friend who was staring at the chair with wide eyes.

"Papa!" she said breathlessly. When I asked what she meant, she indicated that the recliner had been her grandfather's, and that he had spent nearly twelve hours a day in it during the last years of his life. She believed that her dead Papa was "visiting" and was sitting in the chair he had loved so much.

I became so terrified I couldn't move. My friend and I remained there in the dark shaking for about five minutes until the chair slipped back into its normal position. We then we went upstairs to sleep on the floor in the living room. The next morning at breakfast, my friend's mother said that Papa had "visited" again the night before. My friend looked at me and said, "I know, mama, I know."

Heard, But Not Seen

Just because a house is believed to be haunted, it doesn't mean that the living residents will actually come face to face with a ghost, spirit, or apparition. In many cases, a ghost will make itself known without ever showing itself.

My husband's brother and his wife owned a farmhouse that was approximately 100 years old. They bought it from an elderly woman who was entering a nursing home. Her husband had recently died. Soon after they moved into the home, odd events began happening. I can no longer remember the order of the events, but my husband and I lived in close proximity and were kept abreast of the almost daily occurrences.

Often, my sister-in-law would come home from work to find both the TV and stereo playing. Jars of spices would be sitting on the kitchen counter. Various lights would be turned on. A clock that they never wound would suddenly begin ticking.

When she and her husband were downstairs in the basement, the light switch at the top of the stairs would switch off, leaving them in total darkness. At times, when my sister-in-law was home alone, she would hear footsteps upstairs, and a sound that she described as being similar to many wire hangers hitting the hard-wood floor at the same time.

She would gather up her courage to go upstairs, only to find nothing amiss. In one instance my sister-in-law poured herself a cup of boiling tea just before she was about to take a shower. She was alone in the house. Before getting into the shower, she left the full mug on the counter. When she got out of the shower, the mug was moved to a different spot on the counter, and it was completely empty. The outer doors were still locked.

Later, when they owned a cockatoo and a dog, both animals would make a ruckus in the middle of the night for no apparent reason. The dog would also sit at the bottom of the staircase and growl at something apparently at the top of the stairs.

While I was in the living room one evening, the CD player switched on and started flipping through songs. It then just as suddenly turned off.

Another time, my husband was house/pet sitting, and both the TV and stereo switched on and off several times. After my in-laws had a baby, the activity quieted down somewhat. Eventually they moved away, not because of the strange activity, but because he was transferred to another city. They had no strange occurrences in their new house.

A Ghost Takes Action

Sometimes ghosts make themselves known by scaring the living people they come into contact with. This story recounts one of the relatively rare cases when a ghost is reported to have actually injured someone. As with all of these stories, how truthful this story is remains unknown, except of course to the person who is conveying the experience.

I was up at around 2:00 A.M. one morning, which isn't too unusual for me. I spent some time playing around on my computer. Suddenly, I got this strange feeling. The hair on the back of my neck started to prick up and I got a very uneasy feeling. At the time, I thought I was just tired. Then I heard our neighbor's dogs, which are kept in a small fenced-in yard beside their house. They began to bark like crazy.

About this time, I figured there had to be a ghost around, because I recognized the feeling from times when I had visited supposedly "haunted" places before. Well, I walked into the kitchen to get some iced tea out of the refrigerator, and I started feeling weighed down, like someone was pushing on my shoulders.

Of course, I was the only one in the house who was awake. I opened the fridge and poured myself a glass of iced tea. When I closed the fridge, I saw something move out of the corner of my eye, near the sink. When I turned and looked, it looked almost as if the air was rippled near the sink. Then I felt a rush of air and heard a loud "FWOOSH" noise. I felt like someone had just rammed into me.

I flew backwards into the doors of the kitchen closet and fell onto the kitchen floor. When I regained my senses (I think I was

Famous Ghost Stories

How It Happened by Sir Arthur Conan Doyle is a ghost story told from the spirit's point of view. The first sentence tells us that the spirit is telling his story through a writing medium. Therefore, we know up front that the narrator is dead; however, we don't get a feel for his impression of death. As the title implies, the story recounts the accident in which the gentleman dies. Not your typical ghost story, this gives us an account of the gentleman's understanding of his death.

knocked out for a few seconds), I ran out of the kitchen as fast as I could. I got back on the computer and talked to a friend of mine who had experience with this sort of thing. With his help, we managed to get the ghost out of the house.

About five months later, I was in my bedroom with my girlfriend, who was visiting. I suddenly felt an intense pain in my shoulder, as if a wild animal had scratched me. My shoulder felt as if it was burning. My girlfriend looked at my shoulder and there were at least fifteen tiny claw marks on it that hadn't been there a few minutes before.

I started to shake. I then found that I couldn't move. Just as we turned out the light and tried to go to sleep, I saw what looked like tiny black hands coming out of the darkness. My girlfriend was screaming. "They're all around me! They're everywhere!" she screamed. We saw an orange face come out of the darkness and hover there for a few minutes before it disappeared.

A Late-Night Visitor

This short story is a recollection from a woman's childhood. She believes she was visited in the middle of the night by a ghost who entered her bedroom.

Our house was built in the early part of this century, somewhere between 1920 and 1930. I know almost nothing about any of the previous inhabitants, except that the family before mine had been a large one.

I couldn't have been more than six or seven when I saw a ghost for the first time. I awoke late at night needing to go to the bathroom. As I looked toward the door of my room, I saw a man. He looked like a lightly colored line drawing. The image was three-dimensional, but somehow softer. This "man" was floating/standing on the same level as the molding, which ran around the walls, about six inches off the floor.

He seemed to be having a conversation with someone whom I could not see. I was terribly frightened. Plus, I had to go to the

Taking a Ghost Tour

Contact the department of tourism in your city for information about ghost tours. The New England Ghost Tour: Boston Spirits Walking Tour (781-235-7149; *http://members.aol.com/nehaunts*), for example, is a ninety-minute walking tour of Boston's most infamous haunted locations.

bathroom! As I sat staring at him he turned and looked at me. I nearly died of fright. I knew, with childlike certainty, that if I walked by him he would "get" me.

Finally, after what seemed like an eternity, he looked away. I closed my eyes and walked toward the door, opened it, and felt my way to the bathroom. Once I was safely in the bathroom, I opened my eyes. When I went back to my room he was gone.

I never saw this man again, but many times late at night, I would awake from strange nightmares with the feeling that I wasn't alone.

A Paranormal Romance

Mediums who communicate with the other side virtually all seem to agree that spirits (or ghosts) have personalities and emotions. But could a ghost actually have a romantic crush on a living person?

When I was young and still in school, there was a boy who many girls liked. He was very handsome. For a few weeks one month, he came to school in a bothered state. He and I were good friends, so I asked him what was the matter. He told me not to laugh at him, but he thought he had a secret admirer. The problem was, this admirer happened to be a ghost.

I thought he was pulling my leg, but he insisted it was true. He told me how a few times when he was taking a shower and the mirror had become foggy, he'd get out and see a heart drawn in the condensation with the words "[name deleted] loves me" or "[name deleted] is mine," or sometimes just "[name deleted]" in elegant woman's cursive writing.

He said that he sometimes thought he heard female giggling when he'd be getting dressed in the morning. He also sometimes had the suspicion that he was being watched. I believed him, for he was a pretty level-headed guy, not one for making up absurd stories.

I told him to go home and speak as if to himself of a girlfriend, or when he was on the phone, to speak very loudly of a girl he liked. I thought it might make the ghost/girl think he had a girlfriend.

It worked, I supposed, for he never told me anything else about his invisible girlfriend. I am still somewhat amused at the fact that simple crushes can exist in the spirit world.

The Old Lady Who Wouldn't Move On

Like so many encounters with ghosts, this one takes place over many years in an apartment building where an elderly woman died in a tragic fire. Years later, the people who moved into the deceased woman's apartment began to experience some rather strange things.

This occurred over a period of years, since I twice lived at the same address in Maryville, Missouri. In the summer of 1979, several of my college buddies and I took over every apartment in a run-down apartment building. It turns out, everyone who lived in this building had various forms of paranormal experiences, most involving a ghost we've come to know as Lucy. It was a common tie among us, and we formed our own sort of family.

Whenever the dishes would pile up in the apartment that was Lucy's, they would start rattling of their own volition. We'd chuckle about it. While we all had had paranormal encounters, we weren't going to jump at every little creak and groan in an old building.

There was the time we had a party in the building and had nearly seventy-five guests. One of the guests was heard talking to herself in the bathroom. This was odd, but it was odder when she came and asked who the old woman was who had barged in on her in the bathroom. We passed that off too, but a little less quickly. Perhaps she'd had a little too much of the home brew that someone had brought.

One afternoon we were all gathered in Lucy's apartment, and all of a sudden her four-foot-tall, pink-and-black teddy bear flipped from a reclining position in an overstuffed chair to face up and forward, and moved onto the floor. We all stared at this, and this prompted a discussion about poltergeists.

I was a little bit groggy, and was lying back with my eyes closed, listening to the conversation. I suddenly got this vision of an elderly lady, in a faded calico-print dress. Her hair was in a bun and she was wearing those 1950s-style pixie glasses with sparkles in the corners.

As the conversation progressed about the poltergeist theories, she kept shaking her head "no." When the theory came up that the poltergeists know exactly what is going on, where things are, and are simply trying to send a message, the image of the elderly lady made a gesture with a bony index finger and started to shake her head "yes." At that point I opened my eyes and said "Okay." Then I reported to the others what I had just seen.

In 1984, I attempted to go back to college and finish my degree. As it happened, the only apartment available in town was the very same apartment that had been Lucy's. I took it. Nothing outstanding happened at first, so I figured the happenings years earlier could be chalked up to the overactive imaginations of young twenty-year-olds. Perhaps we had some sort of mass hallucination.

A few weeks later, I was going to sleep when I heard a noise in the hall. It was an odd noise, and I went to investigate. I opened the door to a staircase. It was engulfed in flames. I could feel the heat and hear my hair crisping up. I slammed the door and ran for my back door. I tripped and fell face-first on the floor. I must have passed out.

When I woke up, I doubted what I had seen and heard. There was no sign of fire. Two days later, I was talking with my landlord. The back stairs were rather rickety, and I expressed some concern about what would happen if there was indeed a fire. He told me it was funny that I had said something about that.

The apartment building used to have a peaked roof rather than a flat one. There was a fire in the stairwell years earlier. It had acted just like a chimney. An elderly lady had been killed in the center room of the apartment that I was living in.

Famous Ghost Stories

In a Glass Darkly by Agatha Christie tells the story not so much of a ghost, but rather of a vision. The supernatural vision is the catalyst for every action that takes place in the story. A young man visits his best friend at a country home. As he dresses for dinner, a door behind him opens and he witnesses the murder of a woman at the hands of her husband. All this he sees in the mirror. Though this scene could not have possibly taken place, the man is surprised to find the murdered woman and the murderer at dinner that evening.

Guardian Angel

In this retelling of a series of paranormal events, a family that seemed to be tormented by a ghost or evil spirit is ultimately protected by what's believed to be a guardian angel.

These events have happened to a friend of mine for the past ten years. She lives in a nice bungalow, in a middle-class area of Toronto. One night I was at her house and my friend (she was sixteen at the time), her mom, and I were talking about ghosts. Her mom is a down-to-earth, responsible, really nice lady. She began to tell me of things that happened to her and her family within the house.

On one of the first occasions she was renting the basement to one of her cousins. The cousin would constantly complain of the cold. The cousin reported that it was freezing, even in the summer. They ignored her complaints until one night. The cousin came up the stairs and asked the mom to come down for a second. She went down to find that papers and chimes hanging by the window were blowing around uncontrollably.

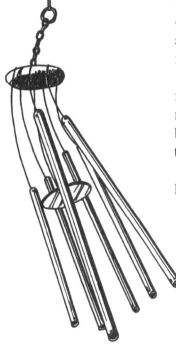

The windows, however, were shut and no fans were around. The mom looked around the room, but couldn't find the source of the draft. Then, the mom screamed, "Stop it!" as if she was talking to or scolding someone. All of a sudden, the wind and cold stopped. The mom and the cousin just looked at each other in disbelief.

The cousin then asked who she was talking to. My friend's mother, however, didn't know. The cold and the draft were soon replaced by an awful stench. It overpowered the cousin, who became physically ill. She ran upstairs (to where my friend was at the time), leaving the mom there alone.

The mom began to pray, because she's very religious and had heard that evil spirits emit awful smells when present. A gust of wind suddenly came back and it broke the windows from the inside out. (It was as if a baseball had been thrown at them.) No one entered the basement for the next few days.

The family called a local priest, who later conducted an exorcism on the house. For the next few years everything was fine. I asked my friend's mom (one night when we were talking), if she was into Ouija boards. She told me that she had this friend who had been able to talk to spirits since she was a little girl, and the two would conduct séances to call "good" spirits for advice.

She continued to tell me that more recently things were "starting up" again in the house. When the family would leave the house, they would come home to a "different house." The fridge would be turned around so the doors would be facing the wall, and bloodstains would sometimes be all over the hallway floors and walls.

Their family dog was also being terrorized. His hair was being pulled out in chunks and he refused to go downstairs where his papers were. This friend of mine suggested that the family set up a camera when they left the house to see what was going on. They put a camera facing the front door.

When they came home a few hours later and looked around the house for any changes, forks and knives were all on the floor and blood was on the repainted walls. They all went up to see the video, but it was just a shot of a closed door. There is no way that anyone could have entered from anywhere else, because they have an alarm (which was untouched), and the windows in the house are way too small for anyone to come in through.

I asked my friend if ever since then things were okay. Her mom then stated that more "bad luck" had come to her family since then. Her mom broke her leg falling down the basement stairs, they lost their business, and they were going to lose their house. My friend's mother told me that when both of her kids went on vacation for a couple of weeks and she was left alone in the house, another unusual event happened.

She was lying down on the couch crying because things were not going well. Then all of a sudden, she felt a warmth all over the house. She looked up and saw a beautiful, bright white light. The light only stayed for a couple of seconds. My friend's mother quickly shut her eyes and opened them again. The light, however, never returned. For the next couple of days, everything in the house smelled like roses, including the basement. My friend's mother is convinced that it was her guardian angel who came to

Famous Ghost Stories

The Presence by the Fire by H. G. Wells tells the story of a man so grief-stricken with the death of his beloved wife that he lives day by day re-counting his memories of their days together. His obsession with her is so strong that he believes he sees her ghost next to the fire. He tells the story to a companion, who has never before believed in ghost tales. However, the honesty with which the story was told made a believer of the companion. Now it is up to the reader to decide the accuracy of the report.

her in her time of need. She said that she had never felt so safe and loved in her life.

Since then, nothing has happened that I know of, and I hope for their sake nothing ever will again.

Apartment Guests

This story involves a man living in an apartment that was once inhabited by an old lady who died in her sleep in the bedroom. This man and his girlfriend continue to experience strange happenings, particularly when they're trying to sleep.

My boyfriend lives in the upper half of an old two-story house, which he rents from a man who owns the house and lives in the lower half. The man who owns the house has always given me the creeps, though he seems nice on the surface.

A friend of my grandmother's once asked my boyfriend where he lived, and when he specified the house, she said an old lady had lived in the upper half, which had been a mother-in-law suite (her son lived in the lower half), and she passed away up there in her sleep a few years ago.

I spend nights there with my boyfriend on weekends, and have always had trouble sleeping, though it is very comfortable. I have often had a strange feeling while lying there, almost as if we were being watched.

I even began to suspect that my boyfriend's "creepy" landlord had set up cameras in there or something. I know it sounds paranoid, but that's how strongly I felt I was being watched. There have been strange occurrences up there at night, and I had always suspected the landlord. I never really thought it could actually be a haunting until recently, though I admit I'm still skeptical.

Anyway, the most recent occurrences have happened at times when the landlord was out of town and nobody else was in the house. Things usually happen late at night, like the time we stayed up to watch a movie. It was about 1:00 A.M. when the movie ended. I got up to rewind the tape. After I hit rewind, there was still sound coming from the speakers, like a faint conversation muffled by static.

I thought maybe the TV was somehow interfering, but when a tape is rewinding, the screen remains blue, it doesn't switch to any channels. I stopped the tape and shut off both the TV and VCR, but there was still sound coming from the speakers. My boyfriend thought it could possibly be the stereo, so he got up and shut it off, but the sounds continued until we finally decided to unplug the speakers.

More recently, I was lying there, awake as usual, and I could hear someone breathing deeply through the nose from across the room. I rolled over and woke my boyfriend, who sat up to listen. I asked if it could be his landlord sleeping, but he said the landlord was out of town. As we listened, the breathing seemed to get closer, as if whoever it was could be right there in the room with us. It suddenly stopped. My boyfriend said he has heard the breathing several times but never knew where it came from.

We settled back down, but were both still awake. About half an hour later, the breathing started again, this time much more clearly, and from the foot of the bed. By the way, if you're wondering, my boyfriend has no pets, and neither does the guy downstairs. Again, it got louder, then stopped. We were so creeped out, we turned on the lights and stayed up the rest of the night. Neither of us can explain what happened.

A Picture Says a Thousand Words

One of the tools used by many paranormal investigators is a standard camera. Many believe ghosts that can't be seen by the naked eye can be caught on film. In this story, a young woman who lives in an old house looks back at her personal photo album and sees some unusual things.

Looking at pictures one day I came across a few with "orbs" and other such "ghosts." (All of these pictures were taken at different times and many with different cameras.) One picture was of me as a baby. I was sitting with my toys on a blanket, in a very old house that my parents and I used to live in. Hovering above my head, in the center of a lamp pole, is a face with shoulders. My husband said he looks a lot like Eddie, the mascot for the band Iron Maiden. The

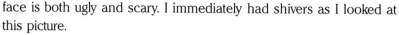

Famous Ghost Stories

Eveline's Visitant by Mary Elizabeth Braddon opens with a duel between cousins over the love of a woman. Andre is slain by Hector and as he lays dying vows to haunt Hector from beyond the grave. As the story progresses, Hector falls in love with Eveline, his only source of happiness. But Eveline is visited daily by the ghost of Andre and becomes entranced by his presence. The ghost follows the couple everywhere seeking vengeance.

face is both ugly and scary. I immediately had shivers as I looked at this picture.

As I viewed this picture, my rational mind said, "Oh no, Lisa, it has to be a flaw in the photo." Well, then I found a second picture, taken at the same exact time and place. It was of me still sitting on the blanket, smiling at the camera. This same face and shoulders were visible, although they were beginning to fade. I began to think that this face was the demon who has been tormenting me for my whole life.

Throughout my life, I have had horrible nightmares and experiences. My brother and I have battles with the devil during our sleep sometimes. I have been visited several times by apparitions, seen while I'm awake. My sister was tormented as well when she was younger, and now my niece seems to be fighting something or someone during her sleep.

I am guessing because of who our ancestors were, but I have heard before that our family had a curse. I keep wondering if this is all part of that curse. When I told my mother about the photos and my experiences, she was in disbelief due to what I think was fear. She told me that God told her not to worry about it. I continue to fight. We all do. I believe demons are real. I believe the demon who has been haunting me has shown himself in my old pictures.

The White Lady

When people report seeing a ghost, it's sometimes after they've been awakened in the middle of the night. This story describes a ghost whose appearance is rather common.

I was only about nine or ten years old when this happened to me. I woke up in the middle of the night to find the noise that aroused me was thunder. Outside was a storm.

I looked over at my desk. Sitting with her back against the drawers was a woman with white hair, a white dress, and white skin. Everything about her appearance was white, and she was glowing.

The sight of this woman didn't frighten me. I was tired, so I fell back to sleep. About two years later, I went to a sleepaway camp. It was a rainy day so we all sat inside telling ghost stories.

One of the counselors asked if anyone had ever heard of the white lady. That's when it struck me . . . I had! He described her, and that is exactly what I saw.

Making Sense of It All

This has been just a small sampling of encounters people just like you have had with ghosts and other paranormal activity. As you can see, these experiences vary greatly. Most people who see, hear, feel, or otherwise experience a haunting find the experience to be a bit scary, but totally harmless. Others find the experience to be extremely unnerving and difficult to deal with. Still others may find these encounters with the paranormal to be comforting, especially if the living person believes they're being "visited" by a departed loved one.

Whether or not these experiences are all 100 percent true is anyone's guess; however, the events described in these stories all seem rather typical of what people from all over the world have reported when it comes to encounters with ghosts and other paranormal activities.

If you've had a paranormal experience that you simply can't explain, try to avoid becoming frightened. The best approach is to seek out the advice and assistance of a recognized and reputable parapsychologist or expert in the field of paranormal events. Several of these experts are interviewed throughout this book.

Some experts suggest trying to make contact with the ghost or spirit you encounter. Speak to it. Ask questions, and if you want it to stop bothering you, try simply ordering it to go away. Most people who experience an unusual presence find that they are in no danger and ultimately discover ways to live in harmony with the entity that inhabits their home.

If you believe you have experienced something unusual, remember that you're probably not going insane! Find someone you trust to share your experience with, then find an expert who can help you. The Internet is an excellent resource for communicating with others who have had similar experiences, because you can be open and honest about what you've experienced, yet maintain some level of privacy.

Chapter Four

Mediums and Channelers

Many people become fascinated with ghosts, spirits, angels, and the concept of life after death after a loved one has died. In fact, many people who report seeing ghosts or apparitions for the first time experience this phenomenon shortly after someone close to them has passed on.

Millions of people believe that those who have died live on in an afterlife and can choose to communicate with the living (often through a medium or channeler). Throughout history, cultures from around the world have believed that the living could communicate with the dead. This is evident among cultures from ancient Egypt, China, and Greece, for example, and in many religions worldwide.

Whether or not you believe in life after death is a purely personal decision that will probably be based heavily on your religious upbringing, personal experiences, and your want or need to better understand death. The human mind is certainly a powerful thing. When combined with forces that are beyond our realm of understanding, who really knows what's possible?

Communicating with the "Other Side"

Some people believe they have the ability to communicate freely with the dead. These people are called "mediums" or "channelers." While some are frauds, unscrupulously preying on the emotional needs of the public, others have a gift that they believe allows them to communicate directly with ghosts or spirits, and these people continue to defy scientific belief and demonstrate their abilities.

Unfortunately, many of the people who choose to use the services of a channeler or medium in order to communicate with a deceased loved one are often experiencing a strong sense of grief, depression, anxiety, or desperation and are easily manipulated or duped by highly skilled con artists. People who offer their "gift" to others in exchange for little or no financial compensation are often the most credible, since these people have nothing to gain.

Typically, a channeler or a medium is used to assist someone in communicating with someone who is deceased.

For this communication to take place, the medium or channeler must make contact with the spirit or ghost of someone who has died, who is believed to now exist within the spiritual plane, which perhaps is heaven or the place where spirits go after death. This place is often referred to as the spirit world or the other side.

A spirit or ghost that uses a medium in order to communicate with someone either verbally or visually is known as a "spirit communicator." Likewise, a spirit or ghost that uses a medium to physically manipulate something on earth is referred to as a "spirit operator."

The spirit or ghost can communicate with a medium or channeler in a number of ways, often involving some form of mental telepathy. The medium typically then verbally communicates with the living people around him or her to pass along messages from the deceased. It is the medium (not the living witnesses) who sees, hears, feels, or senses what the spirit or ghost is trying to communicate. A medium's responsibility is to communicate whatever message the deceased person is attempting to relay without any personal interference.

Before you can actually believe in the work of a channeler or medium (or believe in that person's gift), you must first possess an underlying belief that spirits, souls, and ghosts exist and that any of these are the intelligent consciousness of someone who has moved on to the other side. Next, you must believe that the person you use as a channeler or medium actually has a special ability or psychic gift (and can work as a medium), as opposed to simply having an overactive imagination.

In addition to mediums and channelers, some people believe spiritual guides offer living people a link to once-living beings or spirits that have died. It's also widely believed that anyone can learn to connect mentally with his or her own spiritual guide(s). A spiritual guide is believed by many to be a spirit that watches over a living person and that offers wisdom or guidance. You'll find more information on spirit guides later in this book, but it's widely believed that anyone, with the proper mindset, can communicate with his or her own spirit guide(s). Most experts who

What Is Channeling?

Channeling is the method by which living people are believed to be able to communicate with the dead. During such communication, a spirit temporarily possesses the body of a living person (referred to as a channeler) and is able to communicate with the living. Channelers, like mediums, are believed to possess psychic abilities.

study this phenomenon suggest that people should not allow their desire for answers from the spirit world to overshadow or interfere with their own ability to make decisions pertaining to their lives.

In her book *How to Connect with your Spiritual Guide* (Three Rivers Press), Liza M. Wiemer wrote, "When you receive spiritual guidance, you are being connected to a different state of consciousness. Different states of consciousness can mean your subconscious, your instincts, your soul and even dreams of or contact with departed loved ones." Wiemer explains that death is a transition to a different level of energy vibration. As a result, she believes that departed souls can be thought of as different states of consciousness that, under the right circumstances, ordinary people may be able to contact and receive guidance from.

People tend to use their spiritual guide's assistance to enhance their judgment on important decisions, for example. In her book, Wiemer wrote, "Even though I try to remain alert to guidance, when I have not asked for information directly, sometimes I can dismiss it as 'just' a passing thought . . . When you first try to connect with your spiritual guides, it is natural to question whether you have really received a message from them. You may feel that you're just making up the answer or reflecting your own thoughts. You may even feel that what you are hearing, seeing, or feeling is coming from your Higher Self or, in other terms, your own soul. Sometimes it can be difficult to recognize this difference. But realize that your spiritual guides can give you information that you could not possibly discern on your own."

Many believe that spiritual guides can be contacted without the use of a medium, psychic, or channeler, when a form of hypnotherapy or deep meditation is used to assist someone in reaching an altered state of consciousness. This topic is covered in greater detail in Chapter 5. To communicate with the deceased, however, it's widely believed that a gifted medium, psychic, or channeler must be used. Ordinary people, with no psychic power, often claim to be able to make contact with the spirit world using a Ouija board (talking board) or other tool. You'll find more information on this method of spirit communication in Chapter 6.

Understanding the Gifts of Psychic Mediums and Channelers

Some people believe the ability to communicate with the deceased is a very special gift. It's a gift that only a few people possess and one that can be used to help others in many ways. What you are about to read are interviews with several mediums and channelers who have dedicated their lives to helping people communicate with the deceased. They all believe they have psychic abilities and possess the ability to work as a medium or channeler. Thus, the voices, images, sounds, or thoughts they receive during a reading are from spirits (people who have died).

Several of the people you'll learn about offer their services free of charge; however, the majority perform readings for clients for a living and earn money for their services. If someone is going to charge you for his or her services, make sure that person is credible. The best way to do this is to obtain personal referrals from people you know. Local New Age bookstores in your area can also provide referrals or references.

Whether or not you choose to believe that the mediums and channelers featured in this book actually have a gift that allows them to communicate with people who have died is purely a personal decision on your part. There are certainly plenty of frauds out there looking to prey on people who are suffering emotionally. Be sure that the person you choose to work with is able to provide you with information about yourself and loved ones that is not common knowledge or easily researched. The psychic medium or channeler you work with should do much more than repeat information you initially provide him or her with.

Typically, someone who seeks out the service of a medium or channeler to communicate with a deceased loved one is doing so

What Is a Medium?

A medium is a living individual who has a special gift and believes he or she can act as a bridge between the world of the living and the other side. The medium does not become possessed by the spirit, but is able to convey messages from the other side that "pass through" the person.

as a way to deal with grief, conclude unfinished business, or bring closure to unresolved issues with the person who has died. After participating in a reading, many people who are grieving feel comforted by their experience and are better able to come to terms with their loss.

No matter where you travel in the world, people who call themselves shamans, witch doctors, wise men (or wise women), clairvoyants, clairaudients, psychics, channelers, or mediums can be found. For some reason, these people are able to harness the power of the mind and the energy around them in ways others can't, in order to communicate with the spirit world. While everyone has basic intuition, people who are able to harness their psychic abilities and communicate with the other side have found ways to tap their sixth sense and open their minds to higher levels of consciousness. You're about to be introduced to a handful of those people.

John Holland

Psychic Medium
P.O. Box 400-505, North Cambridge, MA 02140
(617) 747-4491
E-mail: *hollandpsi@yahoo.com*
Web site: *www.psijohn.com*

Even as a small child, John Holland was often found curled up with metaphysical books while other children, including his four siblings, were outside playing. Although Holland knew he had special abilities as a young child, Holland's father was a disbeliever, which forced him to keep his abilities quiet for many years.

How Holland Realized His Powers

Holland doesn't look any different than an ordinary urban professional. He's clean-cut, well educated, and dresses like anyone

Paying To Communicate with the Other Side

You've seen the ads on TV and in the classified sections of newspapers. By dialing a 900 phone number and paying anywhere from $.99 to $9.99 per minute, you too can talk with a psychic or channeler who will help you communicate with a deceased loved one. Unfortunately, some people who advertise their services as psychics or channelers are frauds and are simply trying to capitalize on the grief a potential client is experiencing after the loss of a loved one. As someone looking to utilize the services of a psychic or channeler, you should beware of frauds. Seek out people who come highly recommended by people you know or who work with legitimate organizations. Yes, many people who truly believe they have a gift do charge for their services. You should, however, look to pay a predetermined and flat fee for a session/reading. Anyone who tries to charge extra to communicate with a specific deceased person or who adds fees based on the amount of information provided should be avoided. Agree on a price for a psychic or medium's services in advance, determine exactly what you should expect for your money, and make sure you have realistic expectations.

What Is Clairaudience?

Clairaudience refers to a form of psychic ability that is a result of attunement (the ability to hear sounds or voices normal living people can't). It involves the ability for someone to "hear" or "see" something that doesn't exist in our physical environment or in the physical world as we know it. What someone with clairaudience sees or hears can't be experienced by a typical person using any or all of the five senses. Thus, it's believed a sixth sense (or psychic ability) is used to communicate with spirits.

else living in the suburbs of Boston. What sets Holland apart are his special psychic abilities that continue to draw people to him from all walks of life and from all over the world. As he grew up, Holland spontaneously forecasted events and situations that ultimately helped guide and prepare his clients, thereby empowering them to govern their own destiny. While Holland has strong psychic abilities, he insists that he is not a fortuneteller. He believes he can only show his clients possibilities and choices using his omniscient insight.

Holland believes he was born with special psychic abilities, but it wasn't until he was involved in a car accident several years ago as a young adult that his abilities suddenly became stronger, encouraging him to seek out guidance in harnessing and better understanding his abilities. "What I had pushed away as a child came back, but many times stronger. After the accident, I felt as if I were filled with energy. I think the trauma of the accident opened my chakra centers and I got a full awakening all at once," he said. Understandably, the accident left Holland somewhat overwhelmed and confused by his abilities.

As a young adult, Holland worked at a hotel serving drinks. He would regularly "see things" that pertained to his customers and often share his visions or feelings. It wasn't long before word-of-mouth spread. People would seek him out for personal and business advice. When a customer stepped up to him, he'd simply know personal things about that person and what was happening in his or her life. "I would look at people who stepped up to the bar and I would see images along with them," he recalled. "For example, someone would walk up to me and in my mind, I'd see a map of Europe and I'd somehow know that person was planning a trip to Europe. If I saw in my mind two rings on someone's finger, I'd know they were married twice. I'd see symbols or images and be able to interpret what they meant." Ultimately, he was asked by his employer to refrain from randomly "reading" customers because it sometimes spooked people.

It was Holland's quest for understanding that led him to the United Kingdom, where he studied with some of the world's top mediums and psychics. In 1999, his story was told on an episode of the television series *Unsolved Mysteries*.

Working as a Psychic Medium

Living in North Cambridge, Massachusetts, Holland works part-time as a professional psychic medium, performing readings for clients from his home. The study from which he works is a charming, well-lit room that is sparsely furnished. Two comfortable chairs, one for him and one for his client, are set near a large window. Nearby are several bookcases and plants. The atmosphere is warm and unintimidating.

From his study, Holland performs readings on people from all walks of life, many of whom, he says, are grieving after the loss of a loved one. Unlike many psychic mediums, Holland doesn't advertise his services. Most of his clients come to him through word-of-mouth or after initially visiting his Web site. Another thing that sets Holland apart is that he won't meet with the same client more than once in a six-month period, although he prefers to see clients once a year. His goal isn't to become an ongoing counselor for his clients, but to work as a healer and help them make contact with the spirit world. Once a client reaches a deceased relative, Holland wants his clients to be comforted, but doesn't want them to become "psychic junkies" and begin to rely on their encounters with the spirit world in order to get through their daily lives. Holland believes that his abilities can be used to offer suggestions and guidance as well as comfort and understanding, but it's ultimately up to each individual to come to terms with his or her loss.

Making Contact with the Other Side

When performing a reading, Holland often sees images and hears the voices of spirits in his mind. These spirits seldom take on

a physical form in the real world. He explained that if you visualize what your kitchen at home looks like, for example, or think about your favorite song, you can often see that image or hear the song in your head. As Holland makes contact with the spirit world, the images and sounds appear in his mind in much the same way people can visualize something they're familiar with.

"I don't make contact with the spirits, they contact me," he said. "I don't have control over which spirit makes contact." Holland believes that spirits, just like living people, are made up of energy. When he communicates with the spirit world, the energy of the spirit combines with his own. "The energy from a person doesn't die when the body dies. It simply goes somewhere else," he said.

Before Holland can begin a reading for a client, he must feel comfortable with that client. Typically, a reading will take between thirty and sixty minutes, since Holland is often able to make contact with the spirit world relatively quickly once a reading begins. For this process to work, Holland needs to develop some form of energy connection with his client. This doesn't, however, involve physical contact. During a reading, a client will sit opposite from Holland. If a reading is being done over the telephone, Holland will tap in to the energies of his client's voice.

Throughout his life, Holland has had many unusual experiences relating to his psychic and medium abilities. He said that while everyone has some psychic abilities, few people open their minds enough to tap in to their natural abilities. "It's often easier for people who work in the arts, who are used to using the right side of their brain for creativity, to tap in to their own psychic abilities. While I believe all mediums are psychic, I don't believe that all psychics are mediums."

There are many types of psychic abilities. "Anyone can learn to play the piano, but few people can call themselves pianists. The same is true for someone with psychic abilities. People learn to focus their abilities and use them in different ways," he said.

Often during a reading, once Holland makes contact with a discarnate (another term for a spirit), the messages he receives are personal and directed only to his client. Thus, they are messages

The C.E.R.T. Method

Holland follows the "C.E.R.T. method" for every reading in which he participates. As part of this processes, he attempts to obtain the following information from the spirit he comes into contact with:

- Confirmation—Holland attempts to learn the identity of the spirit, its relationship to the person he's reading, how he or she died, or some other piece of information to clarify to his client who he's in contact with.
- Evidence—Once an identity is established, Holland tries to obtain personal information from the spirit that only that person and his client would know. This could be a nickname, for example, or detailed information about a personal item that was once owned by the spirit that's now in the possession of the client.
- Return—Holland tries to answer why the spirit is making contact with his client and attempts to obtain whatever messages are being conveyed. When a spirit makes contact with the living world, Holland believes it's always for a reason.
- Tie up loose ends—Upon making contact with the spirit on behalf of the client, obtaining evidence and then receiving whatever messages the spirit chooses to convey, Holland ties up loose ends and brings closure to the session.

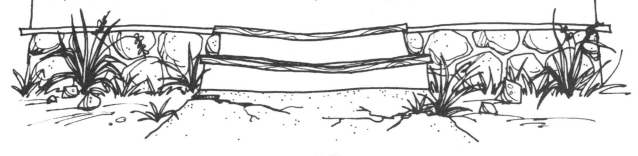

he doesn't always understand himself. It is for this reason that he simply conveys the images and messages he receives from the spirit world, as opposed to trying to interpret them on behalf of his clients.

During one reading, for example, his client was a woman and the spirit he made contact with was also female. The images that came to his mind were that of a spirit who was wearing clothing that didn't match. The colors dramatically clashed. When he conveyed this information to his client, she burst into tears. Holland didn't understand the significance of the mismatched clothing, but his client knew instantly that the spirit was that of her great-aunt, who had been colorblind and when alive always wore outfits that didn't match.

Because he is both clairaudient and clairsentient, Holland is often able to both hear what spirits say as well as physically feel their presence. Sometimes, he hears actual words; other times, he receives more symbolic messages. For some reason that Holland doesn't understand, discarnates tend to come to him and communicate from his left side.

There have been instances, he said, in which he was able to tell how a person died because he received physical sensations from that spirit. For example, there was a time when he was communicating with a spirit who committed suicide and during the reading he felt a tightness around his neck. It turned out the person whose spirit he was communicating with had hung himself. Holland also recalls an instance in which he learned that a spirit died of a heart attack by feeling a tightness in his own chest during a reading. While he is often able to feel things relating to the spirits he communicates with, Holland states that he is simply a middleman between the living and spirit world. The entities he communicates with do not possess his body.

The messages Holland receives aren't always so clear, he stated. During one reading, the word "snowball" kept being communicated to him by a spirit. This made no sense to Holland, but the client understood perfectly. It had been a nickname given to the client by his grandparent, who was now deceased.

What Is Trance Mediumship?

Trance mediumship is a form of mediumship in which the medium shares his or her energy with the spirit through the use of trance. Therefore, the spirit has some control over the communication taking place. This in no way means a full possession is taking place. There are various degrees and strength of trance; and furthermore, different degrees and strength of control.

Holland's Theories

Holland believes spirits choose to make contact with the living for a variety of reasons, but most importantly, he believes it's to demonstrate that there is some form of existence after death and that the love shared by people during life continues after death. Holland stated that ghosts don't spend all of their time following living people around on a daily basis, because he believes they have better things to do. When they're needed or when they choose to, however, Holland says that many spirits have the ability to visit the world of the living and make contact.

"I try to explain to clients, using specifics, what possibilities lie before them or what their potential future might have in store, but I never make decisions for people or tell them specifically what they should do. I believe everyone has free will, so I show them the possibilities or different roads they can take. I offer road signs to watch out for, but I never choose someone's path or try to push the person in a specific direction. It's important to understand that no psychic or medium is ever one-hundred percent accurate," said Holland.

As Holland hears messages from the deceased, he often hears his own voice in his head. If the deceased spoke with a certain dialect or accent, that comes across as Holland telepathically converses with the spirit. As a mental medium, Holland describes the communication process between himself and the spirit world as one where his aura or energy must blend with that of the deceased individual he's communicating with. "I have to heighten my own consciousness while the spirit has to lower their consciousness for communication to take place," explained Holland.

When someone loses a loved one, he or she sometimes visit a medium in order to say goodbye for a final time or to make sure that the deceased relative is, in fact, okay. "People come to me for closure," he said. "I have found that the spirits I communicate with maintain the same personality they had when they were alive. Thus, if someone wasn't good with numbers or finances as a living person, I don't recommend asking that person for financial advice

once they've passed on. People don't transform into super-angels. They're still the same person, they just don't exist in their body any longer."

Holland explained that a lot of energy passes through him as he participates in readings. While this isn't typically physically or mentally draining, he makes a definite point of staying in peak mental and physical shape. No matter what happens during a reading, Holland doesn't become frightened by what he experiences, mainly because he's had his abilities since childhood and believes that throughout his life he has been mentally preparing to do the work he's doing now.

Is There Proof of the Afterlife?

Obviously, some people believe in the afterlife while others don't. Even though every culture and religion throughout history has demonstrated some belief in the afterlife, there is still no scientific proof that spirits continue to live on after death. Holland believes that someday there will be proof. "I think that as mankind continues to develop new technologies, eventually there will be a machine that can tap into and perhaps measure or identify the energy that I believe is what spirits are comprised of," said Holland.

Advice for Those Seeking to Work with a Medium

Before someone chooses to visit a medium, Holland strongly recommends reading several books on mediumship. It's also important to find someone who is legitimate and credible. To do this, Holland suggests obtaining referrals from people you know and trust. "When you actually meet with a psychic or a medium, begin by asking the person to explain how he or she works. Go into the meeting with an open mind. Ask if it's okay for you to record the session or at least take notes. If the psychic or medium says no to this, something is wrong. If you're not comfortable with the person you find, keep looking. Most importantly, whatever happens during the session, stay grounded. Don't expect to find instant answers to all of your problems or expect a miracle to happen. We don't have all of the answers," said Holland.

While it's possible for a psychic or medium to use his or her abilities to "wow" you and tell you information you already know about yourself, a good psychic or medium should be able to help you develop new insight into situations you're facing. Know why you're visiting the psychic or medium and spend time learning everything you can. Knowing what to expect will help you to adjust your expectations accordingly and get the most from the experience.

Most importantly, Holland stated that a psychic or medium should never diagnose medical problems or offer any type of cures. "This is both unethical and illegal, unless the person you're working with is also a licensed medical doctor," he said.

Glenn Klausner

Psychic Medium
Proprietor, Heart and Soul (a metaphysical bookstore)
1400 Colonial Blvd. #19, Fort Myers, FL 33907
(941) 936-5511
Web site: *www.glennklausner.com*

Psychic medium Glenn Klausner was born in the Canarsie section of Brooklyn, New York, in 1971. He first discovered his psychic ability at the age of ten, when he saw an unknown solo artist named Billy Idol, who he had never seen or heard of before, performing a song called "Mony Mony" on a television show called Solid Gold. This was back in October 1981.

Immediately, Glenn turned to his mom and said that his older brother, Phil, who already was a known bass player in a band called Riot, was going to play with this guy Billy Idol. One day in early November 1981, Phil called Glenn and their mother to tell them he just gotten a gig with a solo artist from England named

According to Klausner

According to Klausner, "A Psychic Medium or 'sensitive' is a person who communicates with spirits telepathically in the super-subconscious mind by feeling, hearing, or seeing visual impressions from the other side, which we know as 'heaven.' A medium is able to be completely receptive to the higher frequencies or energies that spirits vibrate on. The spirit impresses the medium's highly subconscious mind with thought to deliver its messages for the one who is getting the reading."

Billy Idol. Idol had just moved to New York and was being managed by Bill Aucoin, who also managed the band Kiss. Glenn asked if he was a blond, spiky-haired guy who was on television a month earlier. Phil said, "Yes, how do you know who he is?" Glenn then shared the information he "knew," which was now validated.

Through his teen years and early twenties Klausner himself spent eight years performing in many bands, such as Masquerade, The Hedgehogs, and Glenn Kidd. During this period, he found his psychic abilities of clairvoyance (clear seeing) and mediumship (communication to the deceased) becoming more pronounced.

Klausner refers to himself as a professional psychic medium. During his teen years, he recalls communicating with all of his deceased grandparents on a regular basis.

As he grew up, Klausner developed his psychic abilities and discovered he possessed clairvoyance as well as the ability to work as a medium. "When I communicate with a spirit, I see images in my mind and hear voices in my mind. I don't see and hear spirits the same way I see and hear living people. In some cases, a spirit will communicate with me using English. Other times, the communication happens through feelings. Each spirit communicates differently with me. I am what people refer to as a mental medium, in that I see and hear things in my mind," said Klausner.

He described his experiences as being like watching a movie inside of his head. Even at an early age, this gift never scared him. He recalls that on a fairly regular basis, things would happen. For example, he'd tell his mother that their neighbor was at the door, and a few seconds later the doorbell would ring and it would be their neighbor.

During his life, Klausner has had the opportunity to work with the FBI as well as local law enforcement officials throughout the country in an effort to solve crimes. Unless the law enforcement officials contact him, however, Klausner is often hesitant to get involved in a situation, due to the skepticism and harsh treatment he has received in the past while trying to share information regarding a crime or unsolved mystery. According to Klausner, in February 1993, while watching the news, he received visual and audio impressions of the people who were responsible for the

A Psychic's Extra Senses

Klausner believes clairvoyance means "clear vision." A clairvoyant is able to see objects, symbols, images, and scenes. For instance, a spirit will show him what he or she looked like while in the physical body or show him a celebrity that he can identify with. A spirit will show him a word, like a family name, to validate that he is in fact communicating with someone related to his client. A clairaudient or audiovoyant means "clear hearing." A clairaudient is able to hear sounds and voices, which is the mind's voice at a higher frequency than the normal human ear, kind of in a sense like an animal hears.

Clairsentience is the feeling or sensing of a spirit's message. Spirits, according to Klausner, can convey emotions regarding how they felt in life or how they are feeling in their passing. For instance, if a person was strangled, the clairsentient will feel his own neck being choked just for a quick second. If it's a heart attack, he or she will feel tightening in the chest for a quick second. It's basically the spirit's way of validating its passing. They also express love or sadness in this way as well, he explained.

Clairalience is "clear smelling" and clairambience is "clear tasting." In these forms Klausner can smell a spirit's perfume or cologne or taste if the spirit smoked or drank.

World Trade Center bombing. He drew a sketch of a twenty-six-year-old Middle Eastern male with the initials "M.S." who was hiding in Jersey City, New Jersey. These psychic impressions took place on the day it happened. Klausner telephoned the FBI and offered this information. A few days later the FBI arrested the exact man he spoke of. In February 1997, Klausner helped recover a kidnapped child alive after seeing the missing girl on the television show *America's Most Wanted.*

Klausner explained that he refrains from watching the news these days and doesn't use his gift to analyze or foretell what's happening in politics. "When I hear about a child being murdered, that's when I tend to use my gift in an effort to assist law enforcement officials. A few years back, there was a murder that happened in my home town and I offered my assistance. However, the law enforcement officials started to believe I was involved with the crime and I had to convince them otherwise," explained Klausner, who tends to offer his assistance to parents of children involved in a crime as opposed to working directly with law enforcement officials unless he is specifically invited to offer his assistance.

In 1996 Klausner was questioning whether he should continue to pursue a career in music or pursue a career working as a professional psychic medium. His guidance came from a priest at St. Patrick's Cathedral in New York City. The validated answer that Klausner needed to be a professional psychic medium came after he spent thirty minutes telling the priest about his life and his psychic experiences. According to Klausner, the priest gave him an odd yet comforting look and said, "Glenn, I believe that God gave you this beautiful gift and that you can talk to departed spirits in heaven and, you are probably meant to share it by guiding, healing, and educating people all over the world." The final thing the priest said was, "Always work with love and light from God, Jesus, and the Holy Spirit." Klausner's answer had arrived, and with no turning back he opened up his practice in May 1996.

By the spring of 1997, Klausner felt spiritually it was his time for change and decided to leave New York. That summer he moved to Florida. Since relocating to Florida, Klausner has been working at a metaphysical bookstore where he does a majority of his readings and has made numerous appearances on local television and radio.

In 1999, Klausner became a licensed and certified minister and member of the Universal Life Church, located in Modesto, California. To date, he has read nearly 10,000 people in the United States in person, on radio, and by telephone.

Klausner—A Psychic Medium

Klausner refers to himself as a psychic medium. "A psychic uses empathic feelings to pick up on things. A medium is able to communicate with spirits. I possess abilities of both a psychic and a medium, plus I'm clairvoyant and clairaudient. I use the term psychic medium to describe myself because many people don't really understand what a medium is, but they do understand what a psychic is," he said.

These days, Klausner focuses his abilities as a medium in order to communicate with spirits. He doesn't try to see into the future for himself or anyone else. However, when he does a reading for someone, if he's asked about the future, he may tap his clairvoyant skills in order to help a client. Klausner reports that he can do a reading for about 97 percent of the people he comes into contact with during his everyday life. One thing that he has learned from the spirit world is that some people are closed off and unwilling to be read.

Conducting a Reading

A reading, according to Klausner, takes place when a client asks him to communicate with a spirit on his or her behalf. Often, Klausner can't control who the spirit is that he communicates with; however, it's always someone who was close to his client. "There are times when a spirit simply doesn't want to communicate with the living person trying to make contact. This happens very rarely. Just as living people have different personalities, I have found that spirits have different personalities. Some are very shy, while others

are much more willing to communicate. Some spirits have trouble communicating with the living. Every situation is different," he explained.

While some mediums need to be in physical contact or in close proximity to their client when performing a reading, Klausner is able to do readings over the telephone or without physical contact with his living client. Whenever possible, Klausner looks into the eyes of his clients to feel their energy. He mainly uses his clients' voice energy when performing a reading.

According to Klausner, a reading begins with a brief discussion with his client. During this discussion, he describes what the client can expect and tries to alleviate the client's concerns or fears. "As the actual reading begins, I simply begin communicating with the spirit and passing along messages to the client. The link with the spirit happens for me as easy as someone turning on the faucet of a sink. I can just sit down, clear my mind, and begin communicating with a spirit or spirits," said Klausner, who stated that he doesn't typically ask who the client is trying to contact. Instead, he opens his mind and sees what spirit(s) makes contact with him.

One client, he recalls, was hoping to communicate with her deceased parents; however, it was her mother-in-law's spirit that made contact. "I have no choice in what spirits I communicate with. The spirits seek me out," stated Klausner, who usually performs readings in either thirty-minute or one-hour sessions. It's often within the first few minutes of a session that he makes contact with a spirit. "Once a spirit contacts me, I try to obtain validation from the client to determine who it is I'm communicating with. The spirit will often give me information that I wouldn't have known simply by talking to the client. Before a reading, I ask the client as little as possible about the spirit he or she is trying to contact," said Klausner.

As a spirit makes contact with Klausner, he tries to learn something about the spirit's identity and what messages it's trying to convey early on to help his clients and obtain validation from the spirit. He stated, "Sometimes, the spirit will communicate important pieces of information in order to identify itself. Other times, the information will be more obscure or even silly. For example, I was doing a reading recently and the spirit kept saying, 'Smell my finger.' I had no idea what this meant, but it turns out that my client's father used to use this phrase often. This was how the spirit identified itself."

No matter what information a spirit conveys to Klausner, he always makes a point to convey that exact information to his client, whether it's positive or negative. "There are certain things that spirits simply won't talk about; however, I never shield information from my clients. Most of the time, I find the spirits are very blunt with their communication. I am often shocked at the things I'm told and compelled to convey to clients. I'll never sugarcoat or fabricate any-thing," he said. While he didn't provide specific exam-ples, he did explain that some deceased people he communicates with don't always have happy and polite messages for those they're passing messages to in the world of the living.

Some of his clients are simply curious as to his abili-ties, while others are deeply grieving and are in search of solitude and comforting. About eight out of ten of his clients have lost someone either recently or several years earlier. If he knows someone is upset as a result of someone's death, Klausner will help the person find closure or comfort through the messages he's able to convey from the spirit world. Most of the people he does a reading for feel a sense of peace and calmness after a reading. "Most people are aware that there's life after death, and helping a living person deal with his or her loss by communicating with the spirit of a loved one is often helpful. If necessary, I also refer clients to organizations that provide counseling or other services for people who are grieving or having trouble coping with their loss," explained Klausner.

While Klausner understands psychology, he is the first to admit that's he is not a counselor. The support he is able to offer people who are grieving or experiencing a difficult time in their lives comes directly from the other side, not from himself. "I never tell people what to do. I simply give them the messages they are meant to hear," he said.

What Is Physical Mediumship?

Physical mediumship is a form of mediumship in which the spirit communicates using not only the consciousness of the medium but also physical energies. In this way, the physical world is affected in ways for all to see.

Klausner Explains Some Common Misconceptions

In the movies, people often see mediums become possessed by a spirit during a séance, for example. Hollywood often shows the medium or channeler taking on a totally different personality as the person's voice and mannerisms change. According to Klausner, this isn't at all how a reading works, at least for him. When he communicates with a spirit, his voice does not change. Once in a while, he said, if the spirit had a Southern accent when it was alive, for example, some of the words he says may convey that accent during a reading, but this isn't typical. Most of the time, the client simply hears Klausner using his normal voice as he conveys messages from the spirit world.

"I am not a physical medium. A physical medium actually invites the spirit into the body, which temporarily takes possession of it. I never allow this to happen, primarily because it's potentially very dangerous. I don't allow a spirit to jump into my body or take over my voice box to talk. Once in a while, a client will mention that my facial expressions change and become similar to the mannerisms of the spirit I'm communicating with, but that doesn't happen too often," said Klausner, who almost always emotionally detaches himself from the readings he performs, as well as from the clients and spirits he communicates with. "If I got caught up in the intense emotions of my clients, I'd never be able to perform the reading. I am always very serious and take my work seriously. If something funny happens, I'll certainly laugh, but remaining emotionally detached is in everyone's best interest," explained Klausner, who said that at times his work can be both physically and emotionally draining.

When he finds himself drained, Klausner stated that it's typically a result of working with the living client, not as a result of communicating with the other side. "It's extremely rewarding for me when someone is comforted by a reading and expresses sincere gratitude. This gives me a strong sense of accomplishment that I am helping to do God's work," stated Klausner.

Famous Psychic

Jeane Dixon (1918–1997) was best known for her prediction of President Kennedy's election to presidency and his death in office. Dixon was also an advisor to very famous and powerful clients, including the Reagans and actress Carole Lombard.

Klausner's Theories

It's Klausner's belief that spirits choose to communicate with the living because they want us to know that life goes on after death. "God never meant to cut off communication with our loved ones. The unfortunate thing is that the physical body simply can't hold out forever. The body is just a shell or temple. It's the soul that's forever. I have found that the spirits never stop loving us and they don't forget us. People think that they do, but that's not true. They still love us as if they were still here," said Klausner.

As a result of his work and abilities, Klausner believes there is nothing to fear from dying. "Spirits want us to live our lives to the fullest, and they want us to know that there's nothing to fear about death," he said.

Nobody, including Klausner himself, truly understands why he has these abilities or what makes them work; however, Klausner knows that his great-grandfather also had special abilities. "Some people are born with special gifts. Some people have the natural ability to be great artists, great writers, great athletes, or great philosophers. I was born with this special ability. I think everyone is born with some type of special gift. Some of us, however, learn to better utilize our gift. I think everyone has some type of psychic ability that stems from the mind and has something to do with energy. The people who harness their psychic ability are willing to open their mind and aren't afraid to listen to their inner voice. People can learn to better tap their psychic abilities by paying closer attention to what's happening around them," he said.

While Klausner's gift may seem difficult for many people to comprehend, he believes his purpose in life is to spread light, love, healing, and understanding, especially to people who have recently lost loved ones. He explained that he treats his work very seriously and never disrespects any of the people who seek him out. "I believe this is a gift that God gave to me and I respect it and deeply value it. What people need to understand about me and people like me is that we're perfectly normal individuals who are blessed with a special gift," he concluded.

One thing Klausner wants people to understand about mediums is that their work isn't exact. He stated, "If you have three mediums in a room reading the same person, each one of the mediums could very well receive a different feeling or different message from the spirit they're communicating with on behalf of the person being read." This is possibly a result of how each medium interacts with the spirit and how the energy associated with that spirit is interpreted.

Marie Simpson

Psychic Counselor / Medium
The Unlimited Thought Bookstore
(210) 525-0693 / Toll-Free: 877-434-2177
Web site: *www.mariesimpson.com*

For more than ten years, nationally known psychic Marie Simpson has studied meditation and psychic development. By a person simply stating his or her name and birthdate, Simpson can provide readings relating to life issues, love, relationships, health, business, and financial matters. She also conducts individual sessions for stress management and improving self-esteem.

Simpson's professional experience ranges from healing groups to metaphysical development and counseling/teaching. She gives private psychic readings at parties, businesses, charity and community events, and many Texas-area psychic fairs. She also has an extensive private practice. Simpson is able to perform readings for clients in-person, over the telephone, or via the Internet.

Her unique psychic readings delve into the past, present, and future and have helped thousands of people, both professionally and personally. After one session, she says, clients express a sense of emotional healing and stress relief. Business clientele use Simpson's services to evaluate employees, operations, and provide guidance for a business's future productivity. Psychologists and psychotherapists use her services to provide insight into their clients' major life issues.

Simpson Is a Gifted Medium

One of Simpson's gifts is mediumship. She is able to read other people in a client's life (living and deceased) and make accurate predictions. "I am clairvoyant. I am able to tune in to other people's energy and tune in to their past, present, and future. I also work as a medium, communicating with spirits on the other side," said Simpson, who began to comprehend her special abilities at the age of eight.

"I assume I was born with my abilities. As a child, I simply thought that everyone had the same abilities as me. At the age of eight, I began to realize my abilities were stronger than those of the average person, but I kept quiet about it for many years," said Simpson.

A Spirit Visits Simpson

The first psychic incidents she remembers were when spirits used to visit her every night as a child. "My grandmother shared a room with me as a child. After she died, almost every night, I experienced a tapping on the headboard of my bed. Being a child, I didn't know what it was, and I grew up being very scared," she recalls. Looking back on her experience now, she believes it was her grandmother trying to communicate with her. Simpson remembers waking up constantly and looking around her room thinking someone was there, only to find the room empty. She was so frightened that she often slept with the covers over her head. "My parents saw I was scared and left the light on for me, but didn't think anything of what little I shared with them about my abilities," she recalled.

As time went on, Simpson recalls being at a public function with one of her best friends. She was able to give her friend information about some of the people at the function that wasn't common knowledge. Simpson's friend gave her a very strange look and began to inquire about how she knew these things without ever being told.

Later, at the age of twenty, Simpson was working at a doctor's office. One day, she was having a discussion with another nurse

Channeling Versus Possession

The gift that mediums and channelers believe they have should not be confused with being possessed. In his book *Unlock Your Psychic Powers* (St. Martin's Press), Dr. Richard Lawrence wrote, "In psychic work, one must be wary of the phenomenon of possession. There is a very thin dividing line between serious psychic interference toward an individual and mental illness. . . . A person cannot be possessed unless there is some form of mental weakness within him or her that can be exploited from the other side."

about their parents dying. "All of a sudden, I got this horrible feeling and insisted that we stop talking about our parents. I looked at my watch and remember that it was 1:33 P.M. We then went back to work. A few hours later, I received a call at work and learned that my father had died suddenly at around 1:30 P.M. that day. My father was about sixty miles away and was not ill," said Simpson.

These were major events that happened early in Simpson's life; however, she recalls thousands of smaller incidents that happened to her on virtually a daily basis. For example, she would always know when the phone was about to ring and who was calling. Simpson said that her former husband would always misplace his belongings, sometimes in very obscure places, yet Simpson would always be able to find things without actually looking. She'd simply be able to sense where the missing objects were.

By studying and learning how to meditate, Simpson slowly discovered how to harness and focus her abilities. "As a clairvoyant and a medium, I can read living people as well as communicate with the spirit world. I don't know why some people who are clairvoyant or psychic don't have the ability to work as a medium. I believe this is a separate gift, but there may simply be fears associated with communicating with spirits," explained Simpson.

How Simpson Conducts a Reading

A typical reading, according to Simpson, lasts between thirty and sixty minutes. When someone visits Simpson for an in-person reading, she'll often hold her client's hand, not out of necessity, but as a way to comfort the client. She'll then ask the client to state his or her name and date of birth. By focusing her energies, Simpson can tune in to a living person. When asked, she also has the ability to make contact with the spirits of loved ones who have passed on. "When I work as a medium, I typically do this as a way to help people heal. My clients are often experiencing grief. To begin a session working as a medium, I'll ask for the name of the person who has died and how long ago that person passed away. I'll then attempt to tune in to that spirit's energy. I can usually see

Famous Medium

Mina Crandon (1888–1941) reached international fame for her talents as a medium. Supported by very influential people, such as Sir Arthur Conan Doyle, Mina held her ground as a powerful medium for several years. However, controversy ensued when magician Harry Houdini set out to expose her as a fraud.

where the spirit is and receive its messages. Sometimes, I'm given very personal messages, such as information that only the client and the spirit would know. Sometimes, a spirit identifies itself through movement or imagery as opposed to verbal messages," explained Simpson.

Once contact is made, Simpson asks her client for questions he or she would like answered. As she communicates with spirits, Simpson says she often sees an entity or a profile of the spirit in the physical world. "That entity communicates with me telepathically. Sometimes, I'll actually hear what a spirit is telling me. Since I can visually see the spirits, I can often read the expressions on their faces," she said.

As Simpson conducts readings, she finds it necessary to pace herself to avoid becoming overwhelmed or becoming too emotionally or physically drained. Like many mediums, she says she often doesn't remember specific things that happen during readings. "This is information that's flowing through me. There is no reason for it to register in my own mind. It's information from the other side that is meant for another person, not me. Also, if I tried to remember everything from every reading, I think I would become overwhelmed quickly. I encourage my clients to record our sessions or at the very least to take notes," she said. After every reading, Simpson works with her client to help the client interpret whatever messages she helped to convey.

Like most mediums, Simpson believes she is communicating with spirits that are comprised of pure energy. When she reads a living person or communicates with a spirit, it's her ability to access that energy that makes what she does possible, although she doesn't truly understand how the process works or why she's able to do what she does. She explained that she doesn't look at her abilities in a logical way, because there's no logical explanation. She is often very surprised by how much she is able to help people.

Many of Simpson's clients are people who are grieving, yet Simpson doesn't work as a psychologist or counselor in the traditional sense. She offers comfort through her work as a medium. Simpson begins a reading by clearing her own mind. She'll often

take a few deep breaths to relax her body and mind. By doing this, she believes she is opening her mind to allow a spirit's energy to enter. This is different than allowing a spirit to actually possess her body or mind, which is something she never permits.

As she communicates with a spirit, Simpson says she's simply working as a bridge between the spirit world and the living world. "I will sometimes take on the former mannerisms of the spirit or use specific phrases the person used to use, but I'm not one of those people who actually takes on the persona of the spirit I'm communicating with," added Simpson.

Despite having the ability to communicate with the deceased, Simpson says she no longer becomes frightened by her experiences. "Every now and then, I tune in to someone who was extremely depressed when alive. When I tune in to this energy, it feels really awful and overwhelmed. This isn't scary, but it's uncomfortable. In this type of situation, I have to make sure that I don't become too overwhelmed by the negative energy," she said.

Simpson Describes Spirits as Having Personalities That Are Memorable

Over the years, Simpson has performed many readings and been in contact with many spirits. She explained that spirits, just like living people, have their own personalities. "Sometimes, they simply don't have a lot to say or they aren't willing to readily communicate. This doesn't happen too often, however," stated Simpson, who rarely feels it's necessary to filter the information being conveyed through her. "Sometimes, I receive information that I intuitively know my client isn't ready to deal with, so I'll convey the information from the spirit very carefully in an attempt to make the overall experience less intense."

When asked about the most intense experience she's had as a medium, Simpson stated, "I recall one woman who I had met with several times. In all of my previous sessions with her, she never discussed her husband. After her husband died, this client came for a session with me. Not knowing anything about him, I tuned in to the spirit of her husband. The spirit explained that he now feels incredibly free and happy, because he's now doing many things that he was never able to do during his lifetime. The spirit wanted his former wife to know how happy he was and that he felt like a kid again because he was running and jumping around. This was profound, because it turned out this client's husband spent the last fifteen years of his life in a wheelchair. This was information I didn't know until the reading."

During the same session, Simpson saw the spirit painting on a large canvas, using his hand as a brush to spread bright colors around the canvas. "He was painting in what seemed like slow motion, using brilliant colors that seemed to appear from his hands. He'd just reach up and colors would appear. The spirit explained that his painting was like life. All we need to do is reach for what we need or want and we can create whatever we want in our life. My client later explained her husband was an artist when he was alive. This was one of the readings that actually made an impression on me," said Simpson.

On another occasion, Simpson recalls working with a client who wanted to make contact with her deceased grandfather. "She wanted so badly to contact the spirit of her grandfather," recalled Simpson. "During a reading, I can't simply choose what spirit I'm going to contact and then obtain the exact information my client wants. It doesn't work like that. If someone gets too anxious, that intense emotion can actually block the flow of energy I need to communicate with the spirit world. Making demands of the spirits seems to put restrictions on the energy. A reading works best if someone doesn't have preconceived expectations or demands. All of a sudden, however, the word 'pumpkin' came into my head. It turned out this was the nickname my client's grandfather had given to her as a child. This was an experience that was very significant to my client."

Every time Simpson makes contact with the spirit world, she says the experience is totally different. This is because every spirit and its flow of energy are different.

Further Reading

If you would like to learn more about mediumship and channeling, consider reading *You, The Medium* written by Raymond G. Berube and Nancy North.

Simpson Communicates with Spirits from Another Dimension

Simpson believes that spirits exist in another dimension. She explained, "There are a number of dimensions in our universe. My feeling is that when our physical body dies, our spiritual body cannot die because it's made up of pure energy, so that energy has to go somewhere. My feeling is that the energy goes into another plane of existence or another dimension. The energy is there and available to us. We can tune in to it using our minds, if we learn how to do it using mental telepathy. I believe everyone has psychic abilities, but for many people, it's an underdeveloped sense. I think some people have trouble believing in spirits and in a medium's ability to communicate with the spirit world because there is no science to support or prove this. Even though mediums have been around throughout history, I think people in general are afraid of our ability, because they don't understand it."

At some point in the future, Simpson believes scientific proof that spirits actually exist in another dimension will be obtained. "There are studies being conducted at major universities trying to answer questions about the existence of spirits and life after death. I am not a scientist, and I have no idea how they'll ultimately obtain the proof so many people want to see, but my feeling is that scientists will learn how to detect a new form of energy, which is the energy that spirits are comprised of. Perhaps the scientists will be able to better study the work of mediums and scientifically explain how we do what we do by studying the energy in and around us," she said.

Sometimes, it's the spirit that chooses to communicate with the living world, according to Simpson, because it doesn't know it's dead or it still need closure on something, even after death. This typically occurs when someone has died very suddenly or unexpectedly, said Simpson. "I believe there's an adjustment process that spirits have to undergo once they die, and sometimes, spirits have trouble making those adjustments, so they stay close to the living world, at least for a while. Some spirits are simply mysterious or they just want to let people know that they're around. I have seen spirits make themselves known in order to protect a former loved one."

One experience Simpson had recently involved working with a client (while he was alive, but seriously ill). Upon this person's death, Simpson began receiving messages from the deceased (her former client) in rather unusual ways. Simpson herself sought out the assistance of another medium, since she won't communicate with the spirit world on her own behalf, and was told by the medium she was working with that her former client was trying to contact her in order to thank her.

"I was told that this former client would somehow contact me from the spirit world in order to thank me. I figured this message would come to me during a dream. Instead, there was this clock in my house that struck every hour. One day shortly after my session with the medium, I came home and the hands of the clock were messed up. This clock was working perfectly, but when I got home, it had stopped at 10:50. I felt psychically that Dennis [the client] had died at 10:50 P.M. This was his way of saying 'hello' to me. I asked Dennis's wife what time he died, and it was at 10:50 P.M.," said Simpson.

What It Takes to Be a Good Communicator

"A good reader will always have the client's best interest in mind. The reader will charge a flat fee and not charge extra in order to make specific things happen. You need to find someone who you trust so you will be comfortable being open and honest with the person you ultimately work with. I've been working as a professional psychic and medium for over ten years. I have count-less references and I work in a reputable place. If you're looking to work with a psychic or medium, look for someone who can provide references," suggested Simpson. "I am not here to make things happen for someone. I am here to offer someone advice or suggestions."

Many paranormal investigators and ghost hunters have managed to capture what they believe to be ghosts or spirits on film or videotape. Simpson has seen many of these photos and believes what's been captured on film is sometimes, but not always, similar

Even Simpson Uses a Medium

Because Simpson doesn't trust the feeling she gets when she attempts to contact the spirit world or tap her psychic abilities for her own benefit, she uses another psychic or medium when her own interests are involved. "I don't know if I can be totally objective if I try to use my abilities for myself. It's too personal and very hard to explain," added Simpson, who tells people who plan to have their own reading done to be open and to find a reader who comes through a reliable referral.

What Is Automatic Writing?

Automatic writing is a method for communicating with the other side. It is one way in which some people who believe they have psychic powers and possess the ability to channel focus their energy to allow the communication to transpire. It involves deep relaxation and meditation. Once the person is relaxed, he or she opens his or her mind to accept messages from the other side.

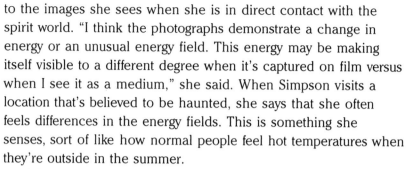

to the images she sees when she is in direct contact with the spirit world. "I think the photographs demonstrate a change in energy or an unusual energy field. This energy may be making itself visible to a different degree when it's captured on film versus when I see it as a medium," she said. When Simpson visits a location that's believed to be haunted, she says that she often feels differences in the energy fields. This is something she senses, sort of like how normal people feel hot temperatures when they're outside in the summer.

Like many other mediums and psychics, Simpson truly respects the abilities she has and takes her gift very seriously. "I feel that people who do have a strong psychic gift have the ability to be extremely helpful to other people," she said, which is why she openly works with clients and shares her gift with others.

Natalie Smith

Psychic Medium, Spiritualist Mystic
P.O. Box 295, Wattsburg, PA 16442-0295
(814) 739-9724
E-mail: Natalie@loveandlight.com
Web site: *www.loveandlight.com*

Natalie Smith began experiencing psychic phenomena in 1989, after having a near-death experience. In the late 1980s, Smith suffered from a life-threatening illness that lasted for more than ten months. She was hospitalized for over three months. As part of her illness, she suffered from an irregular heartbeat, which ultimately caused a cardiac arrest, and also experienced kidney failure. Prior to the cardiac arrest, which was almost fatal, she believes she may have had some psychic abilities, but nowhere to the extent she does now.

These days, Smith has totally recovered from her illness and works as a registered nurse as well as a professional medium. "During the near-death experience, I experienced an enormous love, which engulfed me in a beautiful white/yellow light. I remember that all around me was this light, and I was able to look directly into it. To imagine what this was like, think about looking directly into the sun, but not having it hurt your eyes. Within the light, I met my grandmother who was on the other side. Standing within that light, I could feel God's love. I'm not saying that God was that light, but I could feel him there. At this point, I felt that I was home and that everyone understood me. Communication within this light was done telepathically. When I was brought back to life, I spent several months actually being mad because I was brought back from the other side," she explained.

Smith believes that her mediumship abilities intensified dramatically after her near death experience. "I became able to hear things that normal people couldn't. I feel that I was brought back to use this ability to help other people. I now work closely with people experiencing grief due to the death of a loved one. For example, I help parents understand that when they lose a child, they've lost them in a physical form, but not in a spiritual form," said Smith, who explains that she can see, hear, and sense spirits from the other side when she communicates with them.

What Smith Sees When Communicating with the Other Side

Smith explained that when doing a reading, she often sees in her mind short movies of events that involve the spirits she is communicating with. "What I experience when communicating with spirits is whatever they choose to show me. Not all spirits work the same way. Sometimes I hear messages or music, other times I see images. I never know what to expect," she said.

In addition to sensing and communicating with spirits in her mind, Smith believes she has captured the spirits talking to her using EVP (electronic voice phenomena). During a reading that was recorded by her client, the voice of the spirit she was communicating with using her abilities as a medium was also captured on

the audiotape, despite the fact that this voice wasn't actually heard by the client who was in the room during the reading.

Prior to any reading, Smith communicates with a client via telephone or e-mail, but doesn't gather any personal information other than the client's name and phone number. Smith meditates for about twenty minutes before a reading. During this meditation, she'll also perform automatic writing. This process involves channeling a spirit and having her hand automatically write the messages that come through from the other side. She literally writes down whatever messages pop into her head from the spirit world.

How Smith Conducts a Reading

During an actual reading, Smith explained she uses all parts of her brain. While listening to her client, she also must listen telepathically to the spirit(s) she's communicating with. "A typical reading lasts thirty to sixty minutes," she said. "When I meditate prior to a reading, I spend time praying to God and I ask for help. I ask for help reading the people on the other side and also for help in assisting my client."

No matter what the message is that Smith receives from the other side, she believes it's her responsibility to accurately and honestly convey the information to her clients. She recalls once trying to hold back some information in order to spare her client some grief, which actually angered the spirit she was communicating with. "I wound up just passing along the message that I received word for word as opposed to paraphrasing the message. There have been things that I, Natalie, would never say to someone else, but as a medium, I am passing along messages from the other side, so I feel obligated to share exactly what I receive from the spirits," she said.

When a reading ends, Smith seldom remembers the events that transpired, which is why she always records her readings. She explained that the information from the spirit world flows through her, allowing her to act as a messenger. Periodically, however, she'll remember bits and pieces of her communications with the spirit world. "I believe my conscious mind doesn't remember the events during a reading because the information doesn't pertain to me. If I remembered everything that happened, it would be too emotionally overwhelming for me."

According to Smith, one of the most difficult aspects of her work is communicating with the spirit of a young person who had taken his or her own life. "The first time I ever read someone who had committed suicide, I was shown absolutely everything by the spirit and it was extremely emotionally upsetting. I believe my conscious mind now protects me from events that might be too traumatic if I were to remember them. While a reading is going on, I always try to give my client the opportunity to ask follow-up questions or obtain clarification of a message from the spirit I'm communicating with," said Smith.

Contacting a Deceased Relative

People who seek out Smith to act as a medium often want to know about relatives who have passed on. Her clients often want to know if their loved one is in any pain. "I had one woman who wanted to know if her late husband knew that she really missed him. During the reading, I didn't receive a 'yes' or 'no' response to this question. The message I received was, 'Did you know that I stand by the foot of your bed and watch you sleep, and when you can't sleep, I help you to sleep.' If a client was forced to take a loved one off a respirator, for example, he or she wants to know if that was the right thing to do."

Smith believes the other side, which is where spirits are believed to exist, is a world very much like ours. "I am not happy with the way hell is portrayed. I do not believe that an all-loving and all-powerful God on the other side would love you one minute and punish you the next minute. My opinion is that there is no hell. I believe that if we ask for God's forgiveness for things we've done, God forgives us. Some people, however, go to the

How Does Automatic Writing Work?

All messages are written down using a normal writing instrument and paper. This form of communicating with the other side falls into the area of motor automatism. When this process is used, the mind delivers information by taking control of nerves and muscles of the arm and hand. Professional automatic writers are called autonographists.

other side with lessons they still need to learn. I am a firm believer that there are several levels to heaven," explained Smith, who has "discussed" her beliefs with some of the spirits she has communicated with.

Smith is also a believer in reincarnation. "If someone hasn't learned a lesson while living, they're put back on earth," she said. Smith believes it takes anywhere from seventy-five to 100 years for someone to be reincarnated. However, it's important to understand that there is no such thing as time as we know it on the other side. Smith thinks that everyone has the opportunity to be reincarnated, but most spirits choose to stay on the other side. In other words, they have a choice. Based on her contacts, Smith has discovered that spirits tend keep the same personality they had when alive.

Smith's Theories about Spirits

According to Smith, spirits exist as a form of pure energy. This being the case, when she makes contact with them, she believes it's the spirit that determines what appearance it will take on when it communicates with the world of the living.

After her own near-death experience, when Smith's psychic powers began to intensify, one of her worst fears was that the spirit world would overcome her. "I was afraid that I'd lose a part of myself as a result of spending time on the other side. This hasn't happened, however," said Smith.

While her primary goal in using her mediumship abilities is to assist people in coping with the loss of a loved one, Smith refuses to see each of her clients more than once per six-month period. "I believe it's bad karma to take advantage of someone when that person is grieving. If I am able to make contact with someone's loved one on the other side, there's not much more I'll be able to do for that person a week or two later. I don't believe more can be accomplished by communicating with the same spirit again too soon. My goal is to make people aware that their loved ones on the other side are still close by and looking out for them," said

Smith, who stated that spirits choose to communicate with the living world to finish previously unfinished business.

Advice for Those Seeking to Work with a Medium

When asked to share advice on how clients should prepare if they choose to participate in a reading with a medium, Smith explained that the medium you choose should charge a flat fee. "If a medium asks for more money in order to create a stronger contact with the other side, for example, beware! I recommend that people find a psychic or medium using a word-of-mouth referral," said Smith.

So much of what a medium or channeler does can't be scientifically proven; however, Smith believes that through the study of near-death experiences, mankind will someday be able to obtain a much better understanding of the other side. As a medium, Smith is open to whatever messages she receives from the other side and can focus her abilities to receive those messages. Other times, however, she has learned to shut off her ability so that she can have a somewhat normal life. "I had to learn how to shut off this ability periodically, because I was being bombarded. I would go to the grocery store, for example, and know things about the total strangers I'd come into contact with while I was shopping. I'd know if a woman was being beaten by her husband or if someone's husband was having an affair, and that's information I have no business knowing about people, especially strangers," she said.

For those who aren't committed to believing in life after death or the existence of the other side, Smith offers the following thought: "I have seen the other side. Through my near-death experience I have been to the other side. We definitely go somewhere absolutely wonderful after death. It's a place where we can be at total peace. There is no more pain, grief, or tears on the other side. It's a place where we meet up with our family. The spirits on the other side are not all-knowing, nor is the medium. A lot of the time, the medium works on a need-to-know basis," explained Smith, who doesn't always understand the meaning behind the messages she receives from the other side.

Further Reading

If you are interested in your personal spiritual awakening, check out *You Own the Power*. Written by famous medium Rosemary Altea, this book offers several exercises to help the reader contact the spirit world.

Coping with Grief

The death of a loved one, close friend, or even a pet is an extremely traumatic experience that all of us experience. People deal with death in many different ways. Some people turn to their own faiths, while others try to find meaning in their loss and cope in other ways.

As described in this chapter, people sometimes choose to deal with their grief by seeking out the help of a channeler or medium in an effort to communicate with the deceased. Grieving people often want to say a final farewell, resolve conflicts or differences they had with the deceased, or obtain a better understanding of why the person died.

Whether or not you choose to seek out a channeler or medium to assist you in communicating with someone who has died is a very personal decision. It should be understood, however, that people who experience a tragic loss almost always undergo several stages of grief. Understanding what these stages of grief are, what they mean to you, and how you can deal with them will help you better cope with the tragedy in your life that involves the death of a loved one, whether or not you're able to communicate with that person's ghost or spirit.

The Stages of Grief

Seeking the assistance of a channeler or medium can help people cope with loss; however, there are many other important components to the grieving process. While virtually everyone who experiences grief will experience the following stages, the order in which these stages are experienced will vary based on the individual. Likewise, how long each stage lasts and what triggers the transition from one stage of grief to the next will also vary greatly.

What's important to remember is that these experiences and the feelings and emotions associated with them are all totally normal. If you're experiencing grief and having trouble dealing with the many different emotions associated with it, consider seeking out counseling from a psychologist or psychiatrist who will help you move on with your life and better deal with the loss.

The stages of grief include:

1. **Shock.** Upon learning of a loved one's death, the human body tends to deal with this type of tragedy by going into a state of emotional and sometimes physical shock. This typically happens when a tragic event happens unexpectedly, which causes your own life to instantly be turned upside-down. Many people who experience this equate the feeling to their entire body and emotional state going totally numb. Shock is the body's way of trying to deal with an emotional or physical overload. It's a normal reaction and one that will pass. This state of mind is very different from the medical condition associated with injuries.

2. **Denial.** After learning that a tragedy has occurred, the human mind often can't immediately comprehend what has happened, causing a sense of denial. Denial is a way to temporarily delay having to deal with the emotional impact of coming to terms with someone's death. Experiencing a state of denial for a brief time is normal; however, continuing to deny that a tragedy has occurred isn't healthy or normal.

3. **Anxiety.** This stage of grief involves becoming overly anxious, unable to concentrate on anything, and a general feeling of panic or nervousness about what the future might hold. When someone loses a spouse, for example, he or she may have to deal with leading a totally independent existence for the first time in many years. This can be a scary prospect.

4. **Bargaining.** This is one method by which people try to change something that can't be changed. It often involves

Further Reading

To get a good in-depth look at the life of a famous medium, pick up a copy of *We Don't Die: George Anderson's Conversations with the Other Side* by Joel Martin, George Anderson, and Patricia Romanowski.

trying to "make a deal" with God to somehow reverse the tragedy that has taken place. This is yet another form of denial when it's related to the death of a loved one, for example.

5. **Anger.** Part of the grieving process often involves becoming angry at the person who died or at God for taking the life of someone you cared deeply for. Many people experience a sense of pure powerlessness when dealing with death, becoming angry and frustrated at the situation. People who become angry tend to express this emotion in a variety of different ways, whether it's by taking out their frustration on others who are trying to support them in their time of grief, experiencing an emotional outburst against the person who has died, or temporarily turning against God or their spiritual leader(s). Being able to let out this anger as you experience it will help you come to terms with your loss. Trying to bottle up this emotion can lead to more physical and emotional trauma in your life.

6. **Guilt.** When a loved one dies, especially if it's sudden or unexpected, there are often unresolved issues. Knowing these issues exist can cause strong feelings of guilt to develop. Depending on the circumstances, people may feel guilty for outliving a person, or somehow feel responsible for that person's death. The belief that the death could somehow have been avoided if only something was done or said while the person was alive becomes the premise for guilt to develop. Whether or not there are actually reasons to experience guilt, especially if there are unresolved issues, it's important to find ways of relieving these feelings and coming to terms with the situation.

7. **Depression.** This is the emotion that's most commonly associated with grief and one that virtually everyone will experience. This stage of grief often involves experiencing intense feelings of loneliness and isolation. It's perfectly normal to be sad when someone you love dies; however,

Further Reading

Dr. Elisabeth Kubler-Ross conducts one of the most famous psychological studies on death in her book *On Death and Dying*. Here she explains the five stages of coping with death.

developing an ongoing sense of depression is something that can have long-term physical and mental repercussions. Loss of appetite, inability to sleep, uncontrollable emotional outbursts, feelings of helplessness, and the urge to be alone are all signs of depression. Some people become physically ill as a result of being depressed over an extended period of time. Experiencing these symptoms for a few days or weeks is normal, but if the symptoms persist or intensify, see your doctor.

8. **Acceptance.** Whether it's days, weeks, months, or years after a loss occurs, the grieving process eventually comes to an end when someone begins to accept what has happened and finds the strength to continue on with his or her own life. This doesn't mean that you forget the person who has died or you stop loving that person. It does mean that you come to the understanding that the loved one who has died would want you to go on with your life and be happy. Love is a powerful emotion and one that doesn't die. It's perfectly acceptable and normal to continue loving someone forever, even after that person has died. Instead of focusing on the tragedy of his or her death, begin to focus on the happiness that person brought into your life. Remember the good times and cherish your fondest memories.

While many people find solace and comfort through the use of a medium or channeler to try to communicate with a loved one who has died, there are other resources available to people experiencing grief. Many organizations have been created to help people from all walks of life deal with the grief associated with the loss of a loved one. Even if you're not yet prepared to discuss your feelings with others, many of these organizations offer Web sites and other resources for information that you can read yourself. These organizations include:

- **After Death Project**, *www.after-death.com*. Resources, information, chats, and spiritual help are available here from

the authors of *Hello from Heaven*. This book is a compilation of after-death communication experiences without the aid of a psychic or medium.

- **American Suicide Foundation**, 120 Wall Street, 22nd Floor, New York, NY 10005; 1-800-531-4477. Resources for suicide prevention and the survivors of suicide are available from the group's national office and regional chapters.
- **Bereaved Parents of the USA**, P.O. Box 95, Park Forest, IL 60466-0095; *www.bereavedparentsusa.org*. Self-help guidance for bereaved parents, siblings, and grandparents is offered. This organization offers local chapters, hosts conferences, and publishes newsletters, books, and audiotapes.
- **Center for Attitudinal Healing,** 33 Buchanan Drive, Sausalito, CA 94965; (415) 331-6161. Support is offered to adults and children with life-threatening illnesses and to bereaved families. This organization offers workshops, training sessions, newsletters, plus referrals to more than 100 independent centers worldwide.
- **GROWW**, *www.groww.com*. This is a nonprofit, Internet-based site offering a wide variety of grief and bereavement resources.
- **Mothers Against Drunk Driving** (MADD), 511 East John Carpenter Freeway, #700, Irving, TX 75062; 1-800-GET-MADD; *www.madd.org*. This national organization was created to stop drunk driving and support its victims. There are over 500 local MADD chapters offering victim support groups, training programs, and conferences.
- **National Hospice Organization** (NHO), 1901 North Moore Street, Suite 901, Arlington, VA 22209; 1-800-658-8898; *www.nho.org*. NHO offers referrals to programs, services, and support groups, plus individual and family counseling for the terminally ill and the bereaved.
- **Parents of Murdered Children** (POMC), 100 East 8th Street, B-41, Cincinnati, OH 45202; (513) 721-5683; *www.pomc.com*. With over 400 chapters nationwide, POMC offers self-help for parents, families, friends, and victims of homicide.

- **Samaritans**, (212) 673-3000; *www.samaritansnyc.org*. (Virtually every city in the United States has its own Samaritan hotline with a local telephone number.) This is an all-volunteer, confidential, nonreligious, twenty-four-hour suicide prevention hotline. This nonprofit organization's sole purpose is to provide support to those individuals and groups who are in crisis, have lost someone to suicide, or are feeling suicidal.
- **SHARE Pregnancy and Infant Loss Support**, National Office—St. Joseph Health Center, 300 First Capitol Drive, St. Charles, MO 63301; 1-800-821-6819. This organization offers support to families bereaved by miscarriage, stillbirth, or neonatal death.
- **SIDS Alliance**, 1314 Bedford Avenue, Suite 210, Baltimore, MD 21208; 1-800-221-SIDS; *www.sidsalliance.org*. SIDS Alliance provides support for families who have suffered sudden infant death syndrome (SIDS).
- **The Compassionate Friends** (TCF), P.O. Box 3696, Oak Brook, IL 60522-3696; (630) 990-0010; *www.compassionate friends.org*. TCF offers support for bereaved parents, siblings, and grandparents. The organization has over 600 local chapters and sponsors national and regional conferences, plus offers newsletters, books, tapes, and other resources.
- **The NAMES Project Foundation**, 310 Townsend Street, Suite 310, San Francisco, CA 94107; (415) 882-5500. This is an AIDS support group that sponsors the AIDS Quilt. The organization caters to the needs of people who suffer from AIDS and who are dealing with the loss of a loved one who has died from this disease.
- **Widowed Persons Service** (WPS), 601 E Street, N.W., Washington, D.C. 20049; (202) 434-2260. This division of the American Association of Retired Persons (AARP) offers a wide range of support services for widows and widowers of all ages.

Chapter Five

Past-Life Regression and Contacting Your Spirit Guide(s)

Have you ever met someone new yet had a strong feeling that you've met that person before? Perhaps there was something about that person, on some unexplainable level, that was extremely familiar to you. When visiting a city for the first time, have you ever had the feeling you've been there before, yet you know that in this lifetime it's your first time there? Do you have a habit or a personal trait whose origin you can't explain, yet you can't rid yourself of it?

Many people believe that these situations are clues you have experienced a former or previous life. Using a method of meditation and hypnosis called past-life regression (PLR), some people think you can tap into the memories of your past life (or lives) that have been locked away deep in the recesses of your brain. People who experience past-life regression believe their spirit has lived before, either as a person or animal. Using meditation and hypnosis techniques, many people believe they have the ability to tap the portion of their mind that actually remembers past live(s).

No Scientific Proof Exists, But . . .

Like so many things involving life and death, reincarnation, spirits, and the supernatural, past-life regression is something many people truly believe in, yet it's something that can't yet scientifically be proven. When someone undergoes hypnosis to tap the memories of a past life, is that person in fact unlocking memories from a previous existence, or is that person simply expressing thoughts that are a result of an overactive imagination inspired by the hypnotist?

Some therapists use past-life regression to help clients develop a stronger self-understanding or as a way they can self-heal if they're attempting to overcome something negative. It's important to understand that past-life regression isn't channeling. While in essence you're communicating with "spirits" when you channel or participate in a past-life regression, during a regression, the "spirit" you're communicating with is your own from another lifetime. You're recalling memories that have been blocked out or that for some reason haven't been available to you without assistance.

Many people who believe they've experienced past-life regression equate the actual event to watching a movie in their mind or dreaming, except that when the session is complete, they remember what transpired. This is described by many as feeling as though for a brief time they existed in two places at one time: the present (experiencing their current life) and the past (in a past life).

Shala F. Mattingly (*www.past-life.com*) is a specialist in past-life regression therapy. She is certified in clinical, forensic, and regressive hypnosis, and has maintained a professional practice in Manhattan since 1981.

Mattingly reports that past-life regression therapy is an expedient, effective, and inexpensive technique for accessing the subconscious mind that contains complete knowledge of your personal history throughout time. She stated, "You are a unique blend of a vast number of existences both physical and nonphysical, and your present self is but a minute portion of your totality. More than 75 percent of that which is motivating or restricting you now emanates from memories that were already installed and active within you when you entered this life."

Mattingly believes that most traditional therapies only examine present life memories in the search for understanding and healing, and thus the treatment becomes lengthy, frustrating, and expensive. By examining past-life, between-life, and consciously forgotten present-life memories, many believe it is possible to clarify your current life purpose and remove any stumbling blocks that may be preventing you from achieving the goals you carefully planned prior to your current birth.

Inessa King Zaleski (*www.calmness.com*), another specialist in past-life regression therapy, believes that it can help people discover the reasons for current fears, recurring dreams, and personality tendencies. From this type of therapy, someone can learn to understand more about his or her fears, dreams, and tendencies from past experiences (in past lives), and even let them go forever. Zaleski believes that through exploration of past lives you can easily learn why you are repeatedly entering abusive relationships, why you are born into your particular family,

why you have obsessive behavior(s), and possibly find out what lessons you can learn in your current lifetime.

To explain the possible therapeutic impact past-life regression therapy can have on someone, Zeleski uses the example of a client of hers who was overweight. She explained, "This woman was extremely overweight. She felt a compulsive desire to eat almost constantly and never felt satisfied. She found out that she died from starvation in a past life and was now subconsciously compensating for it." Another client had a strong fear of closed places. "She was unable to drive into a car wash, enter a tunnel, or step into an elevator. When regressed to a past life, she found herself buried alive in a coffin. In those days, when you passed out and they couldn't find your pulse, you were considered dead. In her previous life, this patient had called for help and struggled to get out of her coffin, but with no success. She suffocated to death. After realizing the origin of her fear, she was able to let it go completely," stated Zeleski. Another of her clients was a man who had an unexplainable and severe fear of large bodies of water, yet according to Zeleski, he never lived near a body of water in this life. When this man was regressed into a past life, he found himself eight years old and the only witness to his parents' drowning. Their little boat filled with water while he ran back and forth helplessly on the beach.

Zeleski explained that when you're experiencing past-life regression or PLR, you are led back by the therapist to a different time using hypnosis and relaxation exercises. The goal is to make your body totally relaxed, but to keep your mind fully aware and awake. Your eyes will be closed and you will see and feel that you are in a different time and place. You will be able to talk and answer questions about your experience. A successful subject is anyone with good concentration who is willing to accept and follow suggestions. Although PLR is most effective when guided by an expert who is responding to the subject's individual journey, it can often be successful when guided by an audio recording.

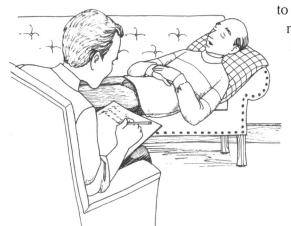

One of the big questions people have when they begin learning about past-life regression is why don't living people (like you and me) remember having lived already? Why isn't this part of our general memory or consciousness? Depending on whom you ask, there are many possible reasons for this.

Rene K. Mueller, a contributor to SpiritWeb (*www.spiritweb.org*), explained that we often judge those who don't live as we do, and blame those who live other lifestyles. We also perceive certain aspects of life differently. "This issue of judging is really important because it's the same mechanism that prevents us from remembering. For example, if you lived a lifestyle or a behavior you currently would judge as unacceptable, you keep this remembrance in your subconscious. Lots of experiences are repeated, not just of past lives, and often we realize that certain happenings are similar. We as souls search for possibilities to realize and then release certain patterns, but we prevent ourselves from remembering consciously the failure, which in truth is not a failure, but nonreleased patterns we keep and we search to understand." In other words, how we act in each of our lives and the behaviors we adopt can and will be repeated, since more often than not we can't remember previous behaviors from past lives. Thus, if we start on a path of poor behavior and making bad decisions, the impact of these actions could have ramifications in later lives.

Understanding Past-Life Regression: The Hypnotherapist's Point of View

The following are in-depth interviews with people who are specialists in past-life regression hypnotherapy and have studied this phenomenon in great detail. Their fascinating firsthand experiences about past-life regression will help you to obtain a greater understanding of how this specialized form of hypnotherapy works and how you might be able to benefit from it.

Past-Life Regression Therapy

Many believe this form of therapy can be used to help people explore a wide range of personal issues, such as:

- Your "between lives" experiences (what happens to you between your lives on Earth)
- Death experiences and beyond
- Healing of grief
- Meetings with spirit guides and deceased loved ones
- Past-life memories that may be affecting your health
- The causes of fear, guilt, anger, or phobias in your present life
- Your choice of parents and other important relationships.

Isa Gucciardi, Ph.D.

(415) 333-1434
E-mail: *isa@depthhypnosiscom*
Web site: *www.depthhypnosis.com*

Isa Gucciardi received her doctorate in transpersonal psychology from Summit University. She is a certified hypnotherapist affiliated with Valencia Healing Arts Center in California, a clinic that provides complementary health care. She holds certificates in transformational healing and hypnotherapy from the Institute of Transformational Healing. Gucciardi is an ordained minister with the Association of the Integration of the Whole Person and a certified Reiki Master. She has been a meditation student of Zen Buddhism for fifteen years and has studied various systems of energy healing. Gucciardi is also a student of advanced shamanism and shamanic healing with the Foundation for Shamanic Studies. In addition to her private practice, she volunteers at the Laguna Honda Zen Hospice Project.

Gucciardi's Interest in Past-Life Regression

Since she was a young child, Gucciardi has been aware of energy and spirits around her. Early in her life, she discovered her psychic abilities and that she is a "natural channel," which allows her to tune in to an energy (or spirit) and be taken over by it, thus enabling the spirit to speak through her. It took many years of study for Gucciardi to learn how to harness her capabilities and better understand the energies or spirits she frequently and easily communicates with.

Her work currently incorporates working as a channeler or medium as well as a hypnotherapist. She works with clients primarily interested in past-life regression. Gucciardi explained that for her entire life, she has been drawn to the study of paranormal phenomena. At a very early age, she vividly recalls receiving simple communications from the trees and plants around her, but it wasn't until her teenage years that she learned how to put the messages or images she was receiving into context.

As a teenager, Gucciardi was able to read her friends and make accurate predictions about them. These days, she describes a person's energy field as being as easy for her to read as a normal book. When working with clients, she taps her psychic skills while working as a trained therapist in order to lead them toward the answers they are seeking about themselves.

What Her Clients Receive from a PLR Session

According to Gucciardi, "The insights gained by allowing the constructs of our conscious mind to rest while we explore other possible realities in hypnosis can bring us to a sense of ourselves which extends far beyond the confines of the conscious mind." Gucciardi explained that past-life regression can bring us beyond where many of us feel hopelessly trapped and can assist us in resolving our imbalances. She added, "We can use the context of a past-life encounter to resolve old 'hauntings' and retrieve parts of ourselves that have been lost in the formation of the constructs of our conscious mind. In doing this, we are able to move into a state of wholeness." She believes this state is not possible if we reject the possibility of other realities beyond what is dominated by the conscious mind.

While Gucciardi appears to be a strong believer in past-life regression, she insists that for this form of therapy to work it should be combined with other forms of therapy, such as depossession or soul retrieval. This is because someone's flashes of past-life content may not always be flashes of his or her own past lives but flashes of an attached entity's past life. She stated, "In the shamanic perspective espoused by Michael Harner, the presence of a violent death within the experience of a past-life regression often indicates such a possession. My clinical experience indicates that this is often, but not always, the case." Thus, some people who believe they are being haunted by past-life experiences may in fact be possessed by outside entities, not at all affiliated with one's past

One Person, Many Lives

According to Zaleski, age regression is the process of going back to a previous time in your current life. Through this process, people often discover repressed memories that impact their subconscious actions and reactions. Past-life regression, however, is age regression taken further back to a previous life. Future-life progression is a progression into a future life. Age progression explores a future time in the current life. "Reincarnation is a belief that we have lived many times before and that our spiritual development evolves with each lifetime. In some religions, reincarnation is part of the belief system," she said.

Hypnosis Explained

Dr. John Gatto, president of the Academy of Professional Hypnosis, explained that hypnosis has been practiced for thousands of years as a bridge to wellness in physical and mental health, relationships, creativity, happiness, and serenity.

"It is a bridge to the future, which is quickly rushing towards us in leaps and bounds. Hypnosis can introduce you to your timeless, ageless self. Hypnosis provides you the opportunity to change the difficult to easy, the complex to simple, and to make the terrors of life manageable. It is a gift to light our way in the dark, to focus on goals and to obtain them."

life. This possession can be misdiagnosed or misinterpreted and can cause ongoing problems in someone's current life.

Through past-life regression, Gucciardi believes people can have a diverse range of experiences. She explained, "There are many types of phenomena that can appear to be either a past- or other-life 'bleed-through' experience or a spirit or entity attachment. Both have the etiology of the repeated encounter with a set of phenomena that appear to be happening in its own context parallel to our conscious waking life reality. Both intrude upon our conscious mind, often without invitation." In other words, the experiences we have in our current lives may be repeated from past lives, yet not remembered or only vaguely remembered. These repeat events happen without our control or conscious effort.

Gucciardi believes that one possible reason for this phenomenon is that these types of uncontrolled or undesired experiences occur when there has been some type of soul loss. She stated that the concept of soul loss has many ramifications. Soul loss can be the loss of vital energy experienced as a result of any kind of physical, emotional, mental, or spiritual trauma. This type of loss creates a vacuum within the energy field. Gucciardi believes that entities, spirits, or past-life reverberations can enter through this vacuum and be experienced by the "host" (the host being the living person). Thus, it's always important to keep an open mind when approaching phenomena that appear to be sapping the vital energy—the energy that makes up someone's spirit. If a spirit is stealing your life energy in order to exist in our living realm, this should be stopped or at least controlled.

Communicating with the Spirit World

When making contact with a spirit as a psychic, Gucciardi stated that she doesn't typically see too much in terms of visual images. She does, however, feel a spirit's presence and often communicates by receiving telepathic pictures or images as opposed to hearing a voice. "Different people have different senses that are active when they're in an altered state. My sixth sense is the most active when I go into an altered state and communicate with spirits. Most living people, including me, are used to seeing and hearing only, so it's unusual to communicate using my sixth sense. I've had to learn how to trust this sense as much as I'd trust my eyes and ears. As I communicate with a spirit, I can physically feel a shift in the energy around me," she explained.

The ability to see, hear, taste, and touch are all senses that humans possess. Those who have the gift of being able to communicate with spirits, for example, are able to tap a sixth sense, which involves the psychic abilities that we may all have.

By inviting the spirit's energy to enter her, Gucciardi is able to read and understand the spirit and obtain the message(s) it's trying to convey. Some people believe that past-life regression allows living individuals to enter into an altered state of mind and communicate with themselves, but from a previous lifetime. However, Gucciardi has discovered that in some cases, the entity that the person communicates with isn't from a past life but an outside spirit that has possessed that person and is feeding off of his or her life energy. "If I discover someone has been possessed by a spirit, I will try to convince the spirit to leave that person and move into the light. In some shamanic practices, the spirit is drawn from the person and transported into a chicken or a pig; however, I believe in helping the spirit enter the light," she said.

Gucciardi's Theories about Spirits

Gucciardi believes there are many different classes of spirits that exist in different realms. There is an upper world, a middle world, and a lower world. Her belief is based on the shamanic model, not the Christian model, which believes in heaven, hell, and limbo. The shamanic model has been discovered and studied throughout history by many cultures, including the Siberians, Africans, and Plains Indians. "Spirits that are connected with hauntings or possessions, I believe, are caught in the middle world. Spirits, such as guides, angelic forces, or God forces, exist in the upper world. To contact these spirits, it's necessary for the

mind to enter into an altered state, through hypnosis, for example," said Gucciardi.

Despite being able to communicate with spirits that she believes are both good and evil, Gucciardi is never fearful of the spirits, because she is aligned with positive spirit guides and energy. "If you are aligned with those energies, nothing can touch you in terms of the negative spirits or the spirits from the lower world. Evil spirits are nothing to be frightened of. Typically, they are simply lost and confused. People who get scared are not grounded in a higher vibration and get drawn into the negative energy," said Gucciardi, who does not agree with the idea of putting up a protective shield when communicating with spirits. She believes this reduces one's own life energy that can better be focused on one's center. By tapping one's spirit guides and harnessing their energy, it's possible for someone to better control their own energy in a positive way. This can be an added barrier of protection against evil spirits.

According to Gucciardi, people who are depressed or otherwise experiencing negative emotional or physical trauma are more apt to become possessed by a spirit. "Spirit guides, however, are available to all of us and are there to offer guidance and assistance. But spirit guides aren't intrusive. They wait for someone to summon them. They will not come into your energy field unless you're open to them. Once someone opens his or her mind and becomes aware of their presence, spirit guides are more than willing to offer guidance and assistance, whether you're participating in past-life regression or simply facing some type of personal challenge," said Gucciardi.

The Difference Between Past-Life Regression and Channeling

According to Gucciardi, past-life regression and channeling (or mediumship) are different. In any of these situations, an extended awareness of one's self is required. She explained, "It's necessary to go into an altered state in order to expand your abilities to perceive and understand other realities. Personally, I don't think there's such a thing as 'past life' when someone participates in past-life regression therapy. I believe the person is experiencing current life experiences that exist in another dimension or reality. I don't think there's linear time in other dimensions. When someone has a past-life experience or reality, that person is tuning in to another part of his or her being, which is living its own life in another dimension." She believes someone can gain a lot of insight by participating in this form of therapy. A person who is having a past-life experience is in many ways channeling the energy of the part of his- or herself that exists in another dimension.

How a Past-Life Regression Session Works

When Gucciardi is working with a client and chooses to use hypnotherapy, she never does so with the intention of exploring "past lives." Instead, she allows the client to subconsciously determine what needs to be accomplished during a hypnosis session. One thing Gucciardi is adamant about is that she doesn't perform what she refers to as "past-life tourism." Unless someone has an issue that needs more clarity in this life, she believes there is no reason to explore other lives.

Gucciardi stated that when someone undergoes past-life regression therapy, what the person actually remembers and can take away from the experience will vary greatly. If someone is facing an issue that is particularly difficult, it make take longer for the person to remember what transpired during a past-life regression session, because he or she is not emotionally ready to accept or face the issues being dealt with. Usually, a person will remember everything that happens, especially what's important to the situation at hand. Gucciardi describes her job as a hypnotherapist as being like an investigator, helping her clients discover the answers they're searching for.

As she guides a client through a hypnotherapy session, especially one that involves past-life regression, Gucciardi is extremely careful not to accidentally place images or thoughts in someone's

Helpful Resources

Past Life Books (*www. eclipsepsychic.com*) is an online bookstore featuring a selection of books about past-life regression. If you're interested in learning more about this form of hypnotherapy, visiting this site is a good start. Another excellent resource for books on this topic can be found at About.com (*http://healing. about.com/health/healing/ library/blbookshelf41.htm*).

mind. Using her psychic abilities, Gucciardi is often able to communicate with her client's higher self in an effort to determine what questions to ask during a session. She stated that her role is primarily to help the client reach an altered state of mind through hypnosis and then to ask questions and act as a guide. "One way to tell if a person is experiencing something real and not something in his or her imagination is that while the person is under hypnosis, he or she will focus on seemingly unimportant or irrelevant issues or details. One of my clients found herself in a room. She was asked to describe the room and what she was experiencing, but she kept focusing in on a bowl that she saw on a table. She became fixated on the bowl," recalled Gucciardi.

Gucciardi Communicates with Spirit Guides

Gucciardi is a strong believer in spirit guides and feels they are always there to offer us assistance. When someone is in an altered state of mind and facing a traumatic or difficult situation, she'll often help the person seek out his or her spirit guide for comfort. She does this by asking her clients, while under hypnosis, if they feel any type of presence around them that is compassionate and kind. Almost every client will answer "yes" to this question. She'll then have the client focus on that presence and ask the spirit guide questions. The questions that are asked come from the client; Gucciardi merely acts as the facilitator.

Based on Gucciardi's experiences and those of her clients, a spirit guide can take on many different forms. "It will typically take on a form that is the most relevant to the person the spirit guide is working with," she said. "They are compassionate energies that seek to relieve suffering and offer guidance. Some spirit guides are spirits in the sense that they were once living humans who have since died. Some spirit guides, however, have never actually existed on the earth plane because they are higher forms of energy."

To make contact with one's spirit guide(s), Gucciardi believes the mind must first enter into an altered state. This is most easily done through hypnosis. She stated that the conscious mind has too many defenses against seemingly abnormal events. The conscious mind is designed to keep someone sane. It tends to filter out a lot of the information that's necessary for contacting spirit guides. As someone begins to feel safer with his or her own being, the person can begin to open his or her mind to allow spirit guides to communicate. Using hypnosis, someone can be brought to a place where he or she feels incredibly safe and relaxed. This allows for easier communication with spirit guides.

Interested in Experiencing Past-Life Regression Therapy?

For people interested in experiencing past-life regression therapy or contacting their sprit guide, Gucciardi suggests that they first ensure that their intentions are worthwhile. "If someone is looking to understand him- or herself at a deeper level, this type of therapy can be beneficial. Before I begin working with a client, I ask the person to clarify his or her intentions," said Gucciardi. "My advice to people interested in this type of therapy is to not be afraid. There is nothing to fear in terms of ghosts or spirits. I have seen clients filled with all kinds of fears because of what they've seen in movies. Hollywood tends to play up the demonic aspect of communicating with spirits, but that phenomenon is very rare in real life. Living people simply can't be invaded or hurt by a demonic entity without their consent. What people need is to have the courage to face whatever it is in their lives that's bothering them. In cases where a spirit does cause trouble for someone, I would say that over 98 percent of the time the spirit didn't do anything negative intentionally." Gucciardi said that the spirits she has come into contact with actually feel strong remorse for their actions once it's brought to their attention that they've done something physically or emotionally harmful to a living person.

Shamans and Animal Spirits

Shamanism, the world's oldest healing tradition, is found in all cultures on earth. Shamans work with their allies—the animal spirits. The Shamanism: Working with Animal Spirits Web site (*www.geocities.com/ ~animalspirits*) is just one informative resource for learning more about animal spirit guides. The Shamanism belief is that all animals are to be honored, as they may possess the spirit of those humans who have died. This theory focuses around reincarnation.

Dr. Bruce Goldberg

45300 Natoma Avenue, Woodland Hills, CA 91364
1-800-KARMA-4-U
E-mail: *karma4U@webtv.net*
Web site: *www.drbrucegoldberg.com*

Dr. Bruce Goldberg received his undergraduate degree in biology and chemistry from Southern Connecticut State College in 1970, graduating magna cum laude. He then went on to earn his doctorate at the University of Maryland School of Dentistry in 1974. He was also trained by the American Society of Clinical Hypnosis in 1975. After completing a general practice residency in dentistry, Dr. Goldberg began both a practice in dentistry and hypnotherapy.

From Dentist to Hypnotherapist

In 1977, Dr. Goldberg developed progression hypnotherapy (taking patients into future lives) as well as his now internationally recognized superconscious mind tap, which is a form of hypnosis. Dr. Goldberg's first book, *Past Lives–Future Lives*, was first published in 1982. Republished by Ballantine in 1988, it has become a classic text on the topic of past-life therapy. It is also the first book ever written on progression hypnotherapy.

In 1989, Dr. Goldberg moved his office to Los Angeles. It was then that he retired from dentistry entirely to build up a hypnotherapy practice. His cassette tapes are sold internationally and have been described as the "cutting edge of New Age techniques."

According to Dr. Goldberg, "There are many types of entities that assist us with our spiritual growth. These perfect beings are referred to as spirit guides or angels. In certain instances, these entities can protect us from physical harm, and can facilitate a major turnaround in our lives."

Are Spirits the Cause of Human Evils and Disease?

Dr. Goldberg believes that there are various types of entities that drain us, requiring that they be confronted and ultimately removed. These entities are very different from spirit guides, and some feel that they can possess a living individual. Dr. Goldberg refers to these negative entities as "superpersonalities." Superpersonalities, he believes, become attached to living people and can directly impact their behavior and overall lives. In some cases, this causes the living person to have a split personality or to behave erratically. This erratic behavior might include demonstrating self-destructive behavior.

Dr. Goldberg has seen individuals somehow connected with a superpersonality suffer from autism, anorexia nervosa, bulimia, emotional instability, insomnia, drug abuse, migraine headaches, depression, and a wide range of other symptoms that would be considered abnormal or out of character for the individual. "This can seem like an almost psychotic behavior, but it's not," he added.

These entities may be what Dr. Goldberg calls remnants of someone's past lives, or they could be the energy from another soul. Whatever their origin, using past-life regression therapy and other forms of hypnotherapy, Dr. Goldberg is often able to help someone connect with—and if necessary remove—these evil spirits or entities. Once removed, Dr. Goldberg feels that the individuals can lead normal lives, often being cured of the negative or self-destructive behaviors that were hurting them.

Types of Superpersonalities

Based on his own research and experience, Dr. Goldberg has documented four primary types of superpersonalities, including:

1. **Poltergeists**—Dysfunctional souls of humans who have died but whose spirit has not entered the white light.
2. **Extraterrestrials**—Beings from another planet that inhabit unwilling humans.

3. **Past-life personalities**—When a past life was very negative, but a current life is very positive, the interaction between lives causes this phenomenon.
4. **Demons**—Demonic entities or energies that were never human.

According to Dr. Goldberg, a superpersonality cannot take possession of a living individual unless that individual allows it to happen. Simple, seemingly nonharmful activities, such as participating in a séance with amateurs or playing with a Ouija board, can bring someone into contact with an evil spirit without the individual being properly protected or aware of what's happening.

Dr. Goldberg's Firsthand Encounters

A rare instance of a past-life personality attempting to possess one of Dr. Goldberg's clients happened to a woman he calls "Teresa," who was visiting a museum while on vacation in Germany. "She was visiting an old castle that has been converted into a museum," explained Dr. Goldberg. "Teresa took the walking tour of the castle, and upon walking up a flight of spiral stairs, she noticed a portrait of a woman who looked exactly like her. This woman in the picture was a resident of the castle who lived over 500 years ago. Teresa was frozen in her tracks. She didn't move for almost forty-five minutes. When Teresa returned home, we did a past-life regression and discovered that in a past life, Teresa was the woman in the portrait. Until she visited that castle, Teresa didn't know of the woman's existence, she had never been to Germany, and was not a medieval scholar. During the time Teresa was staring at the portrait, I believe the spirit of the woman in the picture was attempting to possess her."

Another of Dr. Goldberg's clients was a young woman suffering from anorexia. When this woman looked in the mirror, she didn't see herself. What she saw was the image of an overweight mobster from the 1920s. "When

she saw this image she subconsciously began to starve herself because the image was so overweight and revolting to her. During past-life regression we confronted the mobster, who was also a mur-derer, and ultimately got rid of this entity. Once she came to terms with the mobster's existence she reverted back to her old self and immediately began eating normally again, and soon was brought back to perfect health," said Dr. Goldberg.

Past-life regression is becoming a more common form of therapy performed by hypnotherapists. The subconscious mind, also referred to by many as the soul, is made up what Dr. Goldberg believes is electromagnetic energy or dark matter. What is being done with this form of therapy is accessing the Akashic Record, which is a chart of past lives, future lives, and parallel lives. Someone can access this record and obtain answers regarding what's happening in their current life. The Akashic Record is believed to hold answers about everyone's past, present, and future. Through hypnosis, it's thought that people can access this information and use it to improve their current lives.

When someone does past-life regression, the person will access his or her higher self or superconscious mind. Dr. Goldberg believes that the messages someone receives during this type of therapy are a result of interdimensional com-munication. As a result, the messages aren't always clear. When tapping these other dimensions, Dr. Goldberg often has his clients make contact with their spirit guides or angels as a way to help them understand what they're experiencing and better deal with it.

Our History Is Prewritten

The Akashic Record is the repository of all human experi-ence—past, present, and future. It is a detailed record of every thought and event that has ever occurred, will occur, or could possibly occur. Thus, it is what guides all of our lives.

Anyone Can Experience Past-Life Regression

According to Dr. Goldberg, anyone can experience a past-life regression without the assistance of a hypnotherapist. People can learn to perform self-hypnosis or capture the power of their inner mind. "People can take charge of their life without being dependent on me or any other therapist. My role in this process is that of a trainer. I often call myself the 'social director on the karmic cruise ship,'" he said with a laugh. "My purpose is to introduce people's subconscious minds or souls to their higher self, which is the perfect component of themselves. I can then take them on a guided tour of their Akashic Record, introduce them to one of their spirit guides, or help them communicate with a past life."

We're living in a time when people are affluent, powerful, educated, have easy access to technology, and in general we have everything going for us. "As a whole, we should be happy, but we're not. Today, Prozac is the number one prescribed drug in America, and divorce rates and child abuse statistics are at an all-time high. These are not good signs. I believe people who use hypnotherapy can choose to take the high road and make the most of their lives. Everyone has free will and people choose to be unhappy. I believe the energy people send out is what they get back. If you don't get your act together, you'll attract the same type of people in your life. If you raise your own energy, you'll attract more positive people into your life. Most people just whine and complain, but make no effort to repair the problems in their lives. I believe in empowerment," added Dr. Goldberg.

Past-life regression is just one avenue of therapy available to people, but it's not the ultimate answer. Dr. Goldberg believes that using consciousness-raising techniques can improve someone's life. Simply making contact with past lives won't have any relevance on someone's life unless the person knows how to take advantage of the information and discovers how to raise his or her consciousness and improve upon spiritual growth.

In his book *Past Lives–Future Lives*, Dr. Goldberg recounts many case histories and discusses the implications of karma in our lives, how we are affected by reincarnation, and how hypnosis works. He also dispels the many myths that surround the practice of past/future life hypnotherapy, and points out that this approach is now recognized as a valid means of therapy. Both his book and his overall approach to hypnotherapy follow one primary theme: empowerment.

"People have the power to customize and control their own destiny," said Dr. Goldberg. By regressing to their past lives, they

Self-Help Videocassettes

Hypnotic Times Travel into Past and Future Lives is one of Dr. Goldberg's videocassette programs available for sale from his Web site or by calling 1-800-527-6248. This tape presents actual cases of past-life regression, future-life progression, and superconscious mind taps. It instructs viewers on how to do these techniques themselves.

can resolve problems in their current life. Through energy cleansing (superconscious mind tap), the subconscious mind is raised to a higher level. Through progressions people are able to perceive future options (frequencies) and select their ideal future. They are then programmed to this ideal frequency, allowing them to steer their current life in the exact direction they want it to follow. This process allows people to use hypnosis to fix problems in their lives by better understanding the situation, determining the cause of the problems, then dealing with them head-on.

Dr. Goldberg firmly believes that anyone can use the space/time continuum and hypnotherapy to eliminate potential and past problems and attain their true karmic purpose. "I believe past lives are real. A recent CNN/Gallup poll concluded that 58 percent of all Americans believe in reincarnation," said Dr. Goldberg.

Dr. Goldberg Believes in Spirit Guides

In addition to tapping past lives, Dr. Goldberg is an avid believer in the use of spirit guides. "These guides are perfect. They are much higher on the evolutionary scale than we are, and they're made up of pure energy. They can be used to offer us guidance or to help us overcome challenges we face," said Dr. Goldberg, who helps people contact their own spirit guides through the use of hypnotherapy. He adds, however, that these beings can't force us to do anything, because we all have free will. What they can do is give us options. Contacting one's spirit guide is done using similar techniques as past-life regression. The first step is to help someone's mind access his or her higher self.

When someone undergoes hypnotherapy to contact a spirit guide or a past life, what is seen or heard will vary greatly. "Within someone's mind, I create a comfortable environment in which a client can summon his or her spirit guide or past life. A spirit guide might materialize in someone's mind on a telepathic level and take on the form of a white light, a religious figure, the image of a deceased relative, or a wise old sage, for example," stated Dr. Goldberg, who had one client explain that his spirit guide looked like Obi Wan Kanobi from *Star Wars*.

It's important to understand that while the techniques for summoning a past life and a spirit guide are similar, these are different phenomena. When experiencing a past-life regression, you're communicating with yourself but from another time; a spirit guide is a spirit or entity that isn't you.

Before attempting to experience a past-life regression or contacting a spirit guide, Dr. Goldberg strongly recommends reading at least one or two books on the topic and learning about these phenomena so that you develop an understanding of what it's all about. It's important to go into the experience having realistic expectations. He also recommends using some form of protection when communicating with the spirit world. He stated that white light is the most common protection. This simply means surrounding yourself with a source of white light as you make contact with other entities.

Dr. Goldberg described white light as perfect God energy that offers protection against evil spirits and demonic forces. When experiencing past-life regression or contacting a spirit guide for the first time, Dr. Goldberg explained, "Ideally, it's best if someone works with a professional hypnotherapist at first. What you don't want to do is go to a scam artist or black magic perpetrator, however. You want to work with someone who has a lot of credibility. It's also possible to do this on your own using audiocassette or videocassette programs."

Gene Chamberlain

Hypnotherapist
(256) 880-9653
E-mail: *genecham@ix.netcom.com*

Gene Chamberlain has worked as a hypnotherapist and performed past-life regression therapy on his clients for more than twenty years. He is certified by the Long Island Society of Clinical Hypnosis and the Society of Neuro-Linguistic Programming. He's also a member of the American Metaphysical Doctors Association and a second-degree Reiki practitioner. Gene Chamberlain has a doctorate in metaphysical science.

Chamberlain's Interest in Past-Life Regression

Chamberlain's interest in past-life regression began when he first got married. Both he and his wife wanted to pursue their interest in the paranormal. This interest led him to further explore hypnosis as a way to experience past-life regression.

"I have found that a lot of people hang on to negative behavior patterns based on what is in their past. Sometimes, I believe this includes previous life experiences. For people who don't believe in reincarnation and past-live regression, this type of therapy works well also, because I tell those people that what they experience during their sessions are things that their mind creates based on experiences they've had. When and where those experiences took place, and in what lifetime, I don't know," explained Chamberlain, who said that this type of therapy allows people to re-explore experiences and behaviors within their subconscious, allowing them to better understand those experiences and, if necessary, change negative behavior patterns.

> ### Past-Life Regression Library
>
> Literally hundreds of books have been written about past-life regression and spirit guides. To learn more about these phenomena, using your computer, point your Web browser to Amazon.com (*www.amazon.com*) or Barnes & Noble Online (*www.bn.com*) and do a keyword search, using the phrases "Past Life Regression," "Spirit Guide," or "Spiritual Guide."

The Subconscious Mind and Its Impact on Our Lives

According to Chamberlain, "The subconscious mind *controls* your entire reality. When you have a traumatic experience, it often causes a behavior modification that stays with you. Whether that experience happens in someone's early life or in a past life, it affects the person's behavior. By touching base with a past experience in your subconscious mind, and ultimately by going back to that experience, someone can actually resolve it. Past-life regression

Psychic Self-Help

Dr. Goldberg's book, *Protected by the Light,* offers an excellent primer regarding the various types of psychic assaults that people experience. The information in the book is based primarily on actual case histories from his Los Angeles practice. Dr. Goldberg demonstrates how to "diagnose" and treat psychic attacks with a six-step plan for psychic self-defense. He explains how the vast majority of psychic attacks come from general negativity in the universe (such as from news stories and advertisements), and that the next most common cause of psychic attack (about 7 percent) is from discarnate entities, or ghosts.

allows someone to go back to the force that's controlling the pattern the person wants to change and address that source so that it goes away."

Chamberlain believes that when someone experiences a past-life regression, the person is communicating memories from earlier in life or memories from a previous life, not an actual spirit. "People are communicating and unlocking memories from their own subconscious," he said. The result, in essence, is that someone's conscious mind begins to communicate and interact with his or her subconscious mind.

Some people believe they've had numerous past lives. When Chamberlain is addressing an issue someone is trying to deal with, such as a negative behavior pattern in his or her current life, while under hypnosis, Chamberlain will direct the person to the point in time when that behavior pattern originated. He says this is how people are able to go way back in time during this type of therapy. Their subconscious mind knows when events took place, so by unlocking memories through hypnosis, the person undergoing past-life regression can go back and remember past lives, often in detail.

When someone is overweight, for example, using past-life regression therapy Chamberlain often finds that in a previous life that person was starved to death or seriously malnourished. Another common scenario is that in a past life the person was always forced to clean his or her plate by an overbearing parent. He's also encountered women who were raped in a previous life and are overweight in this life as a result of that trauma. The person considers him- or herself ugly or dirty as a result of the traumatic experience that happened in a past life but that wasn't properly dealt with then.

Based on what Chamberlain discovers as the reasons for someone's negative behavior, he's able to help his clients address those issues based on their true cause, and overcome whatever issues need to be dealt with using traditional therapy techniques. Unless a client is actually trying to overcome or deal with a specific issue, Chamberlain won't recommend past-life regression therapy.

Preparing for Regression Therapy

In order to prepare clients for the regression therapy, Chamberlain uses guided visualization and neuro-linguistic programming techniques to make people comfortable with the difference between what they're actually perceiving in their mind and what they can actually see. This means he hypnotizes his clients, gets them into a state of relaxation, then verbally guides them by helping to create or draw out mental images that are comforting and relaxing.

"People need to understand where images they see during the therapy are coming from and know how to deal with them. After having the client participate in a series of exercises, I can obtain a good understanding of how the person actually perceives things and then go on with the regression," said Chamberlain. This aspect of the therapy involves having the client enter into a state of deep relaxation, which includes having the person release his or her physical awareness of where he or she is and begin to focus on what's coming from the subconscious mind.

Chamberlain stated that clients have the ability to end the past-life regression therapy session if they become uncomfortable or frightened. This can be done simply by opening their eyes. "People can do this any time they want. When someone is hypnotized, that person can't be forced to do anything he or she doesn't want to do," confirmed Chamberlain. "A lot of people are uncomfortable at the thought of being hypnotized, because they're afraid the hypnotist will control them." Knowing what is and isn't possible using hypnosis will help someone better benefit from the experience, without being frightened by it. Often, what people are afraid of are misconceptions.

People under hypnosis have the ability to relive events in their mind. This can include hearing and seeing places they've been, interacting with people they know (or have known), and feeling or even smelling things from their past. During this process, people can talk about events or experiences as if they're

watching them on TV. People tend to remember just about everything from their sessions once they're over.

According to Chamberlain, the whole process takes about ninety minutes. This includes a consultation before the hypnosis actually begins. During this time, Chamberlain prepares his clients for what they're about to experience.

While many people begin to explore their subconscious and truly believe they're reliving or revisiting experiences from past lives, whether or not this is actually the case remains unproven. After all, people who believe they're re-experiencing an event that happened in another lifetime—hundreds or thousands of years in the past—might be "seeing" or "experiencing" something that their overactive imagination has created.

"The idea is that somewhere in their subconscious mind there is something that is causing negative behavior. If people can touch base with that, whether it happened in a past life, as a baby in this life, or never at all, they're touching base with what they believe is the root cause of their problem and they're able to address and deal with it," said Chamberlain. "I'm just a facilitator, allowing people to let go of the physical reality that surrounds them in order to focus on their subconscious mind." Based on this philosophy, Chamberlain firmly believes past-life regression can be a very powerful form of healing therapy, even if this concept of visiting past lives doesn't actually exist.

For some people, past-life regression isn't always an enjoyable experience. Chamberlain stated that people sometimes experience events that are frightening or emotionally painful. To actually overcome a problem or issue, however, Chamberlain believes someone must first face it. "One way to deal with a difficult or traumatic situation during a session is for me to guide the person to relive the experience from a third-person perspective, as a bystander, as opposed to from a first-person perspective as the experiencer," he said.

Hypnotherapists on the Web

If you're looking to work with a hypnotherapist who specializes in past-life regression, point your Web browser to the Past Life Directory (*www.netcomuk.co.uk/~asclepus/PLDirectory.html*) for a partial directory of hypnotherapists listed by state.

No matter what the situation or his clients' beliefs regarding reincarnation and past lives, Chamberlain stated that everyone he has worked with has had things in their lives change for the positive as a result of their session(s) with him. "It's a very profound experience. Once people have been guided through the experience, they can experience past-life regression themselves using audiotapes or videotapes. Once people know what they're doing, they can record their own tapes to guide them through their own regression process. People's subconscious often respond extremely well to the sound of their own voice," added Chamberlain.

Chamberlain is a firm believer in spirit guides and in everyone's ability to contact their spirit guides in order to receive emotional support or guidance. However, he has not combined past-life regression therapy and spirit guide contact.

Hiring a Hypnotherapist

When it comes to using this form of therapy to somehow heal, better understand, or improve yourself, using the right therapist for your personal needs can generate the best possible results. According to Dr. Bryan Knight from the Hypnosis Headquarters (*www.hypnosis.org*), "There is no one hundred percent foolproof method of selecting the right hypnotherapist, any more than there is a guaranteed way to select the right lawyer, physician, accountant, or plumber." He recommends obtaining a referral from a medical physician, family member, or close friend, or by learning of a hypnotherapist from a recognized professional association such as the International Registry of Professional Hypnotherapists.

A doctor can refer you to a hypnotherapist, stated Dr. Knight, but there's no guarantee the person will be suitable for you. Personality factors, particular problems, or differing ideologies may interfere with rapport between the patient/client and the therapist. The same is true for referrals by family or friends.

Dr. Knight warns that people should not be misled by someone's reputation alone. He explained, "A great reputation in

How to Evaluate a Hypnotherapist

Dr. Knight and many other hypnotherapists agree that when looking for a hypnotherapist to guide you through past-life regression therapy, it's important to evaluate how comfortable you feel with the person by asking yourself questions like:

- Do I feel comfortable with the person?
- Do I feel accepted and welcome?
- Does he or she ask a lot about me?
- Does he or she seem interested in my problems?
- Does he or she seem knowledgeable?
- Does he or she treat me with respect?
- Does the hypnotherapist really listen to me?

Dr. Knight also suggests asking the potential hypnotherapist questions, such as:

- Do you have references?
- Do you mind if I tape-record the session?
- Do you use hypnosis yourself?
- How long have you been in practice?
- May I bring someone with me?
- What are your fees?
- What are your professional qualifications?
- What experience do you have with my kind of problem?
- What hypnotherapy associations do you belong to?
- Will you teach me self-hypnosis?

the therapy field is not always based on competence. Sometimes it is fed by publicity and by professional colleagues who have a personal liking for a particular therapist, especially if he or she devotes a lot of time to their organization's interests. The colleagues may be impressed by the therapist's speeches, self-confidence, and self-promotion, not his or her actual success rates working with patients."

While soliciting a reliable referral is certainly helpful, when looking for a hypnotherapist to work with you on past-life regression therapy, it's important to trust your own instincts when meeting with a hypnotherapist for the first time. Dr. Knight recommends spending as much time looking for a qualified hypnotherapist as you would shopping for a new car. "Look for someone with many satisfied clients. Ask the hypnotherapist for written testimonials. Any therapist who has been in business for a reasonable length of time will have letters on file from grateful clients. These will be people who have given permission for their comments to be shown to inquirers. Read and verify them," he advised.

Respectful hypnotherapists do not snap their fingers at you, nor speak in a condescending manner. You should be treated with the respect, and when applicable, the concern, you deserve. Dr. Knight stated, "Lack of respect also applies to improper questions, suggestions, or behavior. And not just about sex. Impropriety also applies to money and morals. In a truly therapeutic relationship you are heard, accepted, understood, and guided to strengthen your inner resources. The hypnotherapist is your ally. Not your friend. Not your business partner. Not your guru. And certainly not your lover."

When you begin working with a therapist, all of the hypnotherapy sessions you participate in should be tailored to your individual needs. No two people or two sets of problems are alike. For a hypnotherapist to better understand you, it will most likely require extensive questioning and the taking of a complete history. It's important to be totally honest with the therapist, which means this must be a person you like, trust, and feel safe with.

Dr. Knight believes that the therapist you choose to work with should know the details of your problem, your family situation, important life events, health condition, fears, and your likes and dislikes. These may be topics you're uncomfortable talking about, but the more a therapist knows, the easier it will be for him or her to provide assistance and guidance.

One thing Dr. Knight recommends watching for is a therapist who constantly tries to make all of his patients/clients fall into a specific category with the same basic diagnosis. He stated, "Some therapists continually find that the origin of all their clients' problems lies in childhood sexual abuse; others find that all their clients' problems arise from past live or birth trauma, etc. Not all of life's distresses arise from one trauma, or indeed, from any trauma. Human beings are far too complex, and life, fortunately, is far too rich for there to be one single cause of everyone's troubles."

Becoming Your Own Hypnotherapist or Past-Life Regression Therapist

Becoming a hypnotherapist is something that almost anyone can do with the proper training, whether you want to treat yourself or others. There are many home-study courses available. Some schools and training centers can also be attended in-person.

For example, The Center for Human Relations (*www.spirit releasement.org/chr/trainings/basicplt.html*) offers a three-day, twenty-two-hour course (9:00 A.M. to 5:30 P.M. daily) that covers the basic techniques of past-life regression therapy. The curriculum of this course includes:

- Hypnotic and nonhypnotic inductions for present-life recall, pre- and perinatal experience, and memories of past lives
- Use of the affect bridge, somatic bridge, and linguistic bridge inductions for uncovering the origin or cause of present-life problems
- Sequence of a past-life regression
- Uncovering techniques for memories of traumatic experiences that contribute to present-day problems
- Elimination of the mental residues from past lives (decisions, assumptions, conclusions, beliefs, and judgments)

- Resolution of the emotional residues from past lives (anger, fear, sadness, guilt, and revenge)
- Healing of the physical residues remaining from past-life traumatic events
- Dual regression, group regression, and couples counseling
- Use of forgiveness in the process of healing past-life traumatic events
- Integration of the results into the present-life situation
- Introduction to soul fragmentation and recovery
- Demonstrations and practice sessions

According to the Center for Human Relations, many people reject the idea of looking into a past lifetime for problems, claiming they have enough troubles in the present life. However, in clinical practice, clients discover that present-life conflicts and problems often stem from traumatic events in previous lifetimes. The Center reports, "Emotional and physical challenges carried over from past incarnations into the present life can be quickly and effectively resolved through past-life regression therapy in far fewer sessions than with conventional therapy. Many physical ailments are considered to be psychosomatic, and these conditions may diminish or cease altogether through past-life regression therapy."

Before you can buy into the concept of past-life regression and how it might be able to solve all of your current life's problems, you must believe in reincarnation. Do you believe that when living beings die they can come back to the world as another living being? The Center for Human Relations suggests that the overall concept of reincarnation involves the possibility of embodiment and re-embodiment of the eternal spirit, the continuation of the soul consciousness, from one physical lifetime to the next physical lifetime in a human body.

Based on its research, the Center reports, "During the course of a human lifetime, the essence of human interaction is often misperceived and misinterpreted then compared with past memories. The conscious mind, or ego, develops false assumptions, draws baseless conclusions, makes faulty judgments and survival-based decisions, all of which are inappropriate to the current situation. These errors of mind (the mental residue) pervert the interactions with other people and lead to emotional residues of anger and resentment, fear, sadness and loss, guilt and remorse, distortions of love and the pain of unrequited or lost love."

Assuming you believe in reincarnation and that as living beings we have the ability to experience multiple lifetimes, what happens to us (or our spirit) in between those lifetimes? The Center for Human Relations explains that in the spirit space between lives, sometimes called the Light, there is a Planning Stage. This is where conditions are designed for the coming physical lifetime. It's believed that prior to embodiment, the beings involved in past interactions work together to develop situations that will allow for the resolution of their residues and the evolvement of inner peace and harmony.

After a being becomes enmeshed in a new lifetime, the greater spiritual reality is somehow forgotten. The planned situations then arise, and free will allows for choices to be made during that lifetime. The Center hypothesizes that some choices lead to resolution and growth. Others lead to fear, perpetuation of the conflict, and persistence and aggravation of the residues. There is no judgment of right or wrong involved in these choices. The outcome affects only those who make the choices.

It is believed that all memories acquired during all of our lifetimes are stored in our subconscious mind. The Center for Human Relations reports, "The deep subconscious mind retains the memories of every thought, emotional feeling, motive, desire, behavior, and full sensory recall of every physical experience from every embodiment, and from the nonphysical experience since the first separation from the Source. The total memory seems to be related to the so-called Akashic Record, the total register of everything which has ever occurred. There is some evidence that the Akashic Record also contains everything that will ever occur."

When someone experiences past-life regression, what they actually experience can have many meanings. The Center for Human Relations teaches that there are four possible levels of meaning when it comes to the experiences people have when undergoing this form of therapy.

Hypnosis Is Just a Tool . . . Not a Magical Cure

According to Dr. Knight, "The truth about success rates in therapy in general is that one-third of clients get better, one-third stay the same, and one-third get worse. Although statistics are hard to come by, it is likely that hypnotherapy has similar long-term success. A person using hypnosis should practice within his or her professional competence. Responsible therapists use hypnosis as a tool. Since it is not in itself a therapy, nor is it a cure-all, you are in better hands if the hypnotherapist is also able to deal with your problem without hypnosis."

First, it is often fun and interesting to explore one's past and to explore what may have happened to us in the past, even though we can't consciously recall these memories. Past-life regression offers the opportunity to jump back in time in an effort to better understand oneself.

Second, this can also be an extremely therapeutic experience. Many emotional problems and conflicts can be effectively resolved through past-life regression therapy, usually in far fewer sessions than with conventional therapy. Many physical ailments are considered to be psychosomatic, and these conditions may begin to diminish or cease altogether with past-life regression therapy.

Third, this type of therapy can be an educational journey into the spiritual reality, the so-called "inner planes" of consciousness. The subject can experience the greater reality of spirit, past, present, and in some cases, future. The person who undergoes this type of therapy can often find a deeper realization in regard to his or her purpose in life (or lives) and obtain a clearer sense of the meaning of relationships and the transpersonal aspects of existence.

Fourth, this type of therapy is an altered-state regression experience, which tends to offer an ineffable feeling of Oneness—of being connected to all and everything in the Universe, being part of God, Goddess, All That Is, the Source.

You Can Do Past-Life Regression at Home

Some people believe you can achieve the same benefits using an audiotape created by a hypnotherapist as participating in an in-person past-life regression hypnotherapy session. Choosing this course of therapy, however, means you won't be supervised during the actual hypnosis session. While this probably isn't dangerous, not having a trained professional guide you through the experience means you'll be on your own throughout the experience, including when you attempt to interpret whatever results you end up with.

If you use an audiotape as opposed to working with a live hypnotherapist, you can purchase prerecorded tapes or have a custom tape created. Gene Chamberlain (*www.gene5.com/si-order.htm*) is one hypnotherapist who creates customized past-life regression audiotapes for customers. Each cassette is designed to help someone deal with a specific topic or issue.

According to Chamberlain, "To relive is to relieve. That is a basic psychological passage that is applied in many disciplines. A past-life regression provides a tool for reliving just about any event that is the root of a pattern. The pattern can be mental or physical. It can be something that needs to be changed or merely understood."

The thesis here is that the mind contains everything we have ever experienced, in all five senses. Although we cannot recall most of our history at will, we can re-experience much of it through simple relaxation and guided visualization techniques, Chamberlain believes. Whereas all five senses are involved, the subconscious mind seems to work better with visual communication. You can communicate without words but you cannot communicate without pictures.

Chamberlain stated that to consciously go back to a time, place, or experience, physical stimuli are set aside, allowing for a cognitive communication to be established between the conscious mind and the subconscious mind. This exploration is achieved through progressive relaxation and a guided visualization process using hypnosis. Neuro-linguistic programming techniques enhance these processes where changes are desired. To do a past-life regression, some purpose has to be determined in advance. Chamberlain, like many therapists, doesn't believe in using this type of therapy for entertainment purposes.

When someone orders Chamberlain's customized audiocassettes, the customer is asked to complete a short questionnaire that delves into the reason(s) why the personalized tape is being created. For example, the client may be asked to describe what he or she would like to work on and how that issue influences or concerns the client.

According to Chamberlain, each of his customized audiotapes is produced using information from the customer's completed questionnaire. Each tape has three main objectives. First, it guides the listener through several exercises to prepare him or her for the regression. Second, it guides the listener into a relaxed state so he or she can easily set aside physical awareness. Third, it directs the

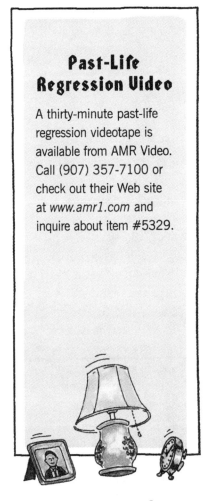

Past-Life Regression Video

A thirty-minute past-life regression videotape is available from AMR Video. Call (907) 357-7100 or check out their Web site at *www.amr1.com* and inquire about item #5329.

Read More about Skeptics

Feeling like a disbeliever? You're not alone. A Skeptic's Bibliography & Bookstore: The James Randi Room (*http://skepdic.com/refuge/randi.html*) is an online directory of books and essays that attempt to disprove virtually every type of paranormal, psychic, and supernatural activity discussed in this book. James Randi was a great magician who used the stage name "The Amazing Randi." Now he works tirelessly writing and speaking in the cause of debunking paranormal claims. He has also established his own foundation (*www.randi.org*).

listener to the experience in his or her subconscious mind that relates to the intended purpose for the regression. "This is done with open communication between the logic and reasoning of the listener's 'here and now' conscious mind and the inert recall from the subconscious mind. This allows you to re-experience the event for self-improvement, understanding, or entertainment."

What the Skeptics Say

Obviously, not everyone believes in past-life regression or the benefits of hypnotherapy. According to Robert Todd Carroll, author and creator of *The Skeptics Dictionary* (*http://skepdic.com*) Web site, past-life regression is the alleged journeying into one's past lives while hypnotized. He states that, "Some hypnotherapists claim to lead their patients to places in their minds where memories of past lives are stored. These therapists claim that past-life regression is essential to healing and helping their patients. Some therapists claim that past-life therapy can help even those who don't believe in past lives. Others have created institutes out of themselves in the search for their patients' past lives."

Carroll added that while it is true that many patients *recall* past lives, it is highly improbable that their memories are accurate. He believes that this is because the memories are from experiences in this life or they are imagined. "Some memories are suggested by the hypnotherapist, but most are probably a mixture of this-life experiences and imagination," added Carroll.

When real-life experiences are mixed with imagined experiences, this is referred to as "confabulation." Carroll believes this provides a tremendous opportunity for therapists looking to exploit their clients. He added, "When it comes to therapists doing this form of therapy, there are at least two attractive features of past-life regression. Since therapists charge by the hour, the need to explore centuries instead of years will greatly extend the length of time a patient will need to be 'treated,' thereby increasing the cost of therapy. Secondly, the therapist and patient can usually speculate wildly without much fear of being contradicted by the facts."

Chapter Six

Ouija Boards and Automatic Writing: Let the Spirits Speak!

Depending on one's beliefs, there are many ways of making contact with the spirit world. Using a psychic medium or channeler is one of the easiest; however, through hypnosis, it's believed that anyone can contact the other side. Of course, some people are lucky enough to simply have ghosts, spirits, or apparitions appear before them, while others seek out these paranormal events by visiting haunted houses, cemeteries, and other places thought to be inhabited by spirits.

While sitting in the comfort of one's own home, many believe it's possible to establish a connection with the other side using a "talking board" or a "channeling board," more commonly known today as a Ouija board. This is a tool that's been in use for centuries. Some of the earliest known Ouija boards were created and used in the sixth century B.C. by a Greek philosopher known as Pythagoras, as well as in ancient China.

The concept behind a Ouija board is rather simple. It's typically a board or flat surface with each letter of the alphabet, the numbers zero through nine, and the words "yes" and "no" printed on it. Using a small pointing device called a "planchette," psychics, mediums, and others experimenting with paranormal phenomena can use this tool in an attempt to summon a spirit and ask it questions. The person (or people) using the Ouija board keeps the tips of his or her fingers lightly touching the planchette so that it can "automatically" move around the Ouija board as if guided by a spirit or paranormal energy. Many believe that once communication with the other side begins, the questions people ask are answered by the spirits, who make the person's hand move the planchette around the Ouija board in order to spell out words or simply answer "yes" or "no" to questions.

The term "Ouija" (pronounced *we-ja*) is derived from the words "oui" (the French word for "yes") and "ja" (the German word for "yes"). The Ouija board was reinvented and introduced to the world again in 1892 by an American named Elijah J. Bond. It was created this time as a fortune-telling game. A few decades before this, two sisters, Kate and Margaret Fox, were major forces behind the emergence of spiritualism in America. These psychic sisters were mediums and worked as intermediaries between the spirit world and the living. The spiritualist movement captured the attention of the public and generated a tremendous interest in one's apparent ability to "talk" or communicate with the deceased.

Much later, in 1966, the American toy manufacturer Parker Brothers released its own version of the Ouija board, also as a fortune-telling game. Today, you can still find Ouija boards, now manufactured by Hasbro, sold at most toy stores.

The Ouija Board Isn't A Toy

While a true understanding of what your future holds may be within reach using a game sold at Toys 'Я' Us or Kaybee Toys, many psychics warn that the use of a Ouija board by people who don't properly understand how to communicate and deal with spirits can be extremely dangerous. In fact, some psychics believe that this fortune-telling tool provides a direct link to the spirit world. They warn that using it could easily lead to the accidental opening of a doorway, through which evil spirits may return to the living world. It's therefore advised that someone never be alone when using the Ouija board, nor should the person be weak or ill, since some believe this provides greater vulnerability for the possibility of possession.

True believers in the power of the Ouija board feel it's the power of the subconscious mind that allows users to tap in to the other side and make contact with spirits. The typical use of this tool involves two people facing each other with the board between them, with their fingers lightly touching the planchette. When used correctly, the planchette will begin to move without consciously being controlled by those touching it. After a question is asked of the spirit(s), the planchette should move from one letter to the next and ultimately spell out an answer, or point to the "yes" or "no" areas of the board.

Using a Planchette with a Ouiji Board

The term "planchette" (pronounced *plan-shet*) is a French word that when translated into English means "little board" or "little plank." This is a tool used in conjunction with a Ouija board.

Those who have experienced the use of a Ouija board have mixed interpretations of their experience. Some believe the board takes on a life of its own, working as a message carrier from the other side. Others see it as nothing more than a game that provides harmless entertainment, just like Monopoly, chess, checkers, or backgammon.

In an article published online entitled "Ouija Board Info," psychic, medium, and healer Del R. Mulroy (*neykomi@winternet.com*) wrote, "The Ouija board is a tool. Like a wrench." It is typically used by ordinary people to channel spirits and communicate with them. Mulroy added, "The art of channeling has been around as long as man. It is a very interesting field. Those who are knowledgeable about it consider channeling to be a wonderful ability, while others, armed with little education about this talent, call it demonic, dark, and even possessed activity."

Unlike some believers in the powers of the Ouija board, Mulroy doesn't believe using this type of challenging tool can result in someone becoming possessed by an evil spirit. He explained, "Always remember that a spirit is energy, and a lot of times, in almost all cases, the spirits that contact is made with are not powerful spirits. Their energy is very ill in strength. Therefore, possession is not even imaginable from the use of a Ouija board." If contact is made with what the user(s) of the Ouija board perceive to be an evil spirit—which, according to Mulroy, is a very rare occurrence—contact should be broken and use of the board temporarily discontinued. When a session with the Ouija board is complete, Mulroy, along with many others who are considered to be experts using this type of tool, strongly suggest that the board be closed properly to ensure the doorway to the spirit world that the Ouija board opened is ultimately shut.

Mulroy explained, "The best advice I can give to people wishing to use a Ouija board is to remain very calm, keep a very open mind to the situation, and set aside your fears. There is nothing to be afraid of. You are simply trying to communicate, using a tool, with a person who has passed on and who would like to communicate with you."

Safety Tip

Some believe that if a pure silver coin is placed somewhere on the Ouija board during its use, no evil spirits will be able to get through. To keep yourself safe, some psychics advise never asking the Ouija board about God or when/how you're going to die. Following these basic tips may help keep evil spirits or entities from using the Ouija board as a way to reach our world.

Ouija Board Operation 101

If you're so inclined to experience using a Ouija board (again, some psychics strongly advise against this), here's how to operate it. Have two people sit facing each other. Place the board on the knees of the two individuals or on a small table placed between the two people. Both people should then gently place their fingers (without using any pressure) upon the planchette, which should be placed near the center of the board. The people actually touching the planchette should allow it to move freely, allowing the spirit (or whatever the driving force is) to move the object, without the conscious mind of the operator being involved.

Let the planchette sit (with fingers upon it) for several minutes as the users sit quietly and focus their mind on a single question. After between one and five minutes, ask a question out loud. The planchette should begin to move, traveling from letter to letter (or number) on the Ouija board to the next, as it spells out the answer to the question at hand. Individual words, phrases, full sentences, or "yes" or "no" answers may result from the planchette moving. It should be understood that the planchette might spell out abbreviated words or use symbolic messages. Be sure to have someone looking on to write down all of the messages communicated from the session. Messages might not make sense right away. Wait until the session is over and then review everything that was received in terms of words, phrases, etc.

One example of how a Ouija board uses abbreviations can be found at The Museum of Talking Boards Web site (*www.museumoftalkingboards.com*), which is one of the best sources of information on Ouija boards available. When describing how the planchette often moves in mysterious ways, here's what was written on the Web site about interpreting what's being communicated: "The planchette first circles aimlessly, but then pauses at one letter followed by several more in quick succession. You string the letters together in your mind as you try to make sense of what you are watching. The word is BALRT. BALRT? What does that mean? Then it hits you. Oh, it says, 'Be a lrt.' Is the Ouija board

What Makes a Ouija Board Work?

So, what makes the planchette actually move? The "scientific theory" is that it's a force known as "ideometer response." This means it's really you, the user, causing the movement, which is being controlled by your subconscious. The spiritualist belief is that when someone uses a Ouija board, the person is channeling a spirit, ghost, or other ethereal being, and it's this entity that's conveying a message to the living. Some spiritualists are such firm believers that they're communicating with the other side that they perform elaborate cleaning rituals before using the tool to help ward off evil forces.

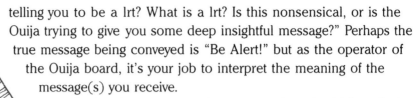

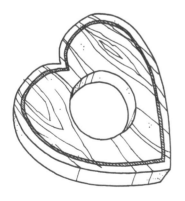

telling you to be a lrt? What is a lrt? Is this nonsensical, or is the Ouija trying to give you some deep insightful message?" Perhaps the true message being conveyed is "Be Alert!" but as the operator of the Ouija board, it's your job to interpret the meaning of the message(s) you receive.

During the process, only one question should be asked at a time, and all questions should be stated clearly. Once the question is asked, everyone involved (including onlookers) should clear their minds and focus only on the question being asked. Some psychics believe that the Ouija board should never be used to answer frivolous or ridiculous questions, as this could anger the spirits.

Experts using this fortune-telling tool recommend that the room where the Ouija board is being used should be kept quiet, with no nearby distractions of any kind. Those who have become skilled at using this tool explain that it takes practice to become proficient, just as it does when learning how to ride a bicycle. The first time you attempt to use this tool, don't become frustrated if nothing amazing happens. Simply clear your mind and keep trying.

Later in this chapter is an interview with an artisan who specializes in creating handmade wooden Ouija boards. Because Seth Thurston treats all of his creations with respect, he says that he's never had any negative experiences using his own boards. He admits, however, that some of his customers have had some rather strange experiences when trying to communicate with the spirit world using a talking board.

Ouija Board Success Stories

Throughout history, people have made incredible claims as to the power of their Ouija boards. For example, according to The Museum of Talking Boards, in the late 1900s, Mrs. John Howard Curran channeled an entity she called Patience Worth and through the Ouija board produced six novels, hundreds of pages of poetry, and a selection of other literary works. It was believed to be Worth who actually wrote the novels but Curran who channeled the information. Another author named Emily G. Hutchings was reported to have contacted the spirit of Mark Twain when she wrote a novel called *Jap Heron*. In more modern times, Iris Maloney is reported to have won $1.4 million in the California State Lottery after picking her numbers using her Ouija board.

An Interview with a Ouija Board Artisan

Seth A. Thurston
Talking Board Artisan
(505) 340-2512
E-mail: *wikd@wikd.net*

Seth A. Thurston is a resident of Farmington, New Mexico, who works part-time designing and handcrafting talking boards for customers around the world. He explained that he's been fascinated by Ouija boards since the age of eleven or twelve; however, his parents wouldn't allow him to have one.

Using a Ouija board became a fixation for Thurston. While Parker Brothers has been selling a Ouija board made from cardboard, based on his research, Thurston discovered that a talking board is far more powerful if it's handcrafted out of wood. When he tried to purchase such a board, he couldn't find one. This caused him to design and create his own wooden talking boards. Because wooden talking boards actually come from nature, it's believed that they contain more natural energy (energy taken from the universe and from the tree from which the board is created) within them.

According to Thurston, when used correctly, a Ouija board can open a portal to another realm via two people's energy. It can then be used to contact spirits on the other side. For a Ouija

Ouija Board in Cyberspace

To experience the power of a Ouija board immediately, point your Web browser to *http://taylor. ieor.berkeley.edu/ouija.* Here you'll find a Ouija board that operates online. Ouija 2000 allows viewers and users to come together and experience the power of a virtual Ouija board with up to twenty others at a time. The computer aggregates the motions players make with the mouse in order to move the planchette on the board's robotic arm. Thus, the answers to questions will appear as if by magic or mystical intervention. No single user can control what the answers will be.

board to work, Thurston believes it must be used by two people simultaneously. Ideally, a special chant should be said as the board is put into use to summon the spirit to the board.

"The board should be placed on both people's knees in order to better utilize their energy. Once a connection with the spirit world is made, the planchette will begin moving by itself. In some circumstances (this is optional), a third person can be present, to work as a scribe and write down each letter that the planchette points to. Many messages that are received will be cryptic and make no sense at first. The scribe should write down everything in a journal, so the messages can be reviewed later and remembered. Often, the messages will actually make sense days, weeks, months, or even years later," he said.

Thurston believes that a Ouija board has the ability to answer any type of question. Unlike some other mass-produced boards, his include the words "hello" and "goodbye" printed on them. These words will help the user determine when a contact with a spirit begins and ends.

One of the misconceptions about Ouija boards is that users can choose the spirit they will make contact with. Thurston explained, "It is thought that if you're a spirit in 'heaven' then you'd have better things to do than to talk with living people via a Ouija board. Thus, it is thought by some that it is mostly evil spirits who are the ones communicating through Ouija boards, because these entities have nothing better to do and they have something to gain."

While Thurston is in the business of handcrafting and selling Ouija boards, he strongly believes there can be danger involved if they are not used correctly. He has had people contact him believing that they were possessed by spirits that made contact through a talking board. For protection, he suggests that people follow protocols outlined by their religious faith. He suggested, "At the very least, someone should take precautions by surrounding themselves with white light. This means doing a visualization of a white light beaming down from above and surrounding the area you're going to have the session in, along with your whole body."

When asked why he believed that the Ouija board actually works, Thurston responded, "Talking boards have been around for so long and have such strong stories behind them, that the power of people's beliefs give the boards the power to open a portal to another realm. I think it's the user's belief in the board that empowers it."

Thurston has created several different styles of talking boards, each of which is handmade. These boards take him several hours each to create, and they're priced starting at $40. Thurston also makes custom boards based on individual specifications outlined by his clients. These talking boards can cost upwards of $300 to $1,000 or more, depending on their intricacy. Some of his custom boards contain jewels, such as inlaid rubies.

For some believers and users of Ouija boards, a handcrafted wooden board better facilitates their connection to the spirit world. However, some people believe a Ouija board created out of paper or cardboard can have the same power. It's really up to the individual. "I believe that my boards make it easier to contact the spirit world," explained Thurston, who stated that once someone takes possession of a board, it must be properly cared for. For example, a board should always be wrapped in a black silk cloth when not in use to keep positive or negative energies from entering it. The board should be stored outside of the bedroom, but in a safe place. It should never be thrown around or treated casually, as you might treat a Monopoly board, for example. "A Ouija board should always be treated with respect and dignity. If you treat the board well, it will treat you the same way," Thurston said.

Thurston has heard about a wide range of problems that have occurred as a result of not properly caring for or using a board correctly. One such problem is progressive entrapment. This means that the board is friendly to you by giving you the answers you need or want, but it slowly entraps you so that using it becomes a habit. People are actually driven to continuously use the board to order to feel satisfied. It becomes like an addiction to cigarettes or alcohol. Once the board does entrap you, the spirits can take advantage of you, according to Thurston, and get what they want from you.

Based on his own work with talking boards, Thurston has never felt as if he were in danger, nor has he ever had a negative

experience using one. "I always honor and respect the board and treat it properly," he said. Some of his customers make it a point to order a Ouija board for the purpose of contacting evil spirits or entities. If Thurston believes that someone will face danger using one of his boards, he will refuse to sell it. Many of the people who contact him to purchase one of his boards tell him specifically why they want to order it. "If someone is looking at a talking board as a tool for revenge, for example, I will not sell one to that person. I try to feel out my customers on the phone before I ship them one of my boards," said Thurston, who admits that after sending out his boards to customers, he occasionally gets one returned because the person who ordered it became uncomfortable using it.

Once someone acquires a Ouija board, it's important that the person feels comfortable with it. It should have images on it that the person can relate to. "If someone fears the board, that's one of the things that could start to cause negative things to happen," said Thurston.

While Thurston has received many letters and phone calls from satisfied customers who share positive stories about experiences they've had with the Ouija board they purchased from him, he admits to hearing some rather bizarre stories as well. For example, he explained that some people choose to hang up their talking board on the wall as artwork when it's not being used. He has received calls from people who say that at exactly the same time every day, during the day or night, the board falls off the wall to the ground. He has also had reports of glasses shattering and beds shaking when one of his boards was in use, or that the users heard strange knocking or banging sounds. These stories, however, have not been substantiated.

Before buying and using a talking board, Thurston strongly recommends that the person do extensive research into what these boards are capable of. "This should not be treated like a game or as an entertaining activity when you're otherwise bored. Owning and using a board should be considered a responsibility. It's a tool, not a game. That's something I can't stress enough," explained Thurston.

Ouija Board Manufacturers

The following companies manufacture Ouija boards:

- The Angel Alliance Network offers a bifold square board featuring an angel design. For more information, call 1-800-211-9516 or visit the organization's Web site at *www.angelalliancenetwork.com*.

- The Psychic Circle has created a talking board that features zodiac symbols and other psychographs from the past. The group also offers The Pathfinder, which is designed to empower you with shamanic wisdom. This board features thirty-six keywords, twelve power animals, eleven sacred stones, twelve plant helpers, and twelve dream symbols, plus the numbers zero through nine and the letters of the alphabet. The Pathfinder uses these signs and symbols to create meaningful, insightful, and intriguing answers to your every question. The Psychic Circle's Magical Message Board can be used to find the answers to all life's questions. Its twenty keywords, forty universal symbols, twenty-six letters, numbers, colors, and Magical Message Indicator let everyone contact their highest spirits. For more information, write to The Psychic Circle, P.O. Box 2299, East Hampton, NY 11937, or visit The Enchanted World Web site at *www.theenchanted world.com*.

- The Clear Channel Board from Destined Soulmates Corporation is another talking board available to more serious users. According to the manufacturer,

"'Clear' indicates that the board is designed to eliminate negative influences that could affect the messages users want to receive. 'Channel' describes the method of receiving these messages through our board. This first edition of the Clear Channel Board is available in a kit including detailed instructions for preparation and use of the board." For more information, call (425) 861-1063.

- Third Eye Concepts is another company that offers a selection of different talking boards, many made from wood or fiberboard. Call (360) 864-8293 or send e-mail to *thirdeye@toledotel.com* for more information.

- The Paper Dragon Gift Shop offers a collection of stunning Ouija boards starting at around $55, along with specially crafted planchettes (sold separately). For more information, visit *www.hollywood artglass.com*.

- Taramisu Custom Channeling Boards offers a selection of handcrafted, solid wood, one-of-a-kind Ouija boards. This company's Web site (*www.channeling boards.com*) also offers extensive information about Ouija boards.

- Cabin Fever (*www.cabinfever.org*) is an online-based dealer of Ouija boards. On this site you'll also find detailed directions for using this type of spirit communication tool.

Thurston is just one of several artists who create and build handcrafted talking boards for customers. If you're looking for a handcrafted talking board, visit the Museum of Talking Boards' Web site (*www.museumoftalkingboards.com/handcrf.html*) for a list of artisans who specialize in creating these tools. To order or request more information about one of Thurston's talking boards, call or e-mail him directly.

Get Your Hands on Your Own Talking Board

Aside from trekking down to your local toy store to pick up a Ouija board manufactured by Parker Brothers/Hasbro (by the way, there's even a glow-in-the-dark version of the product), there are several more serious Ouija board manufacturers. Many of these talking boards, especially the handcrafted ones, are made from wood and sell for $20 to $1,000. The price is often based on how much time and effort is put into the creation of the board along with the quality of the materials. Obviously, if you order a board made from a fine and rare wood and wish to have jewels inlaid in the board, the cost will be higher than if you order a more basic model.

As the Pendulum Swings

People use a wide range of tools for establishing a psychic connection with the spirit world. In addition to Ouija boards, another common tool, particularly useful for obtaining "yes" or "no" answers to your questions, is the pendulum.

According to Pendulums.com (888-4-ASK-BOB, *www.pendulums. com*), "Just as radios pick up information from unseen radio waves, the pendulum is a powerful antenna that receives information from the vibrations and energy waves emitted by people, places, thoughts, and things. Dowsing is best known for locating water, gold, oil, and other minerals, but dowsers have also used pendulum dowsing to find missing keys, eyeglasses, jewelry, and literally anything they put their minds to. Some U.S. marines were taught to use a pendulum in Vietnam to locate underground mines and tunnels. In France, hundreds of physicians have used the pendulum to assist them in making diagnoses using a science known as radiesthesia. For centuries, dowsing has also been called 'divining' because it involves knowing beyond the five senses and predicting the future. The pendulum can also answer any yes/no question and people often call it 'The Truth Teller' because of its accuracy."

Some people believe that the pendulum can create a bridge between the logical and intuitive parts of the mind. It's also believed that this type of tool can connect the user with a higher power, allowing for information to be communicated from a divine source. There's also a theory that a pendulum simply responds to electromagnetic energy that radiates from everything on earth. Just as with most other tools for communicating with spirits (or channeling), nobody knows exactly how or why they work, yet many who have used pendulums, for example, swear they do work.

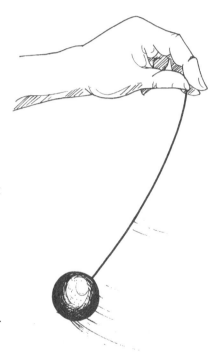

So how do you use a pendulum? Once you've determined what question you want your pendulum to answer, determine the direction for your "yes" or "no" answers. Holding the pendulum in one hand, follow these basic steps:

1. Still the pendulum by holding it in the air from its chain or string, using your thumb and index finger.

2. Say out loud, "Show me YES." This should cause the pendulum to swing in one direction, for example, side-to-side, back and forth, or in circles.

3. After again making the pendulum still, say out loud, "Show me NO." This should cause the pendulum to swing in the opposite direction from a "yes" response.

4. Repeat these steps several times, until you consistently receive the same "yes" and "no" responses from the pendulum.

5. Once you are familiar with how your particular pendulum operates, steady the pendulum once again, then ask your question. When the pendulum starts to move again, it should reveal the answer you seek.

To learn more about pendulums, visit any metaphysical book-shop or New Age store. Many of these shops actually sell pendulums along with books and information on how to use them. One nice thing about this tool is that it can be worn around the neck as jewelry and kept on your person at all times. Some pendulums are made out of precious or semi-precious metals or crystal and look like jewelry. Any string or chain can be connected to the pendulum. They're available in many different shapes, sizes, and designs. Choose one that you personally feel an attachment to based on how it looks and how it feels in your hand.

Automatic Writing

Using nothing but a pen and paper, some mediums believe they can relax their mind and body until a spirit takes control of their hand and starts writing or drawing with it. What results may be the work of a spirit, or it could be the medium's own subconscious or even his or her higher consciousness. This process is called automatic writing or inspirational writing. It involves putting your mind in a receptive state, much as you would when contacting a spirit guide, and using a pen and paper to write down or draw whatever messages or images come to mind.

The process is done without your conscious mind actually thinking about what's being written or drawn on the page. It involves free association and capturing as much information as possible on paper. The information that is communicated through your hand (onto the paper) may be in the form of single words, phrases, sentences, entire pages of text, images, drawings, paintings, or symbols. According to experts, through automatic writing it's possible to:

- Obtain access and insight to your higher self for guidance, advice, or to better expound upon ideas developed in your conscious mind.
- Make contact with the other side and use this process to convey information with a process similar to channeling.
- Unleash your spiritual energy to enhance your creativity.

The Healing from Within Web site (*www.healingfromwithin.com/ Articles/Automatic_Writing/automatic_writing.htm*) provides information about an easy exercise anyone can do to experiment with this process. Begin by following these steps:

1. Find a quiet place and make yourself comfortable.
2. Have a pen and pad of paper ready.
3. At the top of the piece of paper, write down what you would like guidance on. You can seek out general advice or ask a very specific question. (Some experts suggest also writing the date at the top of the paper.)
4. Using meditation, spend a few minutes relaxing and clearing your conscious mind. This is often referred to as centering yourself. Pay careful attention to your breathing and take several slow, deep breaths. Allow your mind and body to relax. The Healing from Within Web site states, "Feel the energy of the earth come up through the base of your spine, up through your entire body, and out through the top of your head, connecting with the universe above. Now imagine that a golden light comes down from above and enters your body through your crown, at the top of your head. Imagine this light flowing down the center of your body, then out through the base of your spine and traveling down to the center of the earth, anchoring you to the earth below."
5. Once your mind is relaxed and open to the opportunity of communicating with your inner self or a spirit from the other side, seek out the guidance you need by asking for it. "When you feel ready, pick up your pen and write down whatever comes to you without stopping. Do not judge, analyze, or evaluate what you have written even if it does not answer your question. Write until your hand is done. When you are finished read what you wrote," explained The Healing from Within Web site.

Online Information

Taramisu's Custom Channeling Boards and Ouija Information Web site (*www.channelingboards.com*) offers a wealth of information concerning channeling boards. You can even order your own custom-made channeling board.

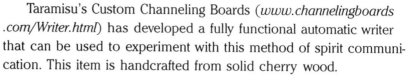

How Automatic Writing Works

When automatic writing is used, it's believed that an entity from another realm brings messages to you through your writing implement. Others have reported not recognizing their own handwriting. It's common when using automatic writing that there will be no punctuation and that words won't always be spelled correctly or fully written out. As someone "communicates" with the other side using this method, it's not always clear who the person is in contact with. It's appropriate to ask questions to determine the spirit's identity.

Taramisu's Custom Channeling Boards (*www.channelingboards .com/Writer.html*) has developed a fully functional automatic writer that can be used to experiment with this method of spirit communication. This item is handcrafted from solid cherry wood.

The company reports that its Automatic Writing Planchette is unlike most others available to the public. "Most vintage designs have two rear legs and the writing instrument is used as the front leg. We found that this does not allow a free movement due to the excessive pressure and friction introduced by the pen being the third leg. This method therefore requires the paper to be fixed to the table in some fashion. Our design utilizes three legs, and a free floating pen. There is no need to secure your paper and you can write right up to the edge of the page."

As with any form of communication with the other side, it's not clear if the messages received through automatic writing are actually coming from a spirit that you're channeling, or if it's only your subconscious mind at work. Obviously, people interpret this phenomenon and the results from it in different ways. If you'd like to learn more about this process, an excellent Web site to visit is *www.automaticwriting.com.*

No matter how you choose to attempt contact with the spirit world, whether it's through past-life regression, channeling, use of a medium (psychic), use of a Ouija board, a pendulum, tarot cards, or any other fortune-telling tool, take whatever information you learn to heart, but don't allow this information to control your life. Everyone is born with free will. The information you believe you obtain from the other side can be used to console you, counsel you, or educate you, but it shouldn't be used to dictate every action you take in life.

When participating in any activities that involve the paranormal, always proceed with caution, taking action only after you've carefully and thoroughly educated yourself. Just as you wouldn't make jokes to someone who is highly religious about his or her belief system, tapping your own abilities to contact the spirit world should be for your personal growth, not for entertainment purposes.

Chapter Seven

Near Death Experiences (NDEs)

Throughout this book, you've been reading about a wide range of paranormal phenomena, much of which involves making contact with the other side—whether it be through actually seeing, hearing, or sensing a ghost, or somehow making direct contact with a spirit or other entity.

What's different about the information in this chapter is that it deals with the belief that some people have actually died, left their physical body, visited the other side, and then have come back to the living. This phenomenon is called having a near death experience (or NDE) and it's much more common than you might think.

One of the things that people who have experienced an NDE have in common is that the majority of people didn't necessarily want or plan it. As the result of an illness or accident, for example, ordinary people have died but have been brought back to life, often through medical intervention. Based on research into this phenomenon, only about one-third of the people who have clinically died and then returned to the living remember anything about their experience. Many simply wake up, as if coming out of a deep sleep, remembering nothing.

Again, there is no scientific proof that NDEs actually happen and that people have been to the other side, only to turn around and return to the living. However, the number of personal accounts from very credible people regarding this phenomenon and the similarities in their experiences can't be ignored. An abundance of circumstantial evidence from all over the world certainly exists.

An NDE Can Happen to Anyone

People who have experienced an NDE aren't necessarily religious, interested in the paranormal, or gifted with psychic abilities. Many lead normal lives until their experience, which they later describe as life-changing. Of those people who do have an NDE, part of almost everyone's experience somehow involves seeing a bright light that is described as all-encompassing. The International Association of Near Death Studies (IANDS) is an organization dedicated to disseminating information and providing networking opportunities in the field of near-death studies. The group's members are comprised of people who have had firsthand experiences, as well as experts in the fields of medicine, psychology, parapsychology, and scientific research.

According to IANDS, near death experiences have occurred throughout history, with documentation dating back thousands of years. A 1982 Gallup poll concluded that in the United States alone, between 8 and 13 million people have had an NDE. One of the things that makes this phenomenon more credible to the average skeptic than other types of paranormal events is that the people who experience an NDE don't often claim to possess some "magical" or "supernatural" power. They have nothing to gain from discussing their experience, and often run the risk of being labeled a freak or nutcase.

Often, the experience people have relating to this phenomenon includes their physical body clinically dying. Their spirit or soul continues on to have a range of experiences. Based on research conducted by IANDS, some of the common experiences during an NDE include:

- Feeling that the "self" has left the body and is hovering overhead. There have been many reports of the experiencer later being able to describe who was where and what happened in the living world during the NDE. The Web site NDEWeb.com (*www.ndeweb.com*) offers more detailed information. The organization believes the experiencer finds him- or herself floating in the air looking down on the activity below. In a hospital room, for example, the experiencer will see doctors and nurses working on his or her lifeless body. The doctors' conversations may be remembered, and the instruments or tools the doctors used may later be identified by the experiencer after he or she is brought back to life. An alternate scenario involves the experiencer leaving the location of his or her lifeless body as the experiencer visits other places or people. Upon being brought back to life, the experiencer may remember, in detail, conversations and

Who Experiences NDEs?

Near death experiences have been reported by people of both sexes, of all ages, all nationalities, and who came from a wide range of religious beliefs (including atheists). While many don't believe a near death experience is proof of reincarnation, many do feel that this phenomenon does demonstrate the spiritual nature of mankind.

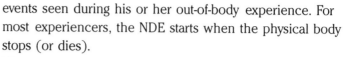

events seen during his or her out-of-body experience. For most experiencers, the NDE starts when the physical body stops (or dies).

- The person experiences traveling through a dark area, sometimes described as a tunnel.

- The experiencer recalls feeling extremely powerful emotions. Sometimes this wave of emotion is described as pure bliss; other times, people have more frightening experiences. Some people actually experience events that scare them, while others are scared by the NDE itself as it changes or challenges their belief system.

- People see "the light." It's often described as a golden white light that experiencers are able to look directly into without it hurting their eyes. Some people describe this light as being almost magnetic in that it draws them in. While some people state that they experience a sense of total peace and love as they approach the light, others believe they witness the fires of hell. No correlation between the person and the NDE they have has yet been established.

- Many experiencers describe receiving a message encouraging them to turn back from the light because it is not yet their time.

- Some people report meeting and actually communicating with deceased loved ones during their NDE. Others report seeing sacred beings or religious leaders.

- Another common occurrence among those who experience an NDE is reliving highlights from their life. People report that their life literally passes right before their eyes.

- During their NDE, some people report feeling that all knowledge is passed through them and that for a brief instant, they are given a true understanding of how the universe works.

- Prior to "waking up" or returning to the world of the living, some people report encountering a barrier or obstacle that keeps them from proceeding further, forcing them to turn back. Some people believe they are actually given a choice and asked if they wish to return to the living.

- Overall, many people describe their NDE as being extremely pleasant and one that totally eliminates any fear of death. Some people, however, report having experiences that are frightening. Different people experience different things. What someone experiences may somehow be connected to their personal belief system, however, this link has not been established or proven.

Without a doubt, once someone has an NDE, it's described as the most intense experience of that person's "life." This experience sometimes alters one's perceptions about life and death, and actually leads to drastic changes in how the person continues to lead his or her life after the experience.

IANDS's research shows that one of the most extraordinary aspects of NDEs is that the underlying pattern seems unaffected by a person's culture and belief system, religion, race, education, or any other known variable. The way in which the NDE is described by the experiencer, however, varies according to the person's background and vocabulary. There is no evidence that the type of experience is related to whether the person is conventionally religious or not, or whether the person has lived a "good" or "bad" life according to society's standards (although an NDE often strongly affects how life is lived after the experience).

While the concept of a near death experience can be traumatic, it's important for experiencers to understand that they're not crazy and they're not alone in their experience. An NDE is an extraordinary experience that happens to normal people. For days, weeks, and even months after the experience, those who have had an NDE often feel frustrated trying to find words to describe it, in part because they're fearful no one else will understand. If you've never had an NDE, hearing about it might be similar to having someone you know return from another country that you've never been to and can't even imagine. IANDS reports, "There are many interpretations of NDEs, and only the individual can decide the

Further Reading

For those interested in near death experiences, the book *Lessons from the Light: What We Can Learn from the Near-Death Experience* written by Kenneth Ring and Evelyn Elsaesser Valarino is a must-read!

meaning of his or her particular experience. One thing is clear, however: An NDE is not a psychotic episode, but its effects are often powerful."

While many people truly believe that near death experiences are real, science has thus far not been able to prove anything. Conventional science deals with objective matters that can be observed, tested, and measured by someone else. An NDE is a subjective experience that only the experiencer has. It can be felt and reported only by the person who has it. It can't be studied, measured, or proved. For this, among other reasons, some people claim that the NDE cannot be scientifically "real."

Conversely, other scientists consider NDEs as scientifically valid as any other intense personal experience. The difference may be that some scientists demand physical proof of reality, while others are less troubled by ambiguity. According to research by IANDS, people who have experienced both an NDE and hallucination say they are quite different, and laboratory work supports this view.

Even though so many people around the world and throughout history have had near death experiences, those who haven't had this type of experience don't necessarily believe this is proof that there's life after death. A more cautious expression, according to IANDS, is that NDEs suggest that some aspect of human consciousness may continue after physical death.

Out of all the people who have had an NDE and are willing to discuss their experience, some express anger or resentment at being brought back to the living world after receiving a preview of what they believe the other side is actually like. Those who are happy about having their life continue often report a changed understanding of what life is all about. This includes losing a fear of death and having major changes in what they perceive success to be. Many who were caught up in financial or career success change their life's focus toward more personal issues. IANDS explains, "Religious observance may increase or lessen, but deepened belief in God or a 'higher power' is almost certain. People say, 'Before, I believed; now, I know.'"

One researcher who has experienced an NDE firsthand stated on the SpiritWeb Web site *(www.spiritweb.org/Spirit/nde-faq.html)*:

"To my knowledge, it is the people who have not experienced an NDE that claim they are unreal. Every NDEer that I have met, knew what they experienced was real . . . The critics of NDEs come mostly from that group of people who believe in a mechanical world—those who believe nothing exists beyond the physical."

Dr. Karl L.R. Jansen, a London-based psychiatrist, wrote, "Recent advances in neuroscience are bringing us closer to a brain-based understanding of the NDE as an altered state of consciousness. This discussion does not address the issue of whether there is life after death, but does argue that NDE's are not evidence for life after death. This would appear to be self-evident on logical grounds: death is defined as the final, irreversible end. The *Oxford English Dictionary* (Sykes, 1982) defines death as the 'final cessation of vital functions.' According to this definition, 'Returnees' did not die—although their minds, brains and bodies may have been in a highly unusual state for a period of time. If these definitions are not accepted, then we need a new terminology to describe these states."

Kevin Williams, a firsthand NDEer (*www.near-death.com*), asserts that there are religious answers that move beyond Christianity, Buddhism, Islam, Judaism, or any other creed and most certainly go beyond the linear explanations of scientific theory. He stated that there is a deeper reason than psychology or physiology for so many to change their lives in response to an experience on the other side of death.

An Interview with Dr. Samuel K. Spitzner

E-mail: *sks@wirenot.net*
Web site: *www.wirenot.net/X*

While nobody truly understands near death experiences from a clinical or scientific standpoint, plenty of highly educated people have dedicated much of their careers to understanding this and other paranormal phenomena as it relates to life after death and one's ability to communicate with the other side.

Dr. Samuel K. Spitzner has been working in the area of paranormal phenomena for over twenty years. He has earned doctorates in metaphysics, philosophy, religion, and divinity. Through his work, he has studied virtually all aspects of the metaphysical realm. He continues to teach and lecture on a range of topics in these fields.

Dr. Spitzner has known for most of his life that he has a latent ability for telepathy. Earlier in life, Spitzner realized he had this gift and wanted to find a place that would help him develop and better understand it. He attended the School of Metaphysics and learned how to develop that side of himself. He ultimately received a bachelor's degree and a master's degree, which started him on a lifelong path of learning and discovery. He currently dedicates much of his time to the study of spirituality, which is the study of becoming a higher spiritual being.

Based on his studies, Dr. Spitzner has become a firm believer in near death experiences. He's also had multiple experiences with ghosts and angels. "The only thing that I have a problem with in regard to past-life regression or near death experiences is the belief that aliens or UFOs are somehow involved. As someone becomes a more spiritual person, he or she focuses on understanding the concept of dying. This is when the being in the physical body within this dimension is given a daily choice. There are people who are capable of visiting and seeing the spiritual realm almost any time they please. This involves a process of deep meditation that virtually simulates death. For most people, an NDE happens when the physical body dies and their conscious mind transforms into a ghost. The NDE is a glimpse into what exists beyond the physical world. I believe the other way to have this experience is through a specialized form of meditation which takes years of practice to master," said Dr. Spitzner.

During this deep, self-induced meditative state, Dr. Spitzner believes he has experienced the same things that people experience during an NDE. Someone who is having an NDE is not in control of the experience, however. He believes the experiencer's mind is being released

to perceive beyond the veils of the physical. By undergoing this type of experience through meditation, Dr. Spitzner believes he is able to remain in control using his psychic abilities.

Based on his experiences and having learned how to enter into this specialized meditative state, Dr. Spitzner has made the decision never to use his psychic abilities to help others communicate with the other side. What he does do is teach people how to reach a higher level of spirituality themselves so that they can make contact with the spirit world on their own.

"By teaching others how to do this themselves, they are forced to take responsibility for it and learn from the experience. Too many people use a channel or a medium simply as a farce. They treat this as a game, and that's very disappointing. If people have a near death experience, they should learn as much as they can about it so that they can learn from the experience and discover ways to incorporate what they learn and experience into their day-to-day lives," stated Dr. Spitzner, who suggests contacting a reputable organization such as IANDS to learn more about NDE phenomena.

At this point, there is no scientific proof of the NDE phenomenon; however, within the next decade or so, Dr. Spitzner believes this will change. Over the past thirty years, he has seen medical science merging with spirituality. There's still a line, but when you get into quantum physics, that's very close to spirituality, because many of the same rules apply. As the field of quantum physics develops more, Dr. Spitzner feels we'll see more of a blending between scientific thinking and spiritual thinking. He hopes this convergence will help us develop methods of achieving the scientific proof that so many people are looking for.

He believes that the American Medical Association (AMA) will eventually change their way of thinking as it relates to near death experiences. Dr. Spitzner added, "For years, the AMA was against the use of herbs for medicinal purposes because it was thought that this form of medicine was hogwash. Only recently has the AMA become more open to the use of herbs, and in some cases actually recommends them. For example, onions have been used for centuries to help people with heart conditions, to clear their

Does Someone Leave His or Her Body During an NDE?

Those who experience an out-of-body experience as part of their near death experience state that when their physical body stops (or dies), something leaves their body and continues on. That something is their spirit, soul, or essence. When the body is brought back to life, the spirit returns to the body, sometimes with a complete memory of what's happened to it.

arteries. Only now is the AMA willing to give this credibility. I believe it's only a matter of time before the way people view near death experiences will change. For years, anything that was wrong with the body was believed to be a physical thing, according to the AMA. These days, doctors are beginning to realize that there are mental attitudes associated with illness and physical disorders, and this is something the AMA is starting to explore."

According to Dr. Spitzner, too many people believe NDEs are both unusual and extremely traumatic in a negative way. He explained, however, that this phenomenon is more common than most people think, and that the majority of people who experience an NDE find it to be extremely positive.

He has found that someone's religion plays absolutely no role in what happens when an individual experiences an NDE. What does have an impact on the experience, however, is the person's spirituality. Dr. Spitzner separates religion and spirituality. Spirituality involves getting in touch with one's inner being and true soul by better understanding his or her God. The more someone is in touch with the inner self, the more the person will understand the NDE phenomenon. He has discovered that people who are deeply religious but not necessarily spiritual have a harder time believing and remembering their NDE, because the church and society may tell them it's wrong. An NDE is neither right nor wrong. He believes the experience simply *is*. "What's right or wrong is what you do with the knowledge acquired after having the experience," said Dr. Spitzner.

Based on research, what's believed to be an NDE can be experienced in one of three ways. The most common is for someone to actually die (to be pronounced clinically dead) and then be brought back to life using medical technology and know-how. Some people have been able to achieve similar experiences to an NDE through the use of certain types of legal, prescription, and/or illegal drugs. This method of inducing an NDE can be extremely dangerous.

Those who are highly spiritual are also able to achieve this experience using a specialized form of meditation that causes the conscious mind and the body to simulate death. It's this latter

Further Reading

The Atlanta Study has become known as a extensive investigation of near death experiences. The book *Light and Death* by Dr. Michael Sabom is one source of documentation of the study's findings.

method that Dr. Spitzner continues to explore. "Through medication, I have become clinically dead for up to five minutes, and then have been able to bring myself back to life, so to speak," he said. While the use of medications and drugs has been used to conduct research into this phenomenon, ordinary people should *not* attempt to invoke an NDE using any type of drug or medication without a doctor's supervision.

My two cents: I can't help thinking that a real NDE seems totally different than a drug-induced simulation . . . one happens to you without you expecting it, and greater spirituality can result; whereas the other is an orchestrated attempt to simulate the experience to gain this greater spirituality. Something just doesn't sound quite right about trying to do this deliberately. I guess I'm not clear on what someone would hope to gain from the experience. If it's greater spirituality, that's within reach without the drugs.

It's only after many years of studying spirituality that Spitzner has been able to achieve the knowledge necessary to successfully use this specialized form of meditation to achieve a near death experience. This practice is definitely not recommended for most people. "Drugs can be used to induce a spiritual awakening that is very similar, if not identical, to what someone who dies on an operating table or of a heart attack will experience. In both cases, the conscious mind is totally pushed aside and loses all control of what happens to one's soul or spirit," stated Dr. Spitzner.

Dr. Spitzner is firm on his belief that a near death experience should not be viewed by anyone as a religious experience. He feels that this phenomenon should instead be accepted as an experience that leads to spiritual growth. It can be used to further the individual's oneness with whomever or whatever his or her creator is envisioned to be.

Dr. Spitzner operates the Archive X Web site *(www.wirenot.net/X)* to help others learn about the paranormal and to provide a forum for people throughout the world to share their experiences. He takes no responsibility for the content that is on the Web site, because what's available on the site is information and firsthand experiences from other people from around the world.

Several firsthand descriptions of the NDEs that people have shared on Dr. Spitzner's Web site are included in the next section.

NDEs: The Firsthand Perspective

Most people who have experienced an NDE are profoundly affected by their encounter with death and what some believe is an afterlife (or at the very least an alternative state of consciousness that has yet to be fully understood). The following are some firsthand accounts from people who have had an NDE. These stories are told in the experiencer's own words.

Like so many others, Paul experienced an NDE firsthand and chose to share his experiences with others looking to understand this somewhat unusual phenomenon.

In January 1971, on a Sunday, I was cooking a late breakfast for my two boys and my mother when I slipped on a spot of cooking oil and fell to my knees in the kitchen. The blow jarred my spine (which had already had one spinal surgery) and I blacked out.

When I awoke I was on my back and paralyzed from the waist down. I was ambulanced to Mercy Hospital and, since my doctor was out of town until the next day, put into bed to wait. In the late afternoon I felt well enough to eat a big meal.

About two hours later, my stomach started to swell enormously and I began to black out. The nurses took me down to an empty emergency room and rounded up the only doctors they could find (presumably there to deliver babies). Despite their efforts, I sank lower and lower. Finally, my respiration and heartbeat stopped.

From their viewpoint, nothing was happening (although no one could figure out why). From mine, however, it was very different.

I went through a dark tunnel with flashing lights toward a bright light. I came out into a sort of cloud-like area. There were beings there, though I couldn't "see" anything. One entity, who I've always called "the greeter" (because he was there to greet me), spoke to me.

We had quite a conversation about my life to date; it was not condemning or retaliatory—just a review. I knew if I chose to go on it was all right. It was like going around a series of light bends. If I went far enough, I couldn't go back—and that was okay. If I did that, however, I wouldn't get the opportunity to raise my children or to experience a type of love I hadn't really known so far.

In the end, I decided to return. When I did so, I found myself instantly in the upper corner of the emergency room watching the doctors trying to figure out what was wrong and how to fix it. It was really quite comical from my point of view. I knew it was my body down there, but I didn't mind. I did have to get back into it, however, and finally did so.

I remember the first thing I heard upon re-entering: One doctor, obviously tired and exasperated, said, "Wow! He's breathing again!" If I had been back more fully to outer con-sciousness I would have laughed out loud! I understood his exasperation: They didn't know why I left, and now they didn't know why (or how) I was back!

Not knowing what to do, they put me back in a room with a nurse stationed beside me. They handed her a pen and paper and told her to write down everything I said. I promptly went to sleep and didn't say a word all night.

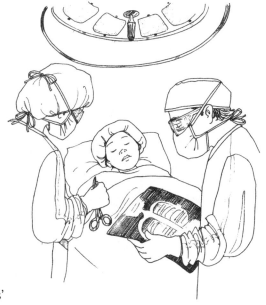

Shortly thereafter, it was discovered I had two injuries, not one. As I blacked out as a result of falling on the oil, I damaged my internal organs. When I ate, the problem got much worse. It was later diagnosed as shock that caused my temporary death.

With therapy, the paralysis let up fairly quickly. Shortly thereafter I entered into a two-year custody fight over my children. I always knew I'd win it, since I had come back to raise them (but I never told the judge or my attorney how I knew it). The doctors passed the experience off as "you had a bad night," but the nuns who read the doctors' reports talked with me about it.

I have now raised the children, and I have experienced the love I always wanted in abundance. I also walk normally, after several spinal operations.

The NDE has changed my life considerably, and continues to have a major effect on me over twenty-five years later. I now totally believe that there is a "there" there, and it's for everyone—not just me, and not just because I belong or don't belong to the "right" religion—whatever that is. God or whatever you choose to call it—Spirit, the Divine All, Whatever—loves us all unconditionally.

The NDE, as wonderful as it is, is a mixed blessing. It can raise more questions than it answers. I was confused about a lot of things for a lot of years, and I felt very alone sometimes. I finally found a group that has helped me a lot. It is called the International Association for Near Death Studies. It is both a scientific and support group for anyone who has had, or is interested in, the near death experience.

In the group to which I belong, two-thirds of the members and participants have never had an NDE, but all have been touched in some way. I would encourage anyone with questions about this phenomenon to find one of these groups.

The next story comes from someone who chose to remain anonymous. This person experienced an NDE as a result of a serious car accident.

I would like to relate an NDE that happened to me about eight years ago. I was seriously injured in a car accident, as a result of which I believe I had an NDE. Immediately following the impact in my car accident, I experienced moving rapidly down a darkened area and being aware of what I believed to be the sensation of a loud wind passing by. This noise was so loud it sounded and felt like a train passing.

Afterwards, I recall lying in what I thought was an open field and feeling both warmth and a bright light totally

Various Religious Views

If you are interested in finding out the different views various religions hold to be true concerning the afterlife, check out Divine Encounters at *www.lovinglight.com.*

surrounding me. I also sensed the presence of my mother, grandfather, and uncle who had passed away several years earlier.

I recall my mother telling me it was not my time and to return. Almost instantly, I was back in the vehicle at the accident scene and in tremendous physical pain. I have never forgotten this experience and have never quite looked at things the same since then. I hope this story may be of interest and hopefully also help in letting others know that life is more than just what we see in our limited earthly existence.

The following person, named Ed, discussed a near death experience that happened to him in 1985 as a result of a heart attack.

I was driving my car to town to catch an airplane in order to go to Anchorage. As I was driving, I saw this woman sitting along the side of the road with her head leaning against the steering wheel.

As I drove by, I ignored her as I didn't want to get involved if she had been raped or molested. A voice in my head told me, as I continued to drive by, "Wouldn't you appreciate it if someone helped you if you had a heart attack?" (At this time mine hadn't happened yet.)

I said to myself, "Sure," so I turned around and went back. As I approached her car, I tapped on the window on the driver's side. She still had her head against the steering wheel. I ask her what she was doing. She replied, "Praying that someone would help me and not rape me."

I asked her what she needed. She explained that she had a flat tire, but didn't know how to change it. I told her I'd help. She seemed nervous because she didn't know me. I told her if she didn't want my help, she could go back and continue to pray to God in hopes he'd send someone else.

She finally gave in and let me help her. I took her to the gas station and she bought a new tire. On the way back I stopped by her car, took the tire out from my trunk, and laid it beside her car. As I was trying to install the new tire onto her

car, I experienced a sudden chest pain and found it very hard to breathe. I went on the driver's side of my car and sat down.

I told the woman that if I passed out, I would appreciate it if she would get me to a doctor. Well, the pain got worse and I exchanged sides with her. She told me I looked blue/gray, and I replied that I felt blue/gray. As time went on, the pain went down my left arm to my little finger. I told her I thought I was having a heart attack. I then saw myself outside of the car and looking through the roof of the car as I was sitting there.

I asked God not to take me now. I had a wife and little girl to take care of. I had a great slamming back to my life here on earth, as if I were slam-dunked back into my body. The woman took me to the doctor. I arrived at the hospital and I saw this buddy of mine. I started to cry, because I knew it would probably be the last time that I would see him in this life.

The doctors took an enzyme count to measure the severity of my heart attack. It was 2,300. A heart attack is considered to be severe or fatal if the results are between 1,500 and 2,000. Nobody can explain how or why I am still alive, with no long-term damage caused by the heart attack. I should be dead; however, I am normal. What did change my life, however, was the NDE.

The following person also chose to remain anonymous; however, what this person experienced is very similar to what many other NDE experiencers have described, only this person didn't ever physically die.

After reading about NDEs, I realized that I had had those weird feelings, only I experienced them without dying or nearly dying. Only a few years ago, I seemed to awaken in the night. I felt weird but very good. I remember it was completely dark. The absence of any sounds added to the eerie feeling.

After a few minutes, I realized that I couldn't move. In fact, after trying hard, I found that I could not feel anything! My body was tingling, but I could not feel its existence. Inside, it felt good and relaxed. I stayed like this for some time thinking that I might have died. I remember being amazed by what I was feeling. The joy ended, however, when I realized that if I was actually dead, I wouldn't have been able to think.

After that realization, I felt like I was plummeting thousands of feet. I awoke in my bed with a thud, as if I had just fallen from the ceiling. During the next few hours, I stayed in bed thinking about what had caused such feelings. Was it merely a dream? To this day, I have tried inducing the same state. I've read articles on the state of mind between the time your conscious mind gives control to your subconscious as you fall asleep. It is said that this state of mind produces the same feelings I felt during my "dream."

I have tried many things from scripts for out-of-body experiences to self-hypnosis, but nothing has worked to recreate the experience.

This next near death experience happened in someone's dream; however, it turned out to became a premonition for a potentially fatal car accident, which this person managed to survive. This person's story demonstrates how people who have an NDE develop a better understanding of death and learn that it shouldn't be feared.

I'm from Dallas, Texas. My near death experience happened last spring, when I awoke from what I thought was a terrible nightmare. During the night, I had an extremely vivid dream. It involved my fairly recently bought sports car.

In my dream, I was driving about a block from my house. It was nighttime. As I came upon a familiar neighborhood, something hit my car, which made it spin out of control. Outside my car was pure darkness—however, the amber lights of my dashboard were extremely bright and were all I could see.

In my dream, I didn't know why I wrecked. I just knew that I was going to die. The death part of my dream was so real—it haunted me for days afterward. I was crushed up against the steering wheel. My whole body was just smashed. Although

Further Reading

The book *Embraced by the Light* written by Betty J. Eadie is a personal account of a near death experience.

it was a dream, I could feel blood in my lungs. I knew I had no chance.

The next day, I told my parents about the vivid realism of the dream. I also said how I was now regretting not getting a safer car, perhaps one with airbags. That evening, I also discussed my dream with my best friend. As some dreams do, this one seemed to stay with me, even when I was awake.

A few weeks later, the dream no longer was plaguing me. One morning I was driving to school. I had left earlier than usual to make up some work. I paused at the top of my street to light a cigarette. I then accelerated quickly to get onto the perpendicular road.

Less than a few hundred feet away, on a decline, a teal van pulled through a stop sign (from the neighborhood in my dream). The van was in my lane. I had no hope of stopping. The roads were wet and my brakes were worthless. I closed my eyes and crouched in a fetal position behind the wheel.

I knew what would happen. It was inevitable. As the car slammed into the van, I remained far away from my body— perhaps to protect myself. So many thoughts flooded my head in that split second. After the cars impacted and settled, the other driver, uninjured, approached my car.

She asked me if I was okay. All I could mumble about was my precognition. Later, I was taken to the doctor and I was all right. I had sustained only relatively minor back problems. However, if I had not decided to just accept my fate when I realized I was going to crash, had I chosen to swerve, the results could have been horrible. I could have had a head-on collision in the opposing lane. I am thankful for the eerie pre-cognition.

The following story describes a childhood experience involving a sudden and rather serious illness. As you'll read, this person had a high fever when the NDE happened.

This is very difficult because my NDE happened thirty years ago, when I was twelve years old. This experience, at the time,

Online Information

If you're interested in learning more, there have been hundreds of books and thousands of newspaper, magazine, and journal articles written about the near death experience phenomenon. For a partial listing of books dedicated to this topic, go to *www.near-death.com/books.html*. Some other excellent resources include:

- Afterlife Knowledge—
  www.afterlife-knowledge.com
- Death and Dying—
  www.death-dying.com

- IANDS—P.O. Box 502, East Windsor Hill, CT 06028-0502; (860) 644-5216; *www.iands.org*
- Insights into the Afterlife—
  www.ettl.co.at/uc/misc/insights.html
- Near Death Experience and the Afterlife—*www.near-death.com*
- Near Death Experience Research Foundation—P.O. Box 36543, Las Vegas, NV 89133; *www.nderf.org*
- Near Death Experiences—
  www.mindspring.com/~scottr/end.html

was very real; although over time, I chose to call it a "dream" until very recently when other "odd" experiences occurred.

But first, here's what happened in my "dream." One day (when I was twelve), I felt ill. Over the course of a few hours, I became even sicker. My aunt, whom I lived with, took my temperature. It was 105 degrees. She sent me to bed. Shortly after closing my eyes, I was awakened by a "swooshing" feeling. I was traveling through a long dark tunnel going upward, like in an elevator, but going so much faster. I was frightened!

At the end of the "ride," I found myself at a place of extreme brightness and warmth. This place exuded such love. I knew I must remain there. Through the brightness, I witnessed many thousands of beings that knew and loved me, and I them.

We communicated in love, not words. In fact, no names were known. I can't explain this. Names were not used. They were not important. Names simply were not a part of this place.

I tried to focus on one individual, but could not. When I tried to bring into focus a "person," I could only clearly see a hand or a foot but never the entire body. I strained to do so and was confused that I could not.

Suddenly a man (who was as clear as a bell) appeared. I could see him fully. He was a big man with a beard and a mesmerizing smile. He looked like a lumberjack. When I focused on one item on him—his teeth, for instance—they were so bright they hurt my eyes. His feet blazed like a golden fire. But the love that came from him to me was extraordinary.

This place was where I belonged. It was like the pieces to a puzzle coming together for me. They all told me in unison (not in words) to look down. I did so and saw a line. They told me not to cross that line. I wanted to know why. They conveyed it wasn't my time yet. This made me sad.

I felt their compassion through the love. They told me my future. It contained two important things I needed to do before I could come back. I was crestfallen, because these things I knew I could not do. Enveloped in their love, they

showed me exactly how I could do them. I was jubilant and anxious to return and perform my tasks.

They told me I would not remember them. Suddenly and quite forcefully I was propelled down the "elevator" trying desperately to hold on to the information; but the further away from "the place" I went, the more I felt it slipping away. The impact awakened me on my bed completely bathed in sweat.

Yes, I know there is a God, but I know he wasn't the lumberjack (he was a special angel though). I know that we're all part of a "puzzle" and that our bodies and even our names are not a part of this place. These things are needed for here, on earth, to accomplish our "tasks." The love in this place, though, is so hard to describe, no words can touch it. I anxiously await the day I can return—when it's my time!

The following person conveyed an experience she had as a child. As you'll read, she is now an adult, and has always been rather religious. This NDE experience happened without this person actually dying a physical death.

This happened when I was seven years old. It was in 1972. When I told what I had experienced to my mother and grandma, they had just said "Forget it, it was just a dream." Now, I knew better. The feelings of rejection stayed with me until a few years ago, when I finally figured out that it was done for me out of unconditional love. Here's what happened.

I had been in a private Christian school for two years. I was convinced that my life path was that of a nun. I didn't know that you had to be Catholic to be a nun. So one night, when I was saying my prayers, I decided that I would go and visit Jesus. I went to sleep and the next thing I knew, I was whooshed out of my body and was floating toward a gray tunnel. The tunnel was beautiful. It was a tunnel of clouds. I knew that I was going to be with Jesus.

The closer I got to the brilliant light, the more love I felt. It was all-encompassing, there was so much emotion I thought that I would burst, but I still wanted more.

When the tunnel opened out, there were three people waiting for me. At first I didn't know who they were. Then, I knew. It was my grandma, great-grandma, and great-grandpa. They were all smiles and had their arms out to hug me. I was so elated. I was home. I never wanted to leave. I finally felt like I belonged somewhere.

Then a beautiful being of light came towards us. I was so happy. I thought that I would finally be with Jesus, but it wasn't Jesus. He was like Jesus, but I knew that it wasn't. He radiated so much love, I didn't care that it wasn't. I went over to hug him and he stopped me. He didn't physically stop me but some force stopped me.

I asked what was wrong. He just looked at me and said, "It's not your time yet. You have to go back." I started to cry because I didn't want to go back. I belonged here. I said, "I'm not going back. I want to stay!" He looked at me and said again "It's not your time."

Then, a force started pulling me backwards, back through the tunnel. I had a sensation of falling. I fell into my body with a thud. I sat straight up. I was crying. I couldn't stop. I didn't want to be here. The feelings of rejection I felt stayed with me for years.

Chapter Eight

The Skeptical Point of View

For every seemingly unbelievable story you've read thus far in this book, there are plenty of people who are true believers; perhaps you're one of them. There are also people who simply don't believe in ghosts, psychic phenomena, or the paranormal. Because there is no hardcore scientific proof that various paranormal phenomena exist, nonbelievers aren't willing to accept anything at face value, such as people's firsthand experiences.

James Randi is just one example of someone who believes that ghosts, spooks, haunts, and other "otherworldly" beings are just a product of people's overactive imaginations. Randi has an international reputation as a magician and escape artist, but these days he is best known as the world's most tireless investigator and demystifier of paranormal and pseudoscientific claims. He has pursued "psychic" spoon benders, exposed the dirty tricks of illegitimate faith healers, investigated homeopathic water "with a memory," and has generally been a thorn in the sides of those who try to pull the wool over the public's eyes in the name of the supernatural.

The James Randi Education Foundation

In 1996, the James Randi Education Foundation (JREF) was established to further Randi's work. The goal of this nonprofit organization is to promote critical thinking by reaching out to the public and media with reliable information about paranormal and supernatural ideas that are so widespread in our society today.

According to Randi, his Foundation's goals include:

- Creating a new generation of critical thinkers through classroom demonstrations and by reaching out to the next generation in the form of scholarships and awards.
- Demonstrating to the public, through educational seminars, the consequences of accepting paranormal and supernatural claims without questioning people's claims.
- Supporting and conducting research into paranormal claims through well-designed experiments utilizing "the scientific method" and by publishing the group's findings.

- Assisting those who are being attacked as a result of their investigations into paranormal claims, by maintaining a legal defense fund available to assist these individuals.

Can psychics really sense hidden secrets and help the police solve crimes? Can astrologers predict the future? Does therapeutic touch practiced by thousands of registered nurses really work? According to Randi, "To date, all existing evidence for the paranormal has been unreliable." As part of its ongoing investigations of paranormal powers and supernatural claims, the JREF has created what he calls "the Million Dollar Paranormal Challenge." To raise public awareness of these issues, the Foundation offers a prize of $1 million in negotiable bonds to anyone who can demonstrate any psychic, supernatural, or paranormal ability, of any kind, under mutually agreed-upon scientific conditions. As you'd expect, there is a lot of criticism as well as interest in JREF's "Million Dollar Paranormal Challenge" as well as the work Randi himself does.

Together with independent scientists, researchers, and statisticians, JREF designs a test for each claim being made. The terms of the test are agreed to in advance by the applicant(s). Applicants, some of whom have been scientists and health care practitioners, have included psychics, dowsers, perpetual motion machine inventors, and many others. So far, no one has successfully proven his or her claim.

For more than thirty years, Randi has examined and tested claims of all kinds, by individuals from all walks of life, from countries all over the world. In the process he has become the world's premiere investigator of psychic and paranormal claims. His investigations have been the subject of many television programs, including *Nova* and numerous network news specials. "Science is the most effective tool we have for discovering the truth about the world around us," stated Randi. "Medieval superstitions and ideas are so prevalent in our society today, they often prevent us from moving forward as rational thinking human beings."

In an effort to support the worldwide community and convey the group's messages, JREF maintains a comprehensive library, awards grants for basic paranormal research, and awards educational

About the JREF

The James Randi Education Foundation's Web site can be accessed by visiting *www.randi.org*. This site offers information about Randi's work trying to debunk frauds. While there is a vast disparity between what psychics, channelers, and mediums believe compared to Randi's beliefs, plenty of circumstantial evidence is available to support both sides of the argument. In reality, there are no right or wrong opinions or answers. You must rely on your own belief system and education, then base your beliefs on the information available.

prizes to teachers and students who demonstrate an exceptional adherence to critical thinking.

When asked about the toughest case he's ever tried to crack, Randi explained, "None have been particularly difficult. The hardest part has always been to get the claimants to state clearly what they think they can do, under what conditions, and with what accuracy. Most are very vague about these aspects, and very few have any notion of how a proper test should be conducted."

Randi explained that the claims made are sometimes simply variations on very old misconceptions or delusions. He stated that there is seldom anything that's a surprise for the group or that requires heavy analysis. In many instances, not enough information is provided by the applicant(s), even though the organization tries to get all the needed data. In some situations, Randi and his coworkers cannot determine what the actual claim might consist of, since the person claiming to be psychic, for example, fails to provide details about what this gift entails and how he or she can demonstrate it in a scientifically controlled environment.

While Randi has met with hundreds, perhaps thousands, of so-called psychics and other people claiming to have paranormal powers or "a gift," he suggests that none of these people have even come close to convincing him or his organization of their legitimacy. Randi stated that he sincerely wishes there were some really challenging offers or claims, just to add some excitement to his job. Unfortunately, he says, it's pretty much the same old material, endlessly repeated.

One of his biggest regrets is that he has been unable to test the high-profile and well-known psychics we all often see on television or on the bestseller list in bookstores. "We can only test persons who either apply to become claimants for the million-dollar prize, or who will actually submit themselves to undergoing proper test procedures. The 'stars' [the psychics one often sees featured on television talk shows, for example] never do this. In fact, they do anything they can to avoid us and our challenge. They would rather just run on about past glories, point to anecdotal evidence, or grandly ignore our genuine offer to test them. The people who do apply are probably honestly convinced of their abilities, and have no fear of discovery," said Randi.

If all of these high-profile psychics are legitimate, Randi asks them why they won't agree to be tested by him and his colleagues. "Where are James Van Praagh, Sylvia Browne, George Anderson, John Edward, and the rest of the current big names? Why hasn't Uri Geller, the professional spoon bender, snapped up this easy cash that my organization is offering? One can only wonder," he stated.

These well-known personalities have mainly chosen to ignore the efforts of Randi and his organization. These people believe that their work and track record speak for themselves. While people like James Van Praagh and John Edwards can't offer solid proof of their abilities, they do have thousands upon thousand of people who acknowledge they've been helped.

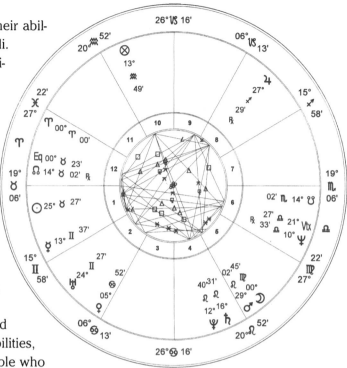

Even if psychics, mediums, and others are all frauds, you might wonder what harm there is in believing what these people say about the afterlife. According to Randi, the potential harm is very real and dangerous. He feels that a belief in such obvious flummeries, such as astrology or fortunetelling, can appear quite incorrectly to give confirmatory results. Randi believes these false results lead to the victim pursuing more dangerous, expensive, and sometimes health-related scams. "Blind belief can be comforting, but it can easily cripple reason and ultimately stop intellectual progress," said Randi.

Randi urges everyone to pursue lines of what he calls "critical thinking" when it comes to the paranormal. One of the goals of his organization is to help young people think more critically about subjects like fortune-telling, psychics, mediums, ghosts, and other paranormal events. He believes that those who have not completely surrendered to careless acceptance of flimflam can be brought to think about their decisions, and in many cases, they can and will change their minds.

When asked if the general public will begin to better deal with psychic frauds, Randi explained, "We think that 'war' will never be won, because the scam artists and the honestly deluded promoters of nonsense are constantly being replaced with others. Though P.T. Barnum never said it, there does appear to be 'a sucker born every minute.' So, we have predators and prey, and that is a natural and expected condition of life."

According to Randi, his organization hopes to teach those whom he believes are unaware of certain facts of the real world. He wants people to be harder prey for the so-called psychic predators, for example, to catch. "There's a difference between winning a 'war' and winning a 'battle.' We win battles every day, such as when someone walks through our doors and announces we've added in some way to their understanding of the world. Every class of kids that we speak to and every audience in any part of the world that listens to what we have to say wins us a battle," he said.

While the people who belong to and support JREF are not necessarily scientists, Randi explained that the people in his organization are skilled in two primary areas: They understand all too well how people are fooled by others, and they know how people fool themselves. Randi suggested that he and those he works with deal with hard, basic facts, and try their best to make those facts known. His objective is to protect people from influences that might obscure the true danger of uncritical thinking. His organization includes a handful of scientific authorities to provide the advice and specialization required to promote the theories of the group.

As for Randi himself, he considers himself a seeker of the truth more than a skeptic. When asked why he doesn't believe in the abilities of psychics and others with special "paranormal" abilities, he stated, "Why don't adults believe in Santa Claus? Actually, I don't believe the evidence is available to support the claims that these people make. There is no hard evidence for any of these claims. There is plenty of anecdotal evidence and a lot of poorly derived evidence that can't be substantiated or verified, but no real evidence. I'm looking for more than people swearing on a stack of Bibles that they've seen, interacted, or communicated with a ghost. Some people identify every dream or thought that passes through their head as reality. I don't think they're dealing in the real world in doing that, but some people can't differentiate."

Whether or not the proof Randi is seeking will ever manifest itself is anyone's guess. Because Randi is extremely cynical when it comes to paranormal phenomena, even if proof did become available, it may not satisfy him. "I can't predict the future, so I have no idea if there ever will be hard evidence that people possess psychic or paranormal abilities," he said.

It's Randi's belief that people want and need these types of phenomena to be real. However, he thinks there is real harm in believing in something that isn't real, just as there is harm in taking heroin. It's his philosophy that feeling better, rather than actually *being* better, is not the answer to life's problems. Randi urges people to deal with the real world, as opposed to escaping into a pretend one.

"When people tell me they're going to see a psychic 'just for fun,' I don't think there's anything fun about it. To me, it's like saying, 'I'm going to do a shot of heroin just for fun.' The people who pass themselves off as psychics, mediums, or other types of fortunetellers are very clever. They know exactly what questions to ask and what to tell you in order to make you feel good about your experience," he said.

Randi explained that at the very start of a reading, and during the time a so-called psychic or medium spends with the client, he or she does what's called a "cold reading." The psychic or medium is not reading what spirits or entities from the other side are saying. During a cold reading the psychic asks the client very specialized questions, usually at a very fast rate, all guised as normal conversation. This is a method by which psychics gather information about their clients, which Randi believes is later repackaged

Randi's Beliefs

James Randi's book, *An Encyclopedia of Claims, Frauds, and Hoaxes of the Occult and Supernatural,* is a comprehensive treatment of definitions, origin, and terminology used by the occultists, parapsychologists, and psychics, done from the skeptical point of view.

during the reading. "Cold reading is a well-organized system of guessing, asking questions, and suggesting. The so-called psychic winds up telling you little or no original information, but in the course of an hour, I've seen literally hundreds of questions be asked. I once clocked a well-known 'psychic' and 'medium' who appears constantly on the TV shows at asking at least one question every fourteen seconds when he was supposed to be offering information, not collecting it. It's all about asking questions and reading someone's body language," stated Randi. "I once saw this same well-known medium take twenty-six guesses to come up with the name of a woman's deceased husband who this medium was supposedly in contact with." Randi also stated that virtually all of the psychics and people with "special abilities" who appear on TV talk shows, for example, refuse to do a reading for an audience member who hasn't been prescreened or interviewed in advance.

So, do all psychics, mediums, channelers, fortunetellers, tarot card readers, and so on use trickery in order to scam their clients? Randi has certainly exposed many people as frauds; however, he has not put every psychic to his test. Many people who truly believe they have a special gift feel no reason to prove it to anyone, including Randi, and therefore don't associate with him or his organization. The reason why Randi and his organization are offering a prize of $1 million to anyone who will come forward and demonstrate proof of paranormal or psychic ability is because he was asked to put his money where his mouth was in order to demonstrate his conviction regarding these issues.

While Randi encourages people to use critical thinking when dealing with paranormal issues, he makes it clear that his focus is to investigate claims of people who promote themselves as having special abilities. He says that he's not in the business of debunking people. "I don't set out to disprove anything. I set out to investigate people's claims. Thus far, we've found that the claims don't check out," he said.

Randi certainly isn't the only person who runs a foundation dedicating to debunking ghost stories and people who claim to have supernatural powers. The New England Skeptical Society (*www.theness.com*) also takes a critical look at whether or not

The Skeptic's Magazine

The *Skeptical Enquirer,* published by the Committee for the Scientific Investigation of Claims of the Paranormal, offers a wealth of information regarding the scientific community's views on the paranormal.

ghosts really exist. This organization's philosophy is that the problem with ghosts is similar to that of UFOs: There are thousands of testimonials from people from all walks of life, but there is no proof or even reliable evidence of their existence.

Proving or disproving the existence of ghosts as true paranormal entities is clearly difficult. The New England Skeptical Society reports that psychical researchers have offered what they consider evidence in the form of photographs, videos, and sound recordings, but none of these are convincing and all are possible to fake. Other known phenomena, such as hallucinations or misidentification, can be influenced by wishful thinking, grief, or loneliness. "Who hasn't wanted a departed loved one to show that he or she is still alive and conscious in some way? Someone who vividly dreams of a departed person can be convinced that he or she has indeed been visited by the soul of a loved one. Another possibility here is hypnagogic or hypnopompic dreams or lucid dreams. These types of dreams are so vivid and lifelike that the dreamer may not be able to distinguish them from the objectively real," reported the organization.

It's the belief of the members in this organization that in some situations, a person, often under extreme stress, can hallucinate a vision of an encounter from a departed loved one or some other supernatural being, who often appears to provide comfort or advice. These experiences, loosely called "visions," seem to be elaborate dramatizations concocted by the unconscious mind of a traumatized person to lend him or her reassurance and a sense of validity to help resolve a major difficulty.

A Few Final Words

Throughout *The Everything® Ghost Book,* you've read all about experts who truly believe in paranormal phenomena. You've read about people who believe they have experienced these phenomena firsthand. For them, there is no doubt that what they experienced was 100 percent real. You've also just read about skeptics who have made a career out of trying to prove that ghosts, hauntings, and

other forms of paranormal phenomena simply aren't real. These people believe that any so-called paranormal experience is the result of a person's overactive imagination or gullibility.

This book makes no claims as to which, if either, of these paths of thinking is accurate or true. We are left with the same questions we began with: Do ghosts really exist? Can people with psychic abilities actually communicate with the dead? Do all of us have psychic abilities that we have yet to unlock? Do ghosts, spirits, and other entities walk among us or visit us from the other side? Do all of us have spirit guides looking out for us? Does the other side exist? Does its believed existence prove that there is life after death?

Perhaps someday these questions will be answered from a scientific standpoint. For now, however, it's important that you develop a belief system that you're comfortable with. Whatever you decide to believe about ghosts and the paranormal, chances are there's no way to prove or disprove your beliefs from a scientific standpoint. From a spiritual or religious perspective, though, many people around the world truly believe in the afterlife and in ghosts.

We all have loved ones who have died, either tragically or from natural causes. We'd all like to believe that when their physical body stopped living somehow, somewhere, their soul, spirit, or essence has lived on and that they're happy, safe, and maybe even watching over us. If these beliefs help you to deal with the emotional trauma and your grief while moving forward with your life, there's probably no reason to believe what the skeptics have to say, especially since, as I've stressed so often, no scientific proof exists. We're living in a country that offers free speech and freedom to practice any religion. Our beliefs are our own. Whether you're dealing with paranormal phenomena or something else, as someone with intelligence and free will, you have the right and ability to believe whatever you wish and aren't required to justify those beliefs to anyone.

If the information provided in this book has piqued your interest, don't hesitate to read any of the hundreds, perhaps thousands, of other books that have been published throughout history that cover the various aspects of the paranormal. Seek out others who have similar beliefs and interests, and never stop trying to learn about topics (paranormal or otherwise) that are of interest to you.

Whether or not we're able to communicate with the other side in order to acquire enlightenment or knowledge, the fact that we are all born with free will and the ability to make decisions allows us to pursue our own dreams, ambitions, and to fulfill our own destinies.

The appendices of this book will help you continue your research into this exciting and extremely interesting topic. Since you probably still have many questions about the topics you've been reading about, use this book as a starting point as you gather additional information that delves deeper into the specific topics you're interested in. Education is a never-ending process. Combine your willingness and ability to learn with the power of the Internet, and you'll be well on your way to becoming a more enlightened person when it comes to topics involving the paranormal. Also, don't let your reading stop here. There are literally hundreds of books available that cover various topics relating to ghosts, haunted houses, psychics, mediums, NDEs, channeling, and other related topics. Visit any bookstore or library, or use an online service (such as Amazon.com, *www.amazon.com* or Barnes & Noble Online, *www.bn.com*) to search for books on topics of interest to you.

Further Reading

The book *Why People Believe Weird Things* written by Michael Shermer covers a wide variety of topics including physics, near death experiences, and abductions.

Glossary

A

age regression—The process of going back to a previous time in your current life through the use of hypnosis.

Akashic Record—A chart of a person's past lives, future lives, and parallel lives.

apparition—The visual appearance of any spirit or unusual phenomenon that doesn't necessarily take on the shape of a human form or that doesn't show signs of intelligence or personality.

automatic writing—A method of communication with the other side that involves using a normal writing instrument and paper.

autonographist—Professional automatic writer.

C

channeler—A person who allows a spirit to temporarily possess his or her body in order for the spirit to be able to communicate with the living.

channeling board—A tool used for communication with the other side. Also known as a Ouija board or talking board.

clairalience—The ability to use smell to receive a spirit's message.

clairambience—The ability to use taste to receive a spirit's message.

clairaudience—The ability to hear sounds to receive a spirit's message.

clairsentience—The feeling or sensing of a spirit's message.

clairvoyance—The ability to foresee the future or to see objects or events that others can't, using only eyes and ears.

collective apparition—An apparition that is seen simultaneously by multiple witnesses.

confabulation—A term used to describe when real-life experiences are mixed with imagined experiences.

D

discarnate—spirit or ghost.

E

ectoplasm—Residue left behind by ghosts or other paranormal phenomena. Many believe that spirits use ectoplasm to materialize.

Electronic Voice Phenomena (EVP)—A term used to describe the noises and voices that are recorded on traditional audio or videotape, but that aren't audible to the human ear—often believed to be voices from the other side.

extrasensory perception (ESP)—An awareness of outside happenings or information not attained through the normal human senses.

G

ghost—A visual manifestation of a soul, spirit, life force, or life energy. Most people use this term to describe the visual appearance of a human being or creature that has died and passed on to the other side.

ghost buster—A person who visits a site that is believed to be haunted with the expressed purpose of eliminating the ghost or paranormal activity from that location.

ghost hunter—A person who investigates and studies ghosts, hauntings, and paranormal phenomena.

H

hypnotherapy—The treatment of an ailment through the use of hypnosis.

M

medium—A person who has a special gift and believes he or she can act as a bridge between the world of the living and the other side.

metaphysics—A field of study dedicated to the nature of reality.

O

orbs—A phenomenon in the shape of a floating ball of light, often thought to be trapped souls.

other side—A term used to describe the spirit world, or the place spirits go after death.

P

paranormal—A term used to describe unusual activity that involves ghosts, apparitions, spirits, hauntings, poltergeists, etc. This term defines anything for which there is no scientific explanation.

parapsychology—The study of phenomena, real or supposed, that appear inexplicable on presently accepted scientific theories.

past-life regression—The act of using trance or hypnosis to visit former lives.

phenomenon—A term used to collectively describe anything that cannot be explained in scientific terms.

physical mediumship—A form of mediumship in which the spirit communicates using both the physical energies and consciousness of the medium.

place memories—Refers to a location that captures energy and uses it to record an image of an event that once happened there and later replays it.

planchette—A pointing device used in conjunction with a channeling board.

poltergeist—A phenomenon that is more often experienced than seen. A poltergeist will often interact with its environment by moving objects, making noises, or making itself known in a variety of other ways.

progression hypnotherapy—The act of visiting future lives through the use of hypnosis.

PSI—A term used to describe psychic ability or power.

psychic—A person who uses empathic feelings to tap into nonphysical forces.

psychokinesis—The ability to move objects using only one's mind.

psychosomatics—A field of study dedicated to the idea that the medical health of a person's body is related to that person's mind and emotions.

R

reincarnation—The idea that a soul can be reborn into a new human body.

residual haunting—A term used to describe a spirit that is trapped in a continuous emotional loop.

S

sixth sense—A term used to describe psychic ability.

soul loss—The loss of vital energy experienced as a result of any kind of physical, emotional, mental, or spiritual trauma.

spirit—Electromagnetic entities in the forms of orbs, mist, vortexes, or shadows, which are the signature of a once-living person who has returned to a specific location.

spirit communicator—A spirit or ghost that uses a medium in order to communicate with someone either verbally or visually.

spirit operator—A spirit or ghost that uses a medium to physically manipulate something on earth.

spirit world—The place spirits go after death.

spiritual guide—A spirit that watches over a living person and that offers wisdom or guidance.

superpersonalities—Negative entities.

T

telepathy—Communication using the mind as opposed to other senses.

trance mediumship—A form of mediumship in which the medium shares his or her energy with a spirit through the use of trance.

V

vortex—A mass of air, water, or energy that spins around very fast creating a vacuum to pull objects into its empty center.

Appendix A

Ghosts, Haunts, and Paranormal Activity on the Web

Okay, there have been no reports that the Information Superhighway is actually haunted; however, there are literally hundreds, perhaps thousands, of Web sites, newsgroups, and Internet-based mailing lists that deal with paranormal activity, ghosts, and hauntings. These Web sites are informational resources created by both professional paranormal investigators as well as amateurs with a sincere interest in the paranormal. While a vast amount of information, so-called "documentation" or evidence of the paranormal, and case studies are available to Web surfers, as you explore these and other Web sites, pay attention to the source of the information and the credibility of each source.

Using any search engine, you can find additional sites relating to the paranormal using keywords like "ghosts," "haunted houses," "spirits," "poltergeists," "paranormal," "parapsychology," "psychic," "hypnotherapy," "past-life regression," "Ouija board," "channeling," "mediumship," or "psychic medium."

The following Web sites, some of which I've mentioned in the book, are useful resources for those who want to discover more about various aspects of paranormal activity. Keep in mind that the opinions and theories expressed on these sites are those of the person or people who have created each site and aren't necessarily based on scientific evidence.

Adventures Beyond
www.adventuresbeyond.com
Adventures Beyond investigates nearly all facets of the paranormal. From ghosts and hauntings to Big Foot and UFOs, Adventures Beyond strives to capture evidence of the paranormal on video. Currently, they have a documentary series including *Chupacabra*, *America's Most Haunted*, *Witches, Ghosts . . . and Phantoms*. Please check the Web site for ordering information.

Alchemy Lab Web Ring
www.webring.org/cgi-bin/webring?ring= alchemylab;list
This Web site is a Web ring for those interested in gaining further knowledge of alchemy, spiritualism, pagan studies, parapsychology, the paranormal, and many more related topics. Some of the member sites include AstroZone, Spagyria, The Alchemist, Parapsychology, Senshen and the Other World, and Haunted Places.

Alien/UFO/Ghost Research Society
www.AlienUFOart.com
The Alien/UFO/Ghost Research Society is dedicated to investigating and documenting paranormal activity. Currently, their Web site contains 130 photographs of the paranormal including ghosts, orbs, and apparitions. The Web site also contains summaries of investigations, ghost stories, and links to additional information.

Alphaland

www.alphaland.com

Alphaland strives to collect evidence of life after death through the use of Electronic Voice Phenomenon. The Web site offers a step-by-step teaching of a method used by Alphaland to record and communicate with inhabitants of the afterlife. This method is quite simple and recommended for those just beginning their exploration into communication with the paranormal.

American Ghost Society

www.prairieghosts.com

The American Ghost Society investigates haunted sites and aids those who believe they are plagued by the paranormal. Their Web site, Ghosts of the Prairie, provides a melange of information regarding haunted sites in the United States, ghost hunting, and resources to further your research into the paranormal.

The American Society for Psychical Research

www.aspr.com

The American Society for Psychical Research is a research organization dedicated to the research and investigation of paranormal activity. Their Web site is a comprehensive resource for finding additional information on parapsychology topics such as near death experiences, out-of-body experiences, ESP, psychokinesis, survival after death, and more.

Amityville Murders

www.amityvillemurders.com

This Web site provides a wealth of information regarding the famous Amityville murders as well as the history of the house at 112 Ocean Avenue. Because there are so many rumors and reenactments of this tragedy, this Web site strives to put the facts out there for the public. Included is a photo gallery, a myths and facts page, and a biography of the members of the DeFeo family.

An Unknown Encounter

www.barcon.com

This Web site allows the viewer to preview clips of paranormal activity caught on video. If you like what you see, you can order the full-length video online. This site also features video equipment for rent and camera crews for hire. If you are interested in video recording paranormal activity, check out this Web site for further information.

Archive X Stories

www.wirenot.net/X

This Web site serves as an archive of stories and articles relating to the paranormal. Featured on this site are ghost stories, near death experiences, stories of angels, out of body experiences, and stories and messages of channeling experiences. The Web site also allows you to post your own story or article if you have an experience to share.

Bay Area Paranormal Research Society

www.rightondesign.com/baprs

The Bay Area Paranormal Research Society investigates and researches encounters with the paranormal. Their Web site features summaries of their investigations, photographs of the paranormal, links to other resources, and tips for ghost hunting.

Bell Witch

www.bellwitch.org

The Bell Witch Web site offers a comprehensive look at information relating to the legend of the Bell Witch of Tennessee. Extensive research and interviews have been conducted in order to compile the information offered on this Web site. Currently, it features the story of the Bell Witch, photographs, resources for additional reading, and opportunities for online chat and message boards.

Celestial Visions School of Metaphyscial Arts

www.cvsma.com

The Celestial Visions School of Metaphysical Arts is dedicated to educating others in the fields of metaphysics and parapsychology. Their Web site will give the viewer a chance to look over the institute's mission statement, as well as introduce you to some of the courses offered by the CVSMA.

Center for Research and Investigation

www.murlin.com/~webfx/ghost

The Center for Research and Investigation is interested in the research of paranormal activity. Their Web site offers four categories: ghosts, ESP, dreams, and aliens. Within each of these categories are opportunities for viewers to check out related stories, both fiction and nonfiction, as well as guidelines for submission of stories.

Center for the Study of EVP

www.ghostshop.com

This Web site is an interesting source of information for those of you curious about Electronic Voice Phenomena. Here you will find guidelines for creating your own microphone for use in picking up EVP, an opportunity to listen to recordings of EVP, facts about this phenomena, and links for more resources to further your study.

Central Indiana Ghost Research

www.geocities.com/Area51/Lair/5865

Central Indiana Ghost Research is a branch of the American Ghost Society. This Web site will introduce you to several resources for information about the paranormal. Included also are photographs, summaries of investigations, and links to additional resources.

Chat Ghosts

www.chattownusa.com/Avenues/Fun/chatghosts

This Web site opens the doors of communication for all of you out there that would like to chat with people expressing the same interest in the paranormal. Share stories, ask questions, play games, find downloads—this Web site is a one stop shop for your paranormal needs.

Connecticut Paranormal Research Soc.

www.geocities.com/Area51/Vault/3384

The Connecticut Paranormal Research Society is a member of the International Ghost Hunters Society. The society researches and investigates paranormal activity. Their Web site offers summaries of investigations, EVPs, ghost stories, a photo gallery, a listing of haunted houses, and links to additional resources.

C.S.I.C.O.P.

www.csicop.org

The Committee for the Scientific Investigation of Claims of the Paranormal is a committee designed to investigate claims of paranormal activity from a scientific standpoint. Their Web site offers a variety of resources for those interested in researching the validity of paranormal experiences. Several articles are featured covering topics such as poltergeist activity, clairvoyance, reincarnation, psychics, and hauntings.

Delaware Paranormal Research Soc.

www.homestead.com/ghostsphere/dprs.html

The Delaware Paranormal Research Society conducts private investigations of paranormal activity. Their Web site offers links to additional resources, ghost stories, and a forum for ghost hunters in which people can post messages, tips, and experiences to share.

Doorway to the Unknown

www.geocities.com/SoHo/Gallery/2638

This Web site offers a wide variety of stories of the paranormal. Essentially, it is broken down into five categories: ghosts, ESP, specters, monsters, and The Hallway, which lists links for additional information. The Web site also offers the opportunity to add your own story of the paranormal to the collection.

Earthbound Ghosts

www.erols.com/rcod

Earthbound is a Web site that offers not only proof about life after death but previews of documented conversations with ghosts. Through the use of a channeler, ghosts are able to tell their tale, most of the time not realizing they are dead. The Web site also offers links to additional resources.

El Paso Ghost Research

www.epgr.50megs.com

El Paso Ghost Research is a society dedicated to investigating and documenting paranormal activity in the El Paso and surrounding areas. Their Web site offers summaries of investigations, theories, and links to additional information.

FATE Magazine

www.fatemag.com

FATE (which is an acronym for Fantastic Adventures and True Experiences) Magazine is a monthly publication featuring true accounts of paranormal activity. The magazine's Web site offers the present month's articles online, as well as guidelines for submissions.

Georgia Haunt Hunters

www.geocities.com/gahaunt

The Georgia Haunt Hunt Team is a research team dedicated to investigating the paranormal. Their Web site gives you instructions on how to request an investigation, become a member of the team, and contact other members.

Ghost Hunters Inc.

www.angelfire.com/tx3/ghosthtml

Ghost Hunters Inc. is interested in the research of paranormal activity. The group conducts investigations and strives to discover scientific proof of the paranormal. Their Web site offers summaries of investigations, ghost hunting tips, stories and photographs, and links to additional information.

Ghost Hunters of Baltimore

www.ghostpage.com

Ghost Hunters of Baltimore is dedicated to researching and investigating paranormal activity. Their Web site offers a wealth of information including a frequently asked questions page, ghost stories and submission guidelines, a listing of haunted sites around the world, information on ghost hunter training courses, and other links for additional information.

Ghost Hunters Society

http://members.tripod.com/GhostHuntersSociety/ Home.htm

The Ghost Hunters Society conducts private investigations and documents paranormal activity. Their Web site offers a frequently asked questions page, true ghost stories and experiences, summaries of investigations, a photograph collection, information for joining the society, and links to additional information.

Ghost Preservation League

http://members.nbci.com/ghostleague

The Ghost Preservation League is dedicated to researching and documenting paranormal activity. Their Web site provides theories, summaries of investigations, photographs, EVPs, a list of services and products available, and links to additional information.

Ghost Research Society

www.ghostresearch.org

The Ghost Research Society is dedicated to the research and documentation of paranormal activity and conducts private investigations. Their Web site offers articles related to the paranormal, photographs, a listing and history of haunted sites, and links to additional information.

Ghosts

www.camalott.com/~brianbet/ghosts.html

This Web site offers those with paranormal experience the chance to tell their tale. Here you will find a collection of stories submitted by viewers, as well as a message board, chatroom, and links to additional information.

Ghosts and Other Haunts

www.go.to/nzghosts

This Web site offers a collection of photographs of the paranormal and a brief description of the circumstances surrounding these pictures. You will also find a collection of ghost stories from both New Zealand and Ireland, as well as several links to additional information.

Ghosts Channel

www.pinn.net/~royaloak/Ghosts.htm

The Ghosts Channel is dedicated to giving people with paranormal experiences the opportunity to tell their stories and ask questions via a chatroom. This Web site also offers a collection of true ghost stories, photographs of the paranormal, and links to additional information.

Ghosts of Ohio

www.greenapple.com/~jas1746/

This Web site is dedicated to paranormal activity in the state of Ohio. Here you will find a collection of ghost stories and legends, a message board, contact information for paranormal investigators in the Ohio area, and links to additional information.

Haunted Chicago

www.hauntedchicago.com

This Web site is dedicated to the research and investigation of paranormal activity in the city of Chicago. Here you will find summaries of investigations, answers to frequently asked questions, photographs of the paranormal, a guide to the equipment used by the investigators, and links to additional information.

Haunted Michigan Guide

www.mlive.com/spooky/michguide.html

This Web page, sponsored by Michigan Live, offers several ghost stories set in Michigan. Stories are categorized by city. The site also offers several links to additional information about the paranormal.

Haunted Philadelphia

www.geocities.com/Tokyo/Harbor/7210

This Web site is dedicated to the research of paranormal activity in the city of Philadelphia. Here you will find true ghost stories, photographs of the paranormal, historical information about Philadelphia, movie reviews, and links to additional information.

Haunted Places

www.haunted-places.com

This Web site is exactly what it sounds like—a directory to haunted sites around the world. Here you will find not only listings of haunted sites, but also links to other organizations dedicated to the research of paranormal activity, a collection of true ghost stories, a bookstore, and media coverage of the paranormal.

Hollywood Hauntings

http://gothic.vei.net/hollywood/

This Web site is dedicated to the research of paranormal activity surrounding Hollywood stars. Here you will find accounts of hauntings and curses plaguing the lives of those involved in the world of entertainment. You can search by celebrity name or location. The Web site also offers links to additional information and a glossary of terms.

Institute of Paranormal Investigations

http://hometown.aol.com/psiexplorer/index.html

The Institute of Paranormal Investigations is interested in helping those plagued by paranormal activity. The organization conducts private investigations and all are kept confidential. Their Web site offers contact information and links to additional information and publications.

International Ghost Hunters Society
www.ghostweb.com

The International Ghost Hunters Society is comprised of several groups and individuals dedicated to the investigation and documentation of paranormal activity. Their Web site offers a wealth of information regarding the paranormal. Included are photographs, videos, articles, stories, EVPs, a home study course, support group information, a recommended reading list, membership information, and links to additional information.

The L.I.F.E. Foundation
www.paranormalhelp.com

The L.I.F.E. Foundation (Living in Fear Ends) is dedicated to helping those who are plagued by the paranormal. This foundation serves as a support group for people in need. The Web site offers articles, media information, procedures for getting help, advice, and links to additional information and help.

Long Island Paranormal Group
www.geocities.com/Area51/Chamber/1182

The Long Island Paranormal Group is interested in the investigation and documentation of paranormal activity. Their Web site offers photographs, EVPs, answers to frequently asked questions about ghost hunting, a recommended reading list, and links to additional information. The society now has a hotline phone number available on their Web site.

Maryland Paranormal Investigators
www.angelfire.com/md/MPInvestigators/index.html

Maryland Paranormal Investigators is a group of individuals interested in the research of paranormal activity. Their Web site offers summaries of investigations, photographs of the paranormal, and links to chatrooms and other investigative groups.

Michigan Ghost Hunters Society
www.tmghs.com

The Michigan Ghost Hunters Society is dedicated to the investigation and documentation of paranormal activity. Their Web site offers a wealth of information including ghost hunting tips, a glossary of terms, photographs and EVPs, summaries of investigations, and links to additional information.

Minnesota Paranormal
www.geocities.com/Area51/Rampart/9114

The Minnesota Paranormal Investigative Group is interested in the investigation of the paranormal. Their Web site offers a recommended reading list, world news relating to the paranormal, and links to additional information.

New Jersey Ghost Hunters Society
www.njghs.net

The New Jersey Ghost Hunters Society is dedication to the research and investigation of paranormal activity. Their Web site offers summaries of investigations, photographs and videos of the paranormal, a listing of haunted sites in New Jersey, and links to additional information. This society is a member of the International Ghost Hunters Society.

Obiwan's Paranormal Page
www.ghosts.org
This Web site offers answers to frequently asked questions concerning ghosts, stories and photographs of the paranormal, a listing of haunted sites, guidelines for ghost story submissions, and links to additional information.

Ohio Ghost Hunters
http://toghs.virtualave.net
The Ohio Ghost Hunters Society is dedicated to the investigation and documentation of the paranormal. Their Web site offers tips on ghost hunting, summaries of investigations, photographs of the paranormal, a listing of haunted sites in Ohio, and information on how to join the society. This organization is a member of the International Ghost Hunters Society.

PA Ghost Hunters Society
http://roswell.fortunecity.com/goldendawn/76/index.html
The Pennsylvania Ghost Hunters Society is interested in the research and investigation of haunted sites in Pennsylvania. Their Web site offers photographs of the paranormal, a recommended reading list, information on becoming a member of the society, and links to additional information. This organization is a member of the International Ghost Hunters Society.

Paranormal Happenings
www.angelfire.com/journal/paranormal
This Web site serves as a place where people with paranormal experiences can share their story. Here you will find guidelines for submitting your story, the stories of others, a recommended reading list, and links to additional information about the paranormal.

Paranormal Investigations
www.swiftsite.com/paranormal_investigation
Paranormal Investigations is an organization dedicated to the investigation of paranormal activity. Their Web site offers photographs and summaries of investigations conducted by the organization.

The Paranormal Network
www.mindreader.com
This is the Web site of famous paranormal investigator Loyd Auerbach. Here you will find a biography of Auerbach in relation to his work with the paranormal, general information about the Office of Paranormal Investigations, and links to additional information.

Phoenix Paranormal Investigations
http://ppi.org.uk
Phoenix Paranormal Investigations is interested in the investigation and documentation of paranormal activity. Their Web site offers summaries and photographs of investigations, information regarding monthly meetings, and links to additional information about the paranormal.

Psychical Research Foundation, Inc.
www.afterlife-psychical.org
The Psychical Research Foundation is an organization dedicated to the scientific research and investigation of the paranormal. Their Web site offers a comprehensive look at the topics studied by the organization including ghosts and apparitions, mediumship and channeling, near death experiences, reincarnation, and poltergeists. It also offers links and publications for further information.

Rent-A-Ghost
www.rent-a-ghost.co.uk
Rent-A-Ghost is exactly what it sounds like—a ghost placement company. Having removed ghosts from other establishments, this company found a client base for installing ghosts in establishments. That said, their Web site offers information on apparition rental, terms and conditions, charges, and links to additional information.

Sightings
www.scifi.com/sightings
This Web site is sponsored by the SciFi Channel, specifically the show *Sightings*. The show investigates paranormal activity. On this Web page you will find a message board in which you can post your own story/article or view the stories/articles of others, a listing of movies and images to download, and links to additional information about the paranormal.

Spooks
www.geocities.com/Area51/Shadowlands/4234
The Supernatural Phenomenon Organization of Kindred Spirits (SPOOKS) Web site offers a photograph gallery, ghost stories, a message board, and links to additional information.

Student Parapsychology Society
www.chelt.ac.uk/su/sps
The Student Parapsychology Society is a society of college students at Cheltenham & Gloucester College of Higher Education interested in the research and investigation of the paranormal. The Web site offers advice, as well as links to additional information.

Texas Ghost Stalkers
www.ghoststalkers.com
The Ghost Stalkers are interested in investigating the paranormal. Their Web site offers tips on stalking ghosts, guidelines for submitting stories, a chat room, links to additional information, and a recommended reading list.

The Society for Psychical Research
http://moebius.psy.ed.ac.uk/~spr/
The Society for Psychical Research strives to discover whether there is life after death through research and investigation. Their Web site offers summaries of research that is currently being conducted, information on educational opportunities, lecture and conference dates, and a listing of publications and links providing additional information.

True Ghost Stories from the Net
www.ghosts.org/stories/stories.html
This is a Web site solely dedicated to true ghost stories. Stories are indexed alphabetically by the story title and also by author name. You will also find guidelines for submitting your own true ghost story if you so choose.

Universal Ghost Guide
http://universalguide.com/myth/
myth-ghosts-4.htm
The Universal Guide offers a compilation of resources and information for those interested in ghosts. The site offers listings of haunted sites, both in the United States and the United Kingdom, as well as stories of the paranormal. You will also find links to societies dedicated to research of the paranormal.

Unsolved Mysteries
www.unsolvedmysteries.com
This Web site is for all of you out there who have a story to tell about paranormal activity. It allows you to post your story and ask questions, whether it be about ghosts, UFOs, ESP, or any other mystery you are interested in. Your story will be added to the archive and others will have an opportunity to respond to it. Or, if you don't have a story of your own, you can feel free to browse the stories of others and respond to their inquiries if you choose. This Web site is not affiliated with the television show.

Warren's Homepage
www.warrens.net
The Warren's New England Society for Psychic Research is dedicated to researching and investigating paranormal activities. Their Web site offers summaries of investigations, photographs of the paranormal, and links to additional information. The society also offers membership. Check out the Web site for more information.

Wisconsin Paranormal Research Center
www.execpc.com/~wisprc/
The Wisconsin Paranormal Research Center is an organization dedicated to the research and documentation of paranormal activity. They conduct private investigations and give lectures on how to become a ghost hunter. Their Web site offers contact information, a procedural breakdown of how an investigation is conducted, and links to additional information.

Appendix B

Haunted Sites

Alabama

Gurney Industries
242 South Court Street, Prattville, AL.
Haunted by the ghost of the mother of a young boy who died there.

Huntingdon College
1500 East FairviewAvenue, Montgomery, AL.
Haunted by the Red Lady who committed suicide in one of the dorms.

Pickens County Courthouse
Located in the Courthouse Square, Carrollton, AL.
Haunted by the ghost of a man who was struck by lightning and died shortly before a lynch mob reached him.

Sturdivant Hall
713 Mabry Street, Selma, AL.
Haunted by several unidentified ghosts.

Whole Backstage Theater
1120 Rayburn Avenue, Guntersville, AL.
Haunted by the ghost of a little boy.

Alaska

Eklutna Village Historical Park
Located on Eklutna Village Road, Chugiak, AK.
Haunted by the ghosts of Eskimos.

Golden North Hotel
Third and Broadway Streets, Skagway, AK.
Haunted by unidentified ghosts, specifically in rooms 23 and 14.

Arizona

Copper Queen Hotel
11 Howell Avenue, Bisbee, AZ.
Haunted by an unidentified ghost.

Hotel Congress
311 East Congress Street, Tucson, AZ.
Haunted by the ghost of a man who died in one of the rooms.

Monte Vista Hotel
100 North San Francisco Street, Flagstaff, AZ.
Haunted by the ghost of a former bellboy.

San Carlos Hotel
202 North Central Avenue, Phoenix, AZ.
Haunted by the ghost of a woman who committed suicide there.

Yuma Territorial Prison State Historic Park
1 Prison Hill Road, Yuma, AZ.
Haunted by the ghost of a woman, as well as a poltergeist.

Arkansas

Albert Pike Memorial Temple
712 Scott Street, Little Rock, AR.
Haunted by the ghost of Albert Pike.

Crescent Hotel
75 Prospect Avenue, Eureka Springs, AR.
Haunted by several ghosts, specifically in rooms 202, 218, and 424 and in the recreation room.

Harding University
900 East Center Avenue, Searcy, AR.
Haunted by the ghost of a woman who is often heard
 playing the piano.

Henderson State University
1100 Henderson Street, Arkadelphia, AR.
Haunted by the ghost of a young woman.

Lyon College
2300 Highland Road, Batesville, AR.
Haunted by the ghost of a girl who committed suicide
 in one of the dorms.

California

Bakersfield High School
1241 G Street, Bakersfield, CA
Haunted by the ghosts of a teenage couple.

Bella Maggiora Inn
67 South California Street, Ventura, CA.
Haunted by the ghost of a prostitute who committed
 suicide in one of the rooms.

Hollywood Roosevelt Hotel
7000 Hollywood Boulevard, Los Angeles, CA.
Haunted by several unidentified ghosts, and one that
 is believed to be the ghost of Marilyn Monroe.

Mariposa Elementary School
30800 Palo Alto Drive, Redlands, CA.
Haunted by the ghost of a young boy accidentally killed
 by a bus.

Moss Beach Distillery Restaurant
140 Beach Way, Moss Beach, CA.
Haunted by the Blue Lady.

Union Hotel
401 First Street, Benecia, CA.
Haunted by the ghost of a woman who committed
 suicide in one of the rooms.

Colorado

Broadmoor Hotel
1 Lake Circle, Colorado Springs, CO.
Haunted by the ghosts of those who lost their lives in
 a fire.

George Washington High School
655 South Monaco Parkway, Denver, CO.
Haunted by the ghost of a former football coach.

Hotel Colorado
526 Pine Street, Glenwood Springs, CO.
Haunted by the ghosts of a little girl and a murdered
 chambermaid.

Melting Pot Restaurant
2707 West Main Street, Littleton, CO.
Haunted by several unidentified ghosts and poltergeists.

Miramont Castle Museum
9 Capitol Hill Avenue, Manitou Springs, CO.
Haunted by the ghosts of a father and his son.

Connecticut

Albertus Magnus College
700 Prospect Street, New Haven, CT.
Haunted by the ghost of a little boy.

Bacon Academy School
611 Norwich Avenue, Colchester, CT.
Haunted by the ghost of a man who died there.

Cyrenius H. Booth Library
25 Main Street, Newtown, CT.
Haunted by the ghost of a young woman who used to
 live there.

Lighthouse Inn
6 Guthrie Place, New London, CT.
Haunted by the ghosts of two women.

Talcott House Bed and Breakfast
161 Seaside Avenue, Westbrook, CT.
Haunted by unidentified ghosts.

Delaware

Blue Coat Inn
800 North State Street, Dover, DE.
Haunted by the ghosts of a young drummer boy and an
 older man.

Woodburn
151 Kings Highway, Dover, DE.
Haunted by several unidentified ghosts.

District of Columbia

Ford's Theatre
511 10th Street Northwest, Washington, D.C.
Haunted by the ghost of John Wilkes Booth.

Old Stone House
3051 M Street Northwest, Washington, DC.
Haunted by 11 ghosts.

Trinity College
125 Michigan Avenue, Washington, DC.
Haunted by the ghost of a former student.

The White House—Lincoln Bedroom
1600 Pennsylvania Avenue Northwest, Washington,
 D.C.
Haunted by the ghost of Abraham Lincoln.

The White House—Rose Bedroom
1600 Pennsylvania Avenue Northwest, Washington,
 D.C.
Haunted by the ghost of Andrew Jackson.

Florida

Carriage House Apartments
2260 University Boulevard North, Jacksonville, FL.
Haunted by the ghosts of former residents, specifically
 apartment 40.

Colony Theater
1040 Lincoln Road, Miami Beach, FL
Haunted by an unidentified ghost.

Flagler College
74 King Street, St. Augustine, FL.
Haunted by the ghost of a woman who committed
    suicide.

Henegar Center for the Arts
625 East New Haven Avenue, Melbourne, FL.
Haunted by an unidentified ghost.

South Dade Senior High School
28401 Southwest 167th Avenue, Homestead, FL.
Haunted by the ghosts of a boy and girl.

Stanna's Restaurant
9 North Central Avenue, Umatilla, FL.
Haunted by the ghost of a young woman who
    committed suicide.

Georgia

Heritage Hall
277 South Main Street, Madison, GA.
Haunted by the ghost of a young child, who is often
    heard crying.

Manget-Brannon Alliance for the Arts
24 Long Place, Newnan, GA.
Haunted by an unidentified ghost.

Pirate's House Restaurant
20 East Broad Street, Savannah, GA.
Haunted by the ghost of a pirate captain who died there.

Public House
605 Atlanta Street, Roswell, GA.
Haunted by the ghosts of a soldier and his wife.

Springer Opera House
103 10th Street, Columbus, GA.
Haunted by several unidentified ghosts.

Telfair Museum of Art
121 Barnard Street, Savannah, GA.
Haunted by the ghost of its former owner.

Hawaii

Chaminade University
3140 Waialae Avenue, Honolulu, HI.
Haunted by the ghost of a former student.

Hilton Hotel
2005 Kalia Road, Honolulu, HI.
Haunted by the ghost of a woman murdered in the
    tower room.

King Kamehameha's Kona Beach Hotel
2490 Kalakaua Avenue, Honolulu, HI.
Haunted by the ghosts of warriors.

Sacred Hearts Academy
3253 Waialae Avenue, Honolulu, HI
Haunted by the ghost of a nun.

University of Hawaii
2600 Campus Road, Honolulu, HI.
Haunted by the ghost of a former student who
    committed suicide.

Idaho

Emmett Middle School
301 East 4th Street, Emmett, ID.
Haunted by the ghost of a former music teacher.

Joyce Building
206 Walnut Street, Genesee, ID.
Haunted by several ghosts including those of an elderly man and a rat.

Illinois

Avon Theatre
805 West North Street, Decatur, IL.
Haunted by the ghost of a former owner.

Hotel Baker
100 West Main Street, St. Charles, IL.
Haunted by an unidentified ghost, specifically the sixth floor.

Madison Elementary School
2435 Maine Street, Quincy, IL.
Haunted by the ghost of a murdered woman.

Red Lion Pub
2446 North Lincoln Avenue, Chicago, IL
Haunted by an unidentified ghost.

Resurrection Cemetery
7201 Archer Road, Justice, IL.
Haunted by Resurrection Mary as well as several other apparitions.

Springfield Theatre Center
101 East Lawrence Avenue, Springfield, IL.
Haunted by the ghost of a former actor that was murdered.

Indiana

Binford Elementary School
2300 East 2nd Street, Bloomington, IN.
Haunted by the ghost of a man wearing a black coat.

Hannah House
3801 Madison Avenue, Indianapolis, IN.
Haunted by several ghosts including those of slaves and a stillborn child.

Highland High School
9135 Erie Street, Highland, IN.
Haunted by the ghost of a little boy.

Warsaw Community Library
310 East Main Street, Warsaw, IN.
Haunted by the ghosts of children.

Willard Library
21 North 1st Avenue, Evansville, IN.
Haunted by the Lady in Gray.

Iowa

American Theatre
108 East Main Street, Cherokee, IA.
Haunted by the ghost of a former owner.

Barn Community Theatre
135 West 8th Street, Dubuque, IA.
Formerly an opera house, it became haunted by
several ghosts when it was renovated as a
community theater.

Coe College
1220 1st Avenue Northeast, Cedar Rapids, IA.
Haunted by the ghost of a former student who is often
heard playing the piano.

Grand Opera House
135 West 8th Street, Dubuque, IA.
Haunted by several unidentified ghosts.

Palmer College of Chiropractic
1000 Brady Street, Davenport, IA.
Haunted by several unidentified ghosts.

Kansas

Eldridge Hotel
701 Massachusetts Street, Lawrence, KS.
Haunted by an unidentified ghost, specifically room
506.

Hutchinson Public Library
901 North Main Street, Hutchinson, KS.
Haunted by the ghost of a woman murdered in the
basement.

McPherson Middle School
700 East Elizabeth Street, McPherson, KS.
Haunted by the ghost of a former construction worker.

Paola High School
401 Angela Drive, Paola, KS.
Haunted by the ghost of a former employee.

Red Rock Elementary School
10468 East US Highway 160, Ulysses, KS.
Haunted by the ghost of a little girl.

Kentucky

Eastern Kentucky University
512 Lancaster Avenue, Richmond, KY.
Haunted by several unidentified ghosts.

Evarts High School
215 Wildcat Drive, Evarts, KY.
Haunted by the ghost of a man who died in the
basement.

Liberty Hall
218 Wilkinson Street, Frankfort, KY.
Haunted by the ghost of a young woman murdered.

Mammoth Cave
Located in the Mammoth Cave National Park,
Mammoth Cave, KY.
Haunted by several ghosts including those of slaves and
a man who was trapped for weeks in a nearby cave.

Speed Art Museum
2035 South 3rd Street, Louisville, KY.
Haunted by the ghost of a woman, as well as a
poltergeist.

Louisiana

Bourbon Orleans Hotel
717 Orleans Avenue, New Orleans, LA.
Haunted by the ghosts of several Confederate soldiers.

Northshore Regional Medical Center
100 Medical Center Drive, Slidell, LA.
Haunted by the ghost of a former maintenance man.

Odin's Inn
3613 18th Street, Metairie, LA.
Haunted by an unidentified ghost.

Sin City
626 St. Philip Street, New Orleans, LA.
Haunted by unidentified ghosts.

Spanish Moon
1109 Highland Road, Baton Rouge, LA.
Haunted by the ghost of a young man.

Maine

Captain Fairfield Inn
8 Pleasant Street, Kennebunkport, ME.
Haunted by the ghost of Captain James Fairfield.

Lucerne Inn
Located on Bar Harbor Road, Holden, ME.
Haunted by the ghosts of a mother and child.

Ogunquit Playhouse
Located on State Road, Ogunquit, ME.
Haunted by the ghosts of soldiers.

University of Maine
5703 Alumni Hall, Orono, ME.
Haunted by an unidentified ghost, specifically a fraternity house on campus.

University of Maine at Farmington
224 Main Street, Farmington, ME.
Haunted by the ghost of a former opera singer, specifically the auditorium.

Maryland

Club Charles
1724 North Charles Street, Baltimore, MD.
Haunted by several unidentified ghosts.

Mount Saint Mary's College
16300 Old Emmitsburg Road, Emmitsburg, MD.
Haunted by several unidentified ghosts.

Paint Branch Home
3120 Powder Mill Road, Adelphi, MD.
Haunted by several ghosts, some of which are those of slaves.

University of Maryland Medical Center
419 West Redwood Street, Baltimore, MD.
Haunted by several unidentified ghosts.

Massachusetts

Central Middle School
1012 Hancock Street, Quincy, MA.
Haunted by the ghost of a girl who was murdered.

Emerson Majestic Theater
219 Tremont Street, Boston, MA.
Haunted by several ghosts including those of a former mayor, a married couple, and a young girl.

First Congregational Church
1 Church Street, Paxton, MA.
Haunted by the ghost of a former minister.

Hammond Castle Museum
80 Hesperus Avenue, Gloucester, MA.
Haunted by the ghosts of former residents and their lovers.

John Stone's Inn
179 Main Street, Ashland, MA.
Haunted by poltergeists, as well as the ghosts of a little girl and Captain John Stone.

Yarmouth Resort
343 Route 28, West Yarmouth, MA.
Haunted by the ghosts of a young girl and a dog.

YMCA
820 Massachusetts Avenue, Cambridge, MA.
Haunted by an unidentified male ghost.

Michigan

Bowers Harbor Inn
13512 Peninsula Drive, Traverse City, MI.
Haunted by the ghost of a woman who committed suicide.

Crestwood High School
1501 North Beech Daly Road, Dearborn Heights, MI.
Haunted by several unidentified ghosts.

Landmark Inn
230 North Front Street, Marquette, MI.
Haunted by the ghost of Amelia Earhart.

National House Inn
102 South Parkview Street, Marshall, MI.
Haunted by the Lady in Red.

Pickle Barrel Inn
10256 Willis Road, Willis, MI.
Haunted by unidentified ghosts.

Ramsdell Theatre Opera House
101 Maple Street, Manistee, MI.
Haunted by the ghost of the theater's founder.

Minnesota

Chanhassen Dinner Theater
501 West 78th Street, Chanhassen, MN.
Haunted by the ghost of a former actress.

Forepaugh's
276 Exchange Street South, St. Paul, MN.
Haunted by the ghosts of Mr. Forepaugh and his lover, both of whom committed suicide.

Guthrie Theater
725 Vineland Place, Minneapolis, MN.
Haunted by the ghost of a former usher who committed suicide.

Lumber Barons
101 Water Street South, Stillwater, MN.
Haunted by the ghost of a Confederate soldier.

Saint Mary's University
700 Terrace Heights, Winona, MN.
Haunted by the ghost of a priest.

Mississippi

Chapel of the Cross
674 Mannsdale Road, Madison, MS.
Haunted by the ghost of a woman visiting her lover's grave.

John Martin's Restaurant
21 Silver Street, Natchez, MS.
Haunted by the ghost of a former prostitute.

King's Tavern
619 Jefferson Street, Natchez, MS.
Haunted by the ghost of a young woman.

The Longfellow House
3401 Beach Boulevard, Pascagoula, MS.
Haunted by the ghost of a slave.

Rowan Oak
Located on Old Taylor Road, Oxford, MS.
Haunted by the ghost of William Faulkner.

Missouri

Historic Missouri Theater
203 South 9th Street, Columbia, MO.
Haunted by the ghost of a former owner.

Plattsburgh High School
800 West Frost Street, Plattsburgh, MO.
Haunted by the ghost of a former student.

Ozark High School
1109 West Jackson Street, Ozark, MO.
Haunted by the ghost of a former student.

Savoy Hotel
219 West 9th Street, Kansas City, MO.
Haunted by the ghost of a woman, specifically room 505.

Springfield Little Theatre
311 East Walnut Street, Springfield, MO.
Haunted by the ghost of a former janitor.

Montana

Carroll College
1601 North Benton Avenue, Helena, MT.
Haunted by the ghost of a man who committed suicide.

Chico Hot Springs Lodge
Located on Old Chico Road, Pray, MT.
Haunted by the Lady in White.

Historic Dumas Brothel Museum
45 East Mercury Street, Butte, MT.
Haunted by the ghost of a woman who committed suicide.

Missoula Children's Theatre
200 North Adams Street, Missoula, MT.
Haunted by a male ghost known as George.

Nebraska

Dana College
2848 College Drive, Blair, NE.
Haunted by the ghost of a man who committed suicide.

Hastings College
800 Turner Avenue, Hastings, NE.
Haunted by the ghost of a former professor.

Scotus Central Catholic High School
1554 18th Avenue, Columbus, NE.
Haunted by several ghosts including those of a nun,
a former student, and a little boy.

State Capitol Building
1445 K Street, Lincoln, NE.
Haunted by an unidentified ghost who is often heard
crying.

York High School
Located 1005 Duke Drive, York, NE.
Haunted by the ghost of a former teacher.

Nevada

Fourth Ward School Museum
537 South C Street, Virginia City, NV.
Haunted by a female ghost.

Goldfield Motel
310 South Sundog Avenue, Goldfield, NV.
Haunted by several ghosts including those of a pregnant
woman and the original owner of the hotel.

Luxor Hotel and Casino
3900 Las Vegas Boulevard South, Las Vegas, NV.
Haunted by the ghosts of two former construction
workers.

Moapa Valley High School
2400 North St. Joseph, Overton, NV.
Haunted by an unidentified ghost.

Parklane Mall
310 East Plumb Lane, Reno, NV.
Haunted by the ghost of a murdered woman.

New Hampshire

Chase Home for Children
698 Middle Road, Portsmouth, NH.
Haunted by several ghosts including that of a young girl
who committed suicide.

Country Tavern
452 Amherst Street, Nashua, NH.
Haunted by the ghost of a murdered woman.

Keene State College
229 Main Street, Keene, NH.
Haunted by Harriet Huntress, the ghost of a woman
who used to live in Huntress Hall.

Fiddler's Choice Music Store
Located on Route 137 North, Jaffrey, NH.
Haunted by poltergeists.

Siam Orchid
158 North Main Street, Concord, NH.
Haunted by unidentified ghosts.

New Jersey

Bernardsville Public Library
1 Anderson Hill Road, Bernardsville, NJ.
Haunted by the ghost of a young woman who is often
    heard crying.

Brass Rail Restaurant
Located 135 Washington Street, Hoboken, NJ.
Haunted by several ghosts, including those in a
    wedding party.

Darress Theater
615 Main Street, Boonton, NJ.
Haunted by several unidentified ghosts.

Elizabeth General Medical Center
655 East Jersey Street, Elizabeth, NJ.
Haunted by the ghost of a baby who is often heard
    crying, as well as a woman dressed in white.

Winterwood Gift Shop
518 Washington Street, Cape May, NJ.
Haunted by the ghosts of two sisters.

New Mexico

Double Eagle
2335 Calle de Guadalupe Street, Mesilla, NM.
Haunted by unidentified ghosts.

Gadsden High School
6301 Highway 28, Anthony, NM.
Haunted by the ghost of a young girl who was
    murdered.

Grant Corner Inn
122 Grant Avenue, Santa Fe, NM.
Haunted by unidentified ghosts, specifically rooms
    4 and 8.

Kimo Theatre
423 Central Avenue Northwest, Albuquerque, NM.
Haunted by the ghost of a young boy who was killed
    backstage.

Rebecca's at The Lodge
601 Corona Place, Cloudcroft, NM.
Haunted by the ghost of a murdered woman.

New York

Bull's Head Inn
2 Park Place, Cobleskill, NY.
Haunted by the ghost of a former resident.

Concordia College
171 White Plains Road, Bronxville, NY.
Haunted by several ghosts, including those of a little
    girl and a former student who was murdered.

Holiday Inn
100 Whitehaven Road, Grand Island, NY.
Haunted by the ghost of a little girl who died in a fire.

Hotel Des Artistes
1 West 67th Street, New York, NY.
Haunted by an unidentified ghost.

Marist College
3399 North Road, Poughkeepsie, NY.
Haunted by the ghost of a young woman murdered by
    her boyfriend.

Mater Dei College
5428 State Route 37, Ogdensburg, NY.
Haunted by the ghost of a nun who committed suicide
and the ghost of a little boy who is often heard
laughing.

Roycroft Inn
40 South Grove Street, East Aurora, NY.
Haunted by several unidentified ghosts.

North Carolina

Appalachian State University
504 Dauphblan Street, Boone, NC.
Haunted by several unidentified ghosts.

Grove Park Inn Resort
290 Macon Avenue, Asheville, NC.
Haunted by the Pink Lady, specifically room 545.

North Carolina School for the Deaf
517 West Fleming Drive, Morganton, NC.
Haunted by an unidentified female ghost.

Western Carolina University
Located on Central Drive, Cullowhee, NC.
Haunted by the ghost of a young woman who
committed suicide in one of the former dormitories.

North Dakota

St. Anne's Guest Home
524 North 17th Street, Grand Forks, ND.
Haunted by the ghost of a woman who committed
suicide.

University of North Dakota
264 Centennial Drive, Grand Forks, ND.
Haunted by the ghost of a legless girl, specifically the
Wilkerson Dining Hall.

Ohio

Akron Civic Theatre
182 South Main Street, Akron, OH.
Haunted by the ghost of a former janitor.

Buxton Inn
313 Broadway East, Granville, OH.
Haunted by the ghosts of the former innkeepers.

Heather Hill Hospital
12340 Bass Lake Road, Chardon, OH.
Haunted by the ghost of a little boy.

Old Stone House on the Lake
133 Clemens Street, Marblehead, OH.
Haunted by the ghost of a little girl, specifically room 11.

Spring Hill School
860 Ormsby Drive, Xenia, OH.
Haunted by the ghost of a former teacher who was
murdered.

United States Air Force Museum
1100 Spaatz Street, Dayton, OH.
Haunted by poltergeists, orbs, and the ghosts of pilots.

Oklahoma

County Line Restaurant
1226 Northeast 63rd Street, Oklahoma City, OK.
Haunted by unidentified ghosts.

Gilcrease Museum
1400 North Gilcrease Museum Road, Tulsa, OK.
Haunted by an unidentified ghost.

Wall's Bargain Center
507 East Main Street, Shawnee, OK.
Haunted by an unidentified ghost.

Young America Corporation
3705 West Memorial Road, Oklahoma City, OK.
Haunted by the ghost of two former employees who
    committed suicide.

Oregon

Oregon State University
2638 Northwest Jackson Avenue, Corvallis, OR.
Haunted by the ghost of a murdered student.

South Eugene High School
400 East 19th Avenue, Eugene, OR.
Haunted by the ghost of a former student.

St. Helens High School
2375 Gable Road, St. Helens, OR.
Haunted by a female ghost.

White Eagle Cafe and Saloon
836 North Russell Street, Portland, OR.
Haunted by several unidentified ghosts.

Pennsylvania

Civil War Library and Museum
1805 Pine Street, Philadelphia, PA.
Haunted by the ghosts of soldiers.

Easton Public Library
515 Church Street, Easton, PA.
Haunted by several unidentified ghosts.

Odette's
Located on South River Road, New Hope, PA.
Haunted by the ghost of a former employee.

Red Rose Inn
804 West Baltimore Pike, West Grove, PA.
Haunted by the ghost of a man hung outside the
    building.

Ship Inn
Route 30 and Ship Road, Exton, PA.
Haunted by an unidentified ghost.

Tannersville Inn
Located on Route 611, Tannersville, PA.
Haunted by a male ghost.

Willow Grove Hotel
655 Main Street, Bethlehem, PA.
Haunted by the ghost of a little girl.

Rhode Island

Belcourt Castle
657 Bellevue Avenue, Newport, RI.
Haunted by several unidentified ghosts.

Colt Elementary School
570 Hope Street, Bristol, RI.
Haunted by a family of ghosts.

Johnson and Wales University
8 Abbott Park Place, Providence, RI.
Haunted by the ghost of a nun.

Providence College
River Avenue and Eaton Street, Providence, RI.
Haunted by several unidentified ghosts.

Salve Regina University
100 Ochre Point Avenue, Newport, RI.
Haunted by the ghost of a little boy.

South Carolina

Airport High School
1315 Boston Street, Cayce, SC.
Haunted by the ghost of the school's first principal.

Battery Carriage House Inn
20 South Battery Street, Charleston, SC.
Haunted by a male ghost.

Coker College
Located on College Avenue, Hartsville, SC.
Haunted by an unidentified ghost.

Lamar High School
216 Darlington Avenue, Lamar, SC.
Haunted by the ghost of a former student basketball player.

South Carolina School for the Deaf and Blind
355 Cedar Springs Road, Spartanburg, SC.
Haunted by the ghost of a former president of the school.

South Dakota

Alex Johnson Hotel
523 6th Street, Rapid City, SD.
Haunted by several ghosts, including that of a former owner.

Belle Fourche High School
1301 12th Avenue, Belle Fourche, SD.
Haunted by the ghost of a former janitor.

Bullock Hotel
633 Main Street, Deadwood, SD.
Haunted by the ghost of the town's first sheriff.

Hill City High School
464 Main Street, Hill City, SD.
Haunted by several ghosts, including that of a former student.

Tennessee

Bijou Theatre Center
803 South Gay Street, Knoxville, TN.
Haunted by an unidentified male ghost.

Orpheum Theatre
203 South Main Street, Memphis, TN
Haunted by the ghost of a little girl.

The Read House
827 Broad Street, Chattanooga, TN.
Haunted by the ghost of a murdered prostitute.

Rocky Top Village Inn
311 Airport Road, Gatlinburg, TN.
Haunted by the ghosts of two murder victims.

Tennessee Wesleyan College
204 East College Street, Athens, TN.
Haunted by several unidentified ghosts.

Walking Horse Hotel
101 Spring Street, Wartrace, TN.
Haunted by an unidentified ghost.

Texas

Catfish Plantation Restaurant
814 Water Street, Waxahachie, TX.
Haunted by the ghost of a woman strangled to death in
the building.

Del Frisco's Double Eagle
812 Main Street, Ft. Worth, TX.
Haunted by the ghost of a murdered man.

Jefferson Hotel
124 West Austin Street, Jefferson, TX.
Haunted by several unidentified ghosts.

Kilgore College
1100 Broadway Boulevard, Kilgore, TX.
Haunted by the ghost of a former student who
committed suicide.

Metz Elementary School
84 Robert Martinez Jr. Street, Austin, TX.
Haunted by the ghosts of children.

St. Anthony Wyndham
300 East Travis Street, San Antonio, TX.
Haunted by several ghosts, including those of a former
employee and a married couple.

Utah

Historical Society
300 Rio Grande Street, Salt Lake City, UT.
Haunted by an unidentified female ghost.

Radisson Hotel
2510 Washington Boulevard, Ogden, UT.
Haunted by a female ghost.

Vermont

White House of Wilmington
178 Route 9 West, Wilmington, VT.
Haunted by the ghost of a former resident.

Winooski High School
80 Normand Street, Winooski, VT.
Haunted by the ghosts of former students.

Norwich Inn
325 Main Street, Norwich, VT.
Haunted by an unidentified female ghost, specifically
  room 20.

Norwich University
158 Harmon Drive, Northfield, VT.
Haunted by the ghost of a student who committed
  suicide.

Southern Vermont College
982 Mansion Drive, Bennington, VT.
Haunted by several unidentified ghosts.

Virginia

Cavalier Hotel
42nd Street and Atlantic Avenue, Virginia Beach, VA.
Haunted by several unidentified ghosts.

Gadsby's Tavern
138 North Royal Street, Alexandria, VA.
Haunted by the ghost of a young woman.

Martha Washington Inn
150 West Main Street, Abingdon, VA.
Haunted by the ghost of a young woman searching
  for her lover.

Wayside Theatre
7853 Main Street, Middletown, VA.
Haunted by the ghost of a former owner.

William Marvin Bass School
1730 Seabury Avenue, Lynchburg, VA.
Haunted by an unidentified ghost.

Washington

Harvard Exit Theater
807 East Roy Street, Seattle, WA.
Haunted by the ghosts of several women.

Oxford Saloon
913 1st Street, Snohomish, WA.
Haunted by the ghosts of prostitutes.

Patsy Clark's Mansion
2208 West 2nd Avenue, Spokane, WA.
Haunted by three unidentified ghosts.

Monticello Middle School
1225 28th Avenue, Longview, WA.
Haunted by the ghost of a little girl who died during
  construction.

Mount Baker Theatre Center
106 North Commercial Street, Bellingham, WA.
Haunted by an unidentified female ghost.

West Virginia

Morgantown Public Library
Located on Grafton Road, Morgantown, WV.
Haunted by an unidentified ghost.

Wisconsin

Bodega Brew Pub
122 Fourth Street South, La Crosse, WI.
Haunted by the ghost of a former owner.

Grand Opera House
100 High Avenue, Oshkosh, WI.
Haunted by the ghost of a former stagehand.

Kozy Korner Restaurant
157 South Knowles Avenue, New Richmond, WI.
Haunted by the ghost of a young boy.

LCO Casino Lodge
13767 West County Road B, Hayward, WI.
Haunted by several unidentified ghosts.

University of Wisconsin
105 Garfield Avenue, Eau Claire, WI.
Haunted by the ghost of the founder of the school's
  theater.

Wyoming

Historic Plains Hotel
1600 Central Avenue, Cheyenne, WY.
Haunted by several unidentified ghosts.

Historic Sheridan Inn
856 Broadway Street, Sheridan, WY.
Haunted by the ghost of a former housekeeper.

Shoshone Bar
159 East Main Street, Lovell, WY.
Haunted by several unidentified ghosts.

St. Mark's Episcopal Church
1908 Central Avenue, Cheyenne, WY.
Haunted by the ghost of a former construction worker.

Sweetwater County Library
300 North 1st East Street, Green River, WY.
Haunted by several unidentified ghosts.

Index

We Have EVERYTHING!

Everything® **After College Book**
$12.95, 1-55850-847-3

Everything® **American History Book**
$12.95, 1-58062-531-2

Everything® **Angels Book**
$12.95, 1-58062-398-0

Everything® **Anti-Aging Book**
$12.95, 1-58062-565-7

Everything® **Astrology Book**
$12.95, 1-58062-062-0

Everything® **Baby Names Book**
$12.95, 1-55850-655-1

Everything® **Baby Shower Book**
$12.95, 1-58062-305-0

Everything® **Baby's First Food Book**
$12.95, 1-58062-512-6

Everything® **Baby's First Year Book**
$12.95, 1-58062-581-9

Everything® **Barbeque Cookbook**
$12.95, 1-58062-316-6

Everything® **Bartender's Book**
$9.95, 1-55850-536-9

Everything® **Bedtime Story Book**
$12.95, 1-58062-147-3

Everything® **Bicycle Book**
$12.00, 1-55850-706-X

Everything® **Build Your Own Home Page**
$12.95, 1-58062-339-5

Everything® **Business Planning Book**
$12.95, 1-58062-491-X

Everything® **Casino Gambling Book**
$12.95, 1-55850-762-0

Everything® **Cat Book**
$12.95, 1-55850-710-8

Everything® **Chocolate Cookbook**
$12.95, 1-58062-405-7

Everything® **Christmas Book**
$15.00, 1-55850-697-7

Everything® **Civil War Book**
$12.95, 1-58062-366-2

Everything® **College Survival Book**
$12.95, 1-55850-720-5

Everything® **Computer Book**
$12.95, 1-58062-401-4

Everything® **Cookbook**
$14.95, 1-58062-400-6

Everything® **Cover Letter Book**
$12.95, 1-58062-312-3

Everything® **Crossword and Puzzle Book**
$12.95, 1-55850-764-7

Everything® **Dating Book**
$12.95, 1-58062-185-6

Everything® **Dessert Book**
$12.95, 1-55850-717-5

Everything® **Digital Photography Book**
$12.95, 1-58062-574-6

Everything® **Dog Book**
$12.95, 1-58062-144-9

Everything® **Dreams Book**
$12.95, 1-55850-806-6

Everything® **Etiquette Book**
$12.95, 1-55850-807-4

Everything® **Fairy Tales Book**
$12.95, 1-58062-546-0

Everything® **Family Tree Book**
$12.95, 1-55850-763-9

Everything® **Fly-Fishing Book**
$12.95, 1-58062-148-1

Everything® **Games Book**
$12.95, 1-55850-643-8

Everything® **Get-A-Job Book**
$12.95, 1-58062-223-2

Everything® **Get Published Book**
$12.95, 1-58062-315-8

Everything® **Get Ready for Baby Book**
$12.95, 1-55850-844-9

Everything® **Ghost Book**
$12.95, 1-58062-533-9

Everything® **Golf Book**
$12.95, 1-55850-814-7

Everything® **Grammar and Style Book**
$12.95, 1-58062-573-8

Everything® **Guide to Las Vegas**
$12.95, 1-58062-438-3

Everything® **Guide to New York City**
$12.95, 1-58062-314-X

Everything® **Guide to Walt Disney World®, Universal Studios®, and Greater Orlando, 2nd Edition**
$12.95, 1-58062-404-9

Everything® **Guide to Washington D.C.**
$12.95, 1-58062-313-1

Everything® **Guitar Book**
$12.95, 1-58062-555-X

Everything® **Herbal Remedies Book**
$12.95, 1-58062-331-X

Everything® **Home-Based Business Book**
$12.95, 1-58062-364-6

Everything® **Homebuying Book**
$12.95, 1-58062-074-4

Everything® **Homeselling Book**
$12.95, 1-58062-304-2

Available wherever books are sold!

Everything® **Home Improvement Book**
$12.95, 1-55850-718-3

Everything® **Horse Book**
$12.95, 1-58062-564-9

Everything® **Hot Careers Book**
$12.95, 1-58062-486-3

Everything® **Internet Book**
$12.95, 1-58062-073-6

Everything® **Investing Book**
$12.95, 1-58062-149-X

Everything® **Jewish Wedding Book**
$12.95, 1-55850-801-5

Everything® **Job Interviews Book**
$12.95, 1-58062-493-6

Everything® **Lawn Care Book**
$12.95, 1-58062-487-1

Everything® **Leadership Book**
$12.95, 1-58062-513-4

Everything® **Learning Spanish Book**
$12.95, 1-58062-575-4

Everything® **Low-Fat High-Flavor Cookbook**
$12.95, 1-55850-802-3

Everything® **Magic Book**
$12.95, 1-58062-418-9

Everything® **Managing People Book**
$12.95, 1-58062-577-0

Everything® **Microsoft® Word 2000 Book**
$12.95, 1-58062-306-9

Everything® **Money Book**
$12.95, 1-58062-145-7

Everything® **Mother Goose Book**
$12.95, 1-58062-490-1

Everything® **Mutual Funds Book**
$12.95, 1-58062-419-7

Everything® **One-Pot Cookbook**
$12.95, 1-58062-186-4

Everything® **Online Business Book**
$12.95, 1-58062-320-4

Everything® **Online Genealogy Book**
$12.95, 1-58062-402-2

Everything® **Online Investing Book**
$12.95, 1-58062-338-7

Everything® **Online Job Search Book**
$12.95, 1-58062-365-4

Everything® **Pasta Book**
$12.95, 1-55850-719-1

Everything® **Pregnancy Book**
$12.95, 1-58062-146-5

Everything® **Pregnancy Organizer**
$15.00, 1-58062-336-0

Everything® **Project Management Book**
$12.95, 1-58062-583-5

Everything® **Puppy Book**
$12.95, 1-58062-576-2

Everything® **Quick Meals Cookbook**
$12.95, 1-58062-488-X

Everything® **Resume Book**
$12.95, 1-58062-311-5

Everything® **Romance Book**
$12.95, 1-58062-566-5

Everything® **Sailing Book**
$12.95, 1-58062-187-2

Everything® **Saints Book**
$12.95, 1-58062-534-7

Everything® **Selling Book**
$12.95, 1-58062-319-0

Everything® **Spells and Charms Book**
$12.95, 1-58062-532-0

Everything® **Stress Management Book**
$12.95, 1-58062-578-9

Everything® **Study Book**
$12.95, 1-55850-615-2

Everything® **Tall Tales, Legends, and Outrageous Lies Book**
$12.95, 1-58062-514-2

Everything® **Tarot Book**
$12.95, 1-58062-191-0

Everything® **Time Management Book**
$12.95, 1-58062-492-8

Everything® **Toasts Book**
$12.95, 1-58062-189-9

Everything® **Total Fitness Book**
$12.95, 1-58062-318-2

Everything® **Trivia Book**
$12.95, 1-58062-143-0

Everything® **Tropical Fish Book**
$12.95, 1-58062-343-3

Everything® **Vitamins, Minerals, and Nutritional Supplements Book**
$12.95, 1-58062-496-0

Everything® **Wedding Book, 2nd Edition**
$12.95, 1-58062-190-2

Everything® **Wedding Checklist**
$7.95, 1-58062-456-1

Everything® **Wedding Etiquette Book**
$7.95, 1-58062-454-5

Everything® **Wedding Organizer**
$15.00, 1-55850-828-7

Everything® **Wedding Shower Book**
$7.95, 1-58062-188-0

Everything® **Wedding Vows Book**
$7.95, 1-58062-455-3

Everything® **Wine Book**
$12.95, 1-55850-808-2

Everything® **World War II Book**
$12.95, 1-58062-572-X

Everything® is a registered trademark of Adams Media Corporation.

**For more information, or to order, call 800-872-5627
or visit everything.com**
Adams Media Corporation, 57 Littlefield Street, Avon, MA 02322

We Have
EVERYTHING®
KIDS'!

Everything® Kids' Baseball Book
$9.95, 1-58062-489-8

Everything® Kids' Joke Book
$9.95, 1-58062-495-2

Everything® Kids' Mazes Book
$6.95, 1-58062-558-4

Everything® Kids' Money Book
$9.95, 1-58062-322-0

Everything® Kids' Nature Book
$9.95, 1-58062-321-2

Everything® Kids' Online Book
$9.95, 1-58062-394-8

Everything® Kids' Puzzle Book
$9.95, 1-58062-323-9

Everything® Kids' Science Experiments Book
$6.95, 1-58062-557-6

Everything® Kids' Space Book
$9.95, 1-58062-395-6

Everything® Kids' Witches and Wizards Book
$9.95, 1-58062-396-4

Available wherever books are sold!

For more information, or to order,
call 800-872-5627 or visit everything.com

Adams Media Corporation, 57 Littlefield Street, Avon, MA 02322

Everything® is a registered trademark of Adams Media Corporation.